Historical, Geographical and Legal Analyses on Dokdo

Northeast Asian History Foundation
Limkwang Tower, 81 Tongil-ro, Seodaemun-gu, Seoul
03739, Republic of Korea

www.nahf.or.kr/eng

ISBN   978-89-6187-399-4   93910

Historical, Geographical and Legal Analyses on Dokdo

NORTHEAST ASIAN
HISTORY FOUNDATION

Disclaimers

• The views expressed here are the authors' own and do not necessarily reflect the position of the Northeast Asian History Foundation.

• "Tokdo" or "Takeshima" mentioned in some articles in this book refers to "Dokdo."

• The articles, except for those originally written in English, were translated by the Center for Interpreting and Translation at Hankook University of Foreign Studies.

Sources of articles in this publication

• Bang, Jong-hyun, "A Day on Dokdo," *Gyeongseong University Newspaper* 13, 1947.

• Shin, Seok-ho, "On Where Dokdo Belongs," *Sahae*, 1948.

• Lee, Byeong-do, "Historical Contemplation of Different Names of Dokdo – the Study of Names; Usando and Takeshima," *Journal of Buddhist History*, 1963.

• Choi, Seo-myeon, "Dokdo as Illustrated on Maps," *Territorial Problems Research* First Edition, 1983

• Han, Cheol-ho, "Survey of Oki by the Japanese Navy Hydrographic Office and its Perception of Dokdo," *Research on Modern and Contemporary Korean History* 65, 2013.

• Song, Byeong-kie, "The declaration of Ulleungdo and Usando (Dokdo) as Foreign possessions by Japanese Dajokan Minister," *Historical Verification of Korea's Sovereignty over Ulleungdo and Dokdo*, 2010.

• Hori, Kazuo, "Japan's Incorporation of Takeshima into Its Territory in 1905," *Korea Observer*, vol. 38, no. 3, Autumn 1997.
  * This article was originally published in Japanese in 1987 under the title "1905年日本の竹島領土編入," 『朝鮮史研究会論文集』(Chosenshi Kenkyukai Ronbunshu), vol. 24, 1987.

• Song, Byeong-kie, "Japan's Annexation of 'Ryanko Island' and Shim Heung-taek's Report to the Korean Government," *Historical Verification of Korea's Sovereignty over Ulleungdo and Dokdo*, 2010.

• Jung, Byung-joon, "A Draft of the Peace Treaty with Japan by the British Ministry of Foreign Affairs, the Formation of the Attached Map (March 1951) and a Reconfirmation of Korea's Possession of Dokdo," *Journal of Korean Independence Movement Studies* 24, 2005.

• Sean Fern, "Tokdo or Takeshima? The International Law of Territorial Acquisition in the Japan Korea Island Dispute," *Stanford Journal of East Asian Affairs* 5, 2005.

• Seichu Naito's article "Territorial Issue between Japan and Korea: Case of Takeshima / Dokdo" was originally published in book form by the Shinkansha Publishing House in 2009.

Contents

7   Hong Seong-keun   Introduction

———— History Knows the Truth ————————————————

20   Bang Jong-hyun   A Day on Dokdo

25   Shin Seok-ho   On Where Dokdo Belongs

40   Lee Byeong-do   Historical Contemplation of Different Names of Dokdo – the Study of Names; Usando and Takeshima

50   Choi Seo-myeon   Dokdo as Illustrated on Maps

61   Song Byeong-kie   Japan's Annexation of 'Ryanko Island' and Shim Heung-taek's Report to the Korean Government

———— Japan Knows the Truth ————————————————

82   Han Cheol-ho   Survey of Oki by the Japanese Navy Hydrographic Office and Its Perception of Dokdo

122   Song Byeong-kie   The Declaration of Ulleungdo and Usando (Dokdo) as Foreign Possessions by Japanese Dajokan Minister

142   Park Byoung-sup   A Study on How the Japanese Government of the Meiji Period Investigated and Disclaimed Jurisdiction over Dokdo

178   Jung Byung-joon   A Draft of the Peace Treaty with Japan by the British
                             Ministry of Foreign Affairs, the Formation of the Attached
                             Map (March 1951) and a Reconfirmation of Korea's
                             Possession of Dokdo

215   Kazuo Hori   Japan's Incorporation of Takeshima into Its Territory
                             in 1905

263   Sean Fern   Tokdo or Takeshima? The International Law of Territorial
                             Acquisition in the Japan–Korea Island Dispute

284   Seichu Naito   Territorial Issue between Japan and Korea: Case of
                             Takeshima / Dokdo – A Critique of the "10 Issues of
                             Takeshima" Published by the MOFA of Japan

Introduction

On March 18, 2016, the Japanese government announced the authorization results for social studies textbooks that will be used in high schools from 2017. References to Dokdo appeared in 27 of the 35 textbooks, or 77%, in history and social geography. Dokdo is an island in the East Sea of the Korean Peninsula, 87.4km southeast of Ulleungdo and 151.7km from Japan's Oki Islands. Since Japan was defeated in World War II, Korea has exercised its effective sovereignty over Dokdo and over 40 Koreans are now living there. Moreover, more than 100,000 tourists from home and abroad visit Dokdo every year. In this light, Koreans are dumfounded by the description of Dokdo as "an inherent territory of Japan" in Japanese textbooks.

References to Dokdo in authorized high school textbooks in 2016 sharply increased, both in content and quantity, from the textbooks authorized in 2012. Such increase is attributable to the Teaching Guide for the Courses of Study for social studies in high schools (curriculum) that serves as a guide for writing textbooks. As the Japanese Ministry of Education, Culture, Sports, Science and Technology (MEXT) revised the Teaching Guide for the Courses of Study, it requires the understanding on Dokdo to be enhanced based on the Japanese government's claim that "Dokdo is an inherent territory of Japan, and Korea is illegally occupying the island." And, Japan's position on Dokdo is simply following the basic position of Japanese Ministry of Foreign Affairs (MOFA) on Dokdo.

The Japanese MOFA website (www.mofa.go.jp) provides detailed grounds for Japan's claims that Dokdo is an inherent part of Japanese territory based on the "Basic Positions on Dokdo." The three bases are as follows. "First, Japan established its sovereignty over Dokdo during the Edo period in the 17th century. Second, Japan reaffirmed its sovereignty over Dokdo through the Japanese Cabinet's decision to incorporate Dokdo into Shimane Prefecture in 1905. Third, Dokdo was not excluded from Japanese territory in the San Francisco Peace Treaty in 1952, which again affirms Japan's sovereignty over Dokdo." Based on the abovementioned three bases, Japanese textbooks also state that "Dokdo is an integral part of Japanese territory."

On the surface, these three bases seem plausible, but they are not logical at all. That is because one single document, the "Dajokan Order of 1877," can single-handedly break the logic of the three grounds above. In 1877, the Dajokan (Grand Council of State), Japan's highest decision-making body during the Meiji period, sent a directive to its subordinate organizations that "regarding Takeshima [Ulleungdo] and one other island [Dokdo]... bear in mind that our country [Japan] has nothing to do with them." The directive is called the "Dajokan Order," which is recorded in an official document of the Meiji government. This directive is a decision made by the highest decision-making body of the Meiji government based on the history of diplomatic negotiations between the Joseon and Japanese government on sovereignty over Ulleungdo (Dokdo) in the late 17th century and the documents of both central and local governments of Japan. It is confirmed, through the directive, that Japan had never established its sovereignty over Dokdo at any time before 1877. In essence, the first basis of Japan's claims that Japan established sovereignty over

Dokdo in the 17th century Edo period is not valid. As the first basis becomes invalid, the other two grounds based on the first cannot be established. Nonetheless, the Japanese government has concealed or disregarded the existence of the "Dajokan Order" so far. Though being the final and official decision made by the Japanese government in the past, the "Dajokan Order" never appears anywhere neither in textbooks nor in the website and pamphlet of the Japanese Ministry of Foreign Affairs.

Numerous studies have been conducted to prove Korea, not Japan, has exercised legitimate territorial sovereignty over Dokdo founded on the Dajokan Order of 1877 and the postwar settlement on Japanese territory by the Allied Powers after the end of World War II. Parts of the results of such studies are compiled in this book. This book contains a total of 12 papers that were published in academic journals or books of Korea, Japan and the United States. As the title of this book implies, these papers provide historical, geographical and legal analyses to demonstrate that Dokdo is an integral part of Korean territory historically, geographically and under international law. The summaries of each paper are as follows.

The first paper is "A Day of Dokdo" written by Bang Jong-hyun, a professor of Korean Language at Seoul National University, and published in Gyeongseong University Newspaper in 1947. Bang Jong-hyun participated as a member of Ulleungdo and Dokdo Investigative Research Team and wrote this paper as a travel essay after exploring Ulleungdo and Dokdo in 1947. Pointing out that Dokdo appears to be made entirely of rocks, he suggests that the name of the island 'Dokdo' might be originated from dolseom in Korean or Seokdo (石島), meaning a rocky island. Noting that residents in Ulleungdo called Dokdo as dokseom, the author who is a scholar of Korean literature and great expert of dialect study reminds that *dol* (stone) was referred to as dok in the regional dialect. This paper served as a pioneering study that found out the name 'Dokdo' originated from dokseom or dolseom in Korean. In addition, this paper provides linguistic bases to demonstrate that Seokdo in the Imperial Decree No. 41 of 1900 is a Chinese translation (漢譯) of dokseom or dolseom, which referred to Dokdo by residents in Ulleungdo. The Imperial Decree No. 41 stipulates that Seokdo [Dokdo] shall be placed under the jurisdiction of Ulleungdo county magistrate (gunsu).

The second paper is "On Where Dokdo Belongs" written in 1948 by Shin Seok-ho, the then-President of Guksagwan (today's National Institute of Korean History). After an actual survey on Ulleungdo and Dokdo in August 1947, the author wrote this paper. During the survey, he discovered and presented Ulleungdo County Magistrate Shim Heung-taek's report of 1906 (copy) kept in Ulleungdo County Office, which is a key record proving Dokdo is an ancillary island to Ulleungdo. The author also introduces the fact, through an interview with residents living in Ulleungdo including Hong Jong-hyun, that Ulleungdo fishermen frequently visited Dokdo to collect seafood and hunt sea lions after the development of Ulleungdo in 1882. Contemplating on the Ulleungdo Dispute, a territorial dispute over Ulleungdo between Korea and Japan, and the Hachiemon Incident where the man named Aizuya Hachiemon was executed for sailing to Ulleungdo by breaking the Japanese government's order in the late 17th century, Shin demonstrates Japan's acknowledgement that Dokdo was an integral part of Joseon territory as an ancillary island of Ulleungdo. In the meantime, the investigative survey on Dokdo by Shin Seok-ho and his company was carried out under the order of An Jae-hong, Civil Administrator of the South Korean Interim Government, which shows that Dokdo was under Korea's administrative jurisdiction. The survey on Dokdo was joined by Director of Japanese Division of the Ministry of Foreign Affairs, an editor and the Ministry of Education and engineer at the Fisheries Bureau from the then Korean government.

The third paper is "Historical Contemplation of Different Names of Dokdo-The Study of Names; Usando and Takeshima" written in 1963 by Lee Byeong-do, a professor emeritus at Seoul National University and historian. With regard to the names Ulleungdo and Dokdo, the islands were called "Ulleungdo" and "Usando" in Korea and "Takeshima (竹島)" and "Matsushima (松島)" in Japan respectively. The author confirms that Dokdo has been an ancillary island of Ulleungdo by pointing out both Korean names and Japanese names referring to the islands came from the same origin. That is, the names Ulleungdo and Usando originated from Uljin-gun of Gangwon Province where the two islands were historically and geographically affiliated. Uljin was called "Ujinya" during the Goguryeo Dynasty and the "U" from Ujinya and "Ul" from Uljin became to refer to Usando (Dokdo) and Ulleungdo respectively. In addition, the Japanese names Takeshima and Matsushima all came from the single origin "Isotakeshima (磯竹島, a high, valiant mountain)." Regarding this, the name "Matsushima (松島, pine tree island)" that used to refer to Dokdo originated from the names of Ulleungdo called in Japan Isotakehima or Takeshima (bamboo island). In conclusion, the author highlights that the two islands are inseparably bound together by a common destiny. He mentions that if Ulleungdo falls under Korea's jurisdiction, then it only stands to reason that its ancillary island Dokdo should be considered Korean territory.

The fourth paper is "Dokdo as Illustrated on Maps" written in 1983 by Choi Seo-myeon, Director of International Korea Research Institute, who has collected and studied maps for a long time. By analyzing ancient Korean, Japanese and western maps that illustrated Dokdo, the author demonstrates that Dokdo has been recognized as an integral part of Korean territory from ancient time. That is, Usando illustrated in Korean maps, Matsushima in Japanese maps and Tchian Chan Tao, Hornet Rock and Liancourt Rocks in western maps all refer to Dokdo, which proves Dokdo is part of Korean territory. He also points out that even through the location and name of Dokdo were marked differently in each map, ancient maps were aimed at reflecting the recognition of people of the time, not designed based on accurate measurement as present. This reflects his usual remark, "ancient maps should be read, not seen."

The fifth paper is "Japan's Annexation of 'Ryanko Island' and Shim Hueng-taek's Report to the Korean Government" written in 2010 by Song Byeong-kie, a professor emeritus of Dankook University. Song Byeong-kie sheds light on Japan's incorporation Dokdo into the Shimane prefecture in 1905 and Ulleungdo County Magistrate Shim Heung-taek's Report of 1906 by discovering historical records in Kyujangkak Archive, Seoul National University and confirms Dokdo has been part of Korean territory. The author points out the fact that the Japanese government renamed the western name Ryanko Island (Liancourt Rocks) to Takeshima for annexing it to Japan shows the Japanese authorities never regarded Dokdo as Japanese territory before 1905. Rather, Japan recognized Dokdo as a Joseon possession, which is supported by Inshu Shicho Gakki (A Collection of Observational Records of Inshu), the oldest Japanese work containing a reference to Dokdo, and the Dajokan Order of 1877 as well as pilots. He also casts doubts that the reason why Japan rushed the annexation of Dokdo during the Russo-Japanese War is because Japan might have determined to secure the island as Japanese territory in preparation for a defeat in the high-stakes battle with the Russian naval fleets. In addition, the paper reveals that the Korean government never remained silent on Japan's illegal annexation of Dokdo through the Report of Ulleungdo County Magistrate Shim Heung-taek who was informed of Japan's incorporation in 1906 and Deputy Prime Minister (Uijeongbu Chamg Daesin) Park Je-sun's Order No. 3.

The sixth paper is "Survey of Oki by the Japanese Navy Hydrographic Office and its Perception of Dokdo" written in 2013 by Han Cheol-ho, a professor at Dongkuk University and historian. By analyzing the Japanese Navy's Hydrographic Office's direct survey on Oki Islands in the late 19th century, Han Cheol-ho points out that Dokdo was consistently excluded from the boundary of the Oki Islands. While the Japanese Navy Hydrographic Office, which was in charge of hydrographic and coastal measurement, had an accurate understanding on the affiliation of islands, it did not include Dokdo as a subject of survey when measuring Japan's coastal areas and the Oki Islands. This reflects, the author explains, Japan's recognition that Dokdo is part of Korean territory, not an ancillary island of the Oki Islands. In particular, the paper examines that when Kimotsuki Kaneyuki, a director of the Japanese Navy's Hydrographic Office who played a key role in incorporating Dokdo to Japan's territory in 1905, took a survey on Japan's northwest coast including the Oki Islands, Dokdo was excluded from the survey area as well. The paper concludes that Japanese sea directories made before 1905 based on the result of Japanese Navy's Hydrographic Office's survey did not mark Dokdo as an ancillary island of the Oki Islands, but illustrated Ulleungdo and Dokdo as one set of islands in the east coast of Joseon, which showed the Japan's recognition of Dokdo as an ancillary island to Ulleungdo.

The seventh paper is "The Declaration of Ulleungdo and Usando (Dokdo) as Foreign Possessions by Japanese Dajokan Minister" in a book Historical Verification of Korea's Sovereignty over Ulleungdo and Dokdo written in 2010 by Song Byeong-kie, a professor emeritus of Dankook University. The author demonstrates that the Meiji government's policies on Ulleungdo including the Dajokan Order of 1877 were influenced by the ban on sailing to Ulleungdo imposed by the Edo Shogunate in the late 17th century. By examining diplomatic negotiations between the Joseon and Japanese government on Japanese people's trespassing to Ulleungdo and illegal logging after 1883, the author sheds light on the historical background of the Imperial Decree No. 41 that stipulates Dokdo shall be placed under the jurisdiction of Uldo-gun (today's Ulleungdo). In this light, the paper concludes both Korea and Japan acknowledged Dokdo is Korean territory based on historical evidences.

The eighth paper is "A Study on How the Japanese Government of the Meiji Period Investigated and Disclaimed Jurisdiction over Dokdo" written in 2015 by Park Byoung-sup, a researcher and representative of "Dokdo=Takeshima

Issue Research Net". After analyzing the background of the Dajokan Order that prescribes "Ulleungdo and one other island have nothing to do with Japan" as well as documents written by the Shimane prefecture and Isotakeshima Rayakuzu (Simplified Map of Istotakeshima), the author proves that "one other island" is Dokdo. He also refutes Japanese studies fraught with contradictions that deny the other island is Dokdo. He also analyzes 12 maps that show changes in the administrative control of each region in Japan from 1871 to 1833 and indicates none of those maps illustrated Dokdo. In conclusion, the paper points out there were many occasions where the past Japanese governments regarded Dokdo as Korean territory, but the island was never viewed as part of Japan prior to 1905. Thus, the author concludes, the Japanese government's argument that Dokdo belongs to Japan does not stand to reason.

The ninth paper is "A Draft of the Peace Treaty with Japan by the British Ministry of Foreign Affairs, the Formation of the Attached Map (March 1951) and a Reconfirmation of Korea's Possession of Dokdo" written in 2005 by Jung Byung-joon, a professor at Ewha Womans University and historian. The author introduces an attached map to the draft of the San Francisco Peace Treaty with Japan by the British Ministry of Foreign Affairs as of April 7, 1951 and points out the British government, as a member of Allied Powers, reaffirmed Korea's sovereignty over Dokdo. He underscores that the British government's draft dated on April 7, 1951 received an official approval by 18 departments under the Foreign Ministry and 13 Ministries as the British government's final and official draft, and it was officially sent to the U.S. government as well as the Commonwealth nations including Canada, Australia and New Zealand. In addition, the attached map was included in the second and third drafts of the Peace Treaty with Japan by the British Ministry of Foreign Affairs, which evidently confirms that Dokdo was excluded from Japanese territory and included as part of Korean territory.

The tenth paper is "Japan's Incorporation of Takeshima into Its Territory in

1905" written in 1987 by Kazuo Hori, a professor at Kyoto University. As
mentioned in the epilogue, the paper critically reviews Historical-Geographical Study of Takeshima written by Kenzo Kawakami in 196 and demonstrates
Dokdo has been historically regarded as an ancillary island to Ulleungdo.
What makes this paper noteworthy is that it is the first paper to discover
and introduce the Dajokan Order of 1877 that prescribes "Ulleungdo and
one other island have nothing to do with Japan." The author points out that
as the Joseon and Japanese government concluded Ulleungdo belonged to
Joseon territory through diplomatic negotiations in late 17th century, Dokdo,
an ancillary island to Ulleungdo, naturally became irrelevant to discussions of
Japan's territory and the Japanese government never paid a special attention
to Dokdo after the Meiji Restoration. In conclusion, though the Japanese
government claims that Japan reconfirmed Dokdo as an inherent part of its
territory through the Cabinet Decision in 1905, the paper proves its obvious
falsehood based on the Dajokan Order of 1877.

The eleventh paper is "Tokdo or Takeshima? The International Law of Territorial Acquisition in the Japan–Korea Island Dispute" published in Stanford
Journal of East Asian Affairs by Sean Fern in 2005. The paper analyzes Korea
and Japan's claims of territorial sovereignty over Dokdo based on theories and
cases regarding territorial acquisition under the international law, drawing a
conclusion that Korea has a stronger claim than Japan. The author reminds us
that Korea never overlooked Japan's illegal incorporation of Dokdo in 1905
as proven by Deputy Prime Minister's Order No. 3, but it had no diplomatic channel to resist due to the deprival of diplomatic rights. The author
also points out Supreme Commander for the Allied Powers Index Number
(SCAPIN) 677 of 1946 excluded Dokdo from governmental and administrative territory of Japan, which shows that Dokdo was evidently acknowledged
as Korean territory by the international community, considering the absence
of Korean diplomats in laying out SCAPIN. On the other hand, Japan's occupation over Dokdo was only temporary during a precarious time of the Japa-

nese colonial era and Japan has failed to present legitimate grounds for proving Japan has occupied the island in the wake of World War II, he explains. The author mentions that as Dokdo issue is closely related to the unfortunate history of the two nations, intervention by the third party might lead to renewed hostilities and further divisions.

Last but not least, the twelfth paper is "Territorial Issue between Japan and Korea: Case of Takeshima/Dokdo (English version was published in 2010)" written in 2008 by Seichu Naito, a professor emeritus at Shimane University and historian. The author provides detailed critiques to each of "10 Issues of Takehima," a promotional pamphlet published by the Japanese Ministry of Foreign Affairs in February 2008. For instance, he refutes Japan's claim that Japan established its sovereignty over Dokdo by 17th century in the pamphlet by saying it does not make any sense because the ban on sailing to Ulleung-do by the Japanese government was issued in 1696. He also notes that the Japanese government only fails to provide logical grounds for its claim that Dokdo is an inherent part of Japanese territory. The author harshly criticizes the pamphlet for raising wrong historical awareness and intentionally omitting historically important facts including the Dajokan Order. He confesses that his strong criticism for the Japanese government, despite being a Japanese national, starts from a keen desire to save Japanese people from being swayed and humiliated by the Ministry's pamphlet full of errors.

After finishing a brief introduction to 12 papers in this book, Professor Seichu Naito's ardent appeal lingers in my mind. As a Japanese scholar who studies the history, he almost cries out to protect his own country's honor by underscoring "Japan needs to face squarely and respect historical facts." I hope the readers of this book can relate to his sincere appeal.

I would like to recommend you to read other articles, not included in this book, that offer in-depth analysis on Dokdo such as "Legal Issues Related to

Sovereignty over Dokdo and Its Maritime Boundary" by Professor Jon M. Van Dyke, "Japan's Island Problem" by Professor Alexis Dudden and "Cases Concerning Sovereignty over Islands before the International Court of Justice and the Dokdo/Takeshima Issue" by Professor Nico J. Schrijver and Researcher Vid Prislan.

In closing, the papers in this book do not necessarily reflect the views of the Northeast Asian History Foundation. In order to protect the copyrights of authors, the terms are used as they were originally used in papers. For example, "Dokdo" is the official English spelling for the island, but other terms such as Tokdo or Takehima are used in papers written by American or Japanese scholars. Of course, both Tokdo and Takeshima refer to Dokdo. In addition, some papers use the term "dispute" to explain issues regarding Dokdo, which might create confusion that there is a dispute over Dokdo. However, we decided to leave those terms intact in protection of the author's copyrights. Nonetheless, it is our firm position that Dokdo is an integral part of Korean territory historically, geographically, and under international law, and no territorial dispute exists regarding Dokdo.

Hong Seong-keun

Director of the Dokdo Research Institute,
Northeast Asian History Foundation

History Knows the Truth

A Day on Dokdo

Bang Jong-hyun

Professor, Seoul National University

Dokdo, the controversial island that captures our interest! We decided to explore Dokdo (獨島) before looking around the interior of Ulleungdo (鬱陵島).

On August 22nd at 3 a.m., an impressive number of over 80 people, including our group of 60 members, the Governor of Ulleungdo (鬱陵島司), and about a dozen Ulleungdo community leaders were supposed to leave from Dodong.

Our bustling footsteps echoed through the early morning calm in the coastal village, while a crisp sky with some twinkling little stars stretched out against the sounds of unusually gentle sea waves.

The peak of Seonginbong rose high to form Ulleungdo, of which records trace back to the Silla Dynasty (57 BC-935 AD). Seonginbong has stood still, witnessing Silla General Isabu (異斯夫) conquer the island [then, Usanguk (山國, Usan State)] with wooden lions about 1,500 years ago and the settlement of people on the island forbidden in the early Joseon Dynasty. Arriving at the waters off Dokdo, the destination of our journey, four and a half hours after departing from Dodong, we exclaimed with delight as if we had discovered a new island. Observed from the vessel, Dokdo consists of two separate islets, not a solitary island. Passing in front of Seodo (西島, West Island), our ship stopped from a distance between Seodo and Dongdo (東島, East Island). On top of Seodo, a large object that looked like a dog crouched down with its ears perked up, as if it would immediately bark at strangers. The peak of Seodo bulges in the shape of a pointed tip of a triangle.

Rowing a boat towards Dongdo, I found that rocks were raised high above the sea surface as if they were coarsely built artificial structures made of stones and cement to be easily crushed.

We got off the boat there and began to climb to the west cliff of Dongdo. On the right side, there was an open-ended cave, through which we could see the other side, and crystal clear water ran deep below. Sagongbawi Rock stood alone between Dongdo and Seodo, and behind it, Sajado lay with a large cave at its bottom that opened to three sides. It was quite unique to see so many open-ended caves, which are rarely seen in other places. We unloaded our luggage on the inclined coast covered with pebbles, which were swept and piled inwardly from the sea by waves, while crumbling rocks were falling from the top of the west cliff into the waters. After finishing our lunch, we decided to climb the cliff.

As it is not so tall but quite steep, a hasty climber could touch the wall with his nose. There was hardly a place to put my foot, while the rocks for hand holds crumbled easily and the creepers were too fragile to clutch. We barely managed to climb to the top, where not a pointed tip but an empty, rounded crater awaited us. While Baeknokdam Crater is located on the top of Mt. Halla, the crater of Dongdo sits deep down beneath the water level. This means that Dongdo is a hollowed-out island. On the surface of the rocky shell, a thin layer of soil had developed on the top, where only soft grasses, not any tall trees, grew. When asked about the number of flora species growing on Dokdo, Do Bong-seop, Dean of the College of Pharmacy, answered that there are merely 35-36 species of flora.

Getting on the boat again, four to five of us sailed towards Seodo, but it was impossible to climb it as the cliff was too steep. Instead, going around the island, we looked around for potable water, only to fail. Yet, there were three caves. In front of them, a square-like formation, large enough to accommodate hundreds of people, stretched so that it would be possible to stroll along it when waves are gentle.

This was when I thought about the origin of the name Dokdo.

As it consists of two islands, Yangdo (兩島) or Daedo (對島) would be a more appropriate name, not Dokdo, which means a solitary island standing alone. However, Daedo sounds like Daemado (對馬島). Considering Yangdo (Japanese still use this name today), its Korean version *duseom* contains *du*, which may sound similar to *dok* of Dokdo. However, it may be a stretch to interpret the name of Dokdo as such. Therefore, the first step should be to interpret *dok* as meaning something with the same phonetic sound.

Under this assumption, considering the interior of the island, which is empty with water on the floor, *dok* reminds us of the *dok* (water jar) that we normally use at home. As they look so similar in terms of their substance, nobody could say that it is wrong to liken the island to a water jar.

Yet, considering its external appearance, it is not reasonable to compare the island to a water jar. At the same time, it is more common to name islands after their topologies, and Dokdo may not be an exception. Even if it can be associated with a water jar, the formation of the two islands does not befit such a case in terms of appearance.

Moreover, Jukdo (竹島), which the Japanese currently use or used to call the island as documented in *Jibong Yuseol* (芝峰類說, Topical Discourses of Jibong), sounds far from its current name. In archaic consonants, the *juk* of Jukdo is pronounced *dyuk*, which may have possibly evolved into *duk*. However, such a transformation has only happened in the western dialect, not in the dialect of the island.

Therefore, after reasoning as above, I concluded that these seemed not to be the original meanings of its name.

Lastly, I thought about whether the name of the island originated from the meaning of Seokdo (石島), which could be called *dolseom* or *dokseom* in Korean. To prove this, there are two key points to solve: whether Dokdo appears to be made only of rocks; and in which dialect *dol* is pronounced as *dok*. If these are solved, Seokdo would be the most feasible interpretation of the name of Dokdo. First, Dokdo is made entirely of rocks, with little soil present. Second, *seok* (石) is pronounced as *dok* in the coastal villages of South Jeolla Province. For instance, *jeolgu*[1] is referred to as *dogutong*; *gi* (碁) as *dol* or *badok*;[2] and *dadeumidol*[3] as *dadeumidok*. Reflecting these examples, therefore, the name of the island originated from the meaning of Seokdo, which is *dokseom*, as the names of places on Ulleungdo did as well.

However, this reasoning is simply to explain that Dokdo or Dokseom (which it is currently called) could be from the meaning of Seokdo. This is only an assumption, and it would not be easy to clarify the original intention of the name.

Let's go back to the topology of Dokdo, which I explored. Simply put, it can be described as a mass of rock. It is made purely of rock with many open-ended caves. Its interior is empty and its outside is steep, while high winds constantly stir waves. There is hardly a place to plant any vegetables, let alone build a house. It would not be too much to say that it looks worthless and useless based on the observation of the island.

However, the waters off the island are reportedly rich with well-known sea animals and fish. According to *Seonghosaseol* (星湖僿說, Treatises on Practical Topics), one of the sea life species living on Dokdo was the sea lion (可支魚), which lived between the rocks and had no scales but a tale. While it clearly had four limbs, its rear legs were short and it could not move fast on the land but could swim swiftly. It made a sound similar to that of a child. As

---

1   *Jeolgu* refers to a traditional Korean mortar usually made of stone.—Trans.

2   *Gi* refers to stone (*dol*) or the play of go (*baduk*), and *badok* is the old Korean name of *baduk*.—Trans.

3   *Dadeumidol* refers to a traditional Korean block of stone used for pounding cloth on.—Trans.

it has flesh rich with oil, it was extracted and used for lighting. One member of our group caught three sea lions and brought them back as specimen. With just a glimpse, I believe, any lay person would say it is not a fish but a seal. It tastes similar to pork, and its fur is so smooth that it could be used as a valuable item. As experts assert that it is different from a seal, it must be a sea lion as described in *Seonghosaseol*.

In the waters or on the rocks near Dokdo, it is easy to spot sea lions that can be as big as a cow or as small as a dog. Only when considering the various sea life of the waters of Dokdo, can we realize its significant hidden value. Therefore, it is a blessing for Korea to have the island, which will be very useful in this regard.

Praying for a brighter future for the island in our minds, we got on the vessel and headed for Ulleungdo after 4 p.m. (This draft is the journal entry for a day and part of the report on the journey to Ulleungdo. On Korean Thanksgiving Eve, 1947)

<1947, *Newspaper of the Preparatory Department*, Gyeongseong University, no. 13>

On Where Dokdo Belongs

Shin Seok-ho

President, Guksagwan

(present National Institute of Korean History)

1. Preface

2. Topography and Resources of Dokdo

3. Name of Dokdo

4. Sambongdo and Dokdo

5. Dokdo and the Issue of Territorial Ownership over Ulleungdo

6. Development of Ulleungdo and Dokdo

7. Japan's Usurpation of Dokdo

8. Dokdo, after Japan's Annexation

9. Conclusion

1. Preface

In the summer of last year, the territorial issue between Korea and Japan over Dokdo (獨島) became a high-profile media story. The uninhabited island, located in the middle of the East Sea, or N 37°14′18″ and E 131°52′22″, lies 49 nautical miles southeast of Ulleungdo (蔚陵島). Throughout history, the island had been a part of Korean territory as belonging to Ulleungdo. However, in the wake of the Russo-Japanese War, Japan forcibly incorporated Dokdo into its territory, and since that time, the island has been regarded as falling under the jurisdiction of the main island of Japan. As we have broken out of Japan's yoke, today it is imperative for us to reclaim the island. Under the order of Civil Administrator An Jae-hong, I conducted a field survey of Dokdo over the course of some two weeks from August 16th of last year with Chu In-bong, Head of the Japanese Division of the Ministry of Foreign Affairs, Lee Bong-su, an editor at the Ministry of Education, and Han Gi-jun, an engineer at the Fisheries Bureau. Based on the research, I would like to clearly demonstrate through this paper that Dokdo was originally a part of Korea.

2. Topography and Resources of Dokdo

Dokdo consists of two main islands, Dongdo (東島, East Island) and Seodo (西島, West Island), surrounded by dozens of scattered islets and rocks. If observed from the seabed of the East Sea, which is some 2,000 *sim*[1] in depth, it rises above the sea surface in the shape of a candle stick with a pointed tip. Situated 200 meters away from each other, Dongdo and Seodo are tiny volcanic islands spanning some 1.5 and 1 nautical miles, respectively. The latter is about 150 meters high. The former is a hollowed-out island with a complete crater sitting on its top like an empty bowl. At the bottom of the crater, seawater flows in and out from the east wall. As Dongdo is made entirely of volcanic rock, not a single tree grows in its soil, except for sparsely scattered overgrown brush. Due to marine erosion, its slope features steep rock cliffs, thereby making the island difficult to climb. Around a number of oddly-shaped caves on

---

1   1 *sim* is equivalent to 1.83 meters.—Trans.

the cliffs and nearby rocky islets, sea lions (可支), also referred to as *otdosei* (海驢) in Japanese, live in flocks. A host of kelp, abalone, conch, sea cucumber, and sea urchin grow attached to the rocks on sea floor, while squid, mackerel, halibut, and other species of fish are abundant in the surrounding waters. The only space for a vessel to dock is between Dongdo and Seodo. On the western side of the former, a gravelly field stretches for over 100 *pyeong*[2] where the sites of houses built in the past by the residents of Ulleungdo as well as the Japanese remain. It may be possible to climb the island from here, but not everyone is able to do so due to its slippery slope of 60 degrees. There is also a flatland as wide as dozens of *pyeong* on the southern part of Dongdo which is difficult to access, because of its location and strong sea winds. According to *Joseon Engan Suiroshi* (朝鮮沿岸水路誌, Hydrographic Chart of Korea) and residents on Ulleungdo, a small amount of fresh water is produced from the southwestern area of Seodo, but I could not find it despite investigating several areas. In general, humans cannot permanently settle on Dokdo as it has neither flatland nor drinking water. However, it is still quite significant in terms of the fishery industry and military purposes.

3. Name of Dokdo

Although no clear record has been found describing the origin of the name of Dokdo, the phrase "Dokdo, part of the administrative district of Ulleungdo" appears in the report of the County Magistrate of Ulleungdo (鬱陵郡守) from the 5th day of the 3rd lunar month in the 10th year of Gwangmu (AD 1906), which is found in the Ulleungdo County Office. This implies that after Ulleungdo was developed in the 18th year of King Gojong's reign (AD 1881) during the Joseon Dynasty, its settlers seemed to name the island Dokdo as it stood solitarily in the middle of the East Sea. However, since the 9th year

---

2   1 *pyeong* is equivalent to 3.3 square meters.—Trans.

of Gwangmu (AD 1905, 38th year of Meiji), when Japan occupied the island during the Russo-Japanese War, the name of Dokdo disappeared from the current nautical charts and began to be replaced by others like the Japanese name of Takeshima (竹島), the French name of Liancourt, and the British name of Hornet. Since the 19th year of King Sukjong's reign, the Japanese used to call Ulleungdo Takeshima, but during King Gojong's reign (Japan's Meiji era), they renamed it Matsushima (松島) and then began referring to Dokdo as Takeshima. Renowned Japanese botanist Nakai Takenoshin (中井猛 之進) and historian Tsuboi Kumezo (坪井 九馬三) groundlessly claimed that the Japanese people of Oki Island (岐島) had called Dokdo Rantou (卵島), [i] which the late professor Tabohashi Kiyoshi (田保橋潔) of Keijo Imperial University eloquently refuted, proving its falsehood in his paper "Response to the Teachings of Dr. Tsuboi on the Name of Ulleungdo" published in *Seikyu Gakuso* (青丘學叢, Quarterly Journal of Articles), No. 4. The name Liancourt was named after the French whaling ship, which came across the island in the 15th year of King Heonjong's reign (AD 1849), while the name Hornet was from a steamer of the British China Fleet, which came across the island in the 6th year of King Cheoljong's reign (AD 1855). [ii] Despite that there are four names to refer to Dokdo as such, it was originally called Sambongdo (三峰島) during King Seongjong's reign in the Joseon Dynasty, and Japan acknowledged that the island was Korean territory during King Sukjong's reign. More recently, it is still most frequently used by the people of Ulleungdo as it belongs to Korea.

4. Sambongdo and Dokdo

Seongjong Sillok (成宗實錄, Annals of King Seongjong's Reign) included a number of reports on Sambongdo, especially in the records from the 2nd to the 12th years of King Seongjong's reign (AD 1471-1481). At that time, the island in the East Sea was regarded as a mirage. However, as a number of people from Gangwon and Hamgyeong Provinces reportedly went to the island to evade conscription and taxation, a navigation ban was imposed on it. At the same time, inspection and patrol forces were organized and dispatched to locate it several times, only to fail in their missions. However, Lee Geuk-gyun, Governor of Yeongan (Hamgyeong) Province [永安道(咸鏡道)觀察使], sent an expedition of 12 members including Kim Ja-ju of Yongheung, who succeeded in observing it. In *Seongjong Sillok*, there is a report by Kim Ja-ju as follows:

> The Ministry of Defense reported, "Kim Ja-ju from Yeongheung stated, 'In order to locate Sambongdo, the Governor of our Province decided to send an expedition of 12 people, including me and Song Yeong-ro as well as Kim Heung, Kim Han-yeong, and Lee Oeulmang, who had visited the island, by allowing the use of five merchant ships. On September 16, our ships departed from Onggumi, Gyeongseong and sailed towards the island… On the 25th, we docked our ships 7-8 *li*[3] west of the island. In the north, there were three rocks, islets, and small rocks in a row. There was one big island at the center, along with another smaller one, and seawater flowed in and out of both of them. Some 30 objects that looked like humans stood between them, which made us hesitant and frightened to approach closer. This is why we drew sketches of the islands.' Last year, Park Jong-won set sail from Gangwon but failed due to the winds. However, Kim Han-gyeong and his expedition departed from Onggumi, Gyeongseong and succeeded again in reaching the island and returning with sketches. Therefore, if we embark on another expedition following their course, I believe we will locate the island. I would like to ask for your permission to select and send one person with a talent both in literary and martial arts on an expeditionary mission to the island in April of next year, when the warm breeze blows." This request was granted.[iii]

---

3   1 *li* is equivalent to 392.7 meters.—Trans.

The expedition of Kim Ja-ju was not able to land on the island but only observed it from 7-8 *li* (some 3 kilometers) to the west. What they saw was exactly the same Dokdo as we know it today. For instance, the three rocks standing in a row to the north that Kim Ja-ju described are the ones rising high to the northwest of Seodo. He also mentioned islets and small rocks, which correlate with the numerous islets between Dongdo and Seodo. The central island he mentioned refers to Seodo, while the smaller one in the west is a rocky islet rising high to the southeast of Dongdo. These features are all similar to the formations of Dokdo. Kim also commented that seawater flowed in and out, which is also identical to the conditions on Dokdo. He said that he saw thirty objects that looked like humans between the islands, seemingly mistaking sea lions as such. In short, by around 480 years ago (at the end of 15th century, King Seongjong's reign), Korean people had already discovered Dokdo and named it Sambongdo. However, back then, since authorities imposed a travel ban on the island as well as Ulleungdo, it disappeared from history for over 400 years until Ulleungdo was redeveloped in the 18th year of King Gojong's reign.

5. Dokdo and the Issue of Territorial Ownership over Ulleungdo

Over 250 years ago, during King Sukjeong's reign, Korea was engaged in a diplomatic row with Japan over the sovereignty of Ulleungdo for several years. To explain its relation to Dokdo, I would like to briefly outline the developments of the dispute, while explaining details later in another paper. It is indisputable that Ulleungdo was Korean territory throughout history, having been called Usanguk (于山國) during the Three Kingdoms Period in Korea (BC 57 - AD 668) and Ulleungdo (鬱陵島), Ulleungdo (蔚陵島), Ureungdo (芋陵島), Ureungdo (羽陵島), Mureungdo (武陵島), or Mureungdo (茂陵島) during the Goryeo Dynasty (AD 918-1392). In the wake of the invasion of the Jurchens during King Hyeonjong's reign in the early Goryeo Dynasty (11th century), residents of the island evacuated to the mainland of Korea, seemingly leaving the island uninhabited from that point.[iv] From the end of the Goryeo Dynasty to the founding of the Joseon Dyansty (14th century), a number of people living in the coastal areas of Gangwon Province moved to Ulleungdo. However, it was not easy to access the island as it was far away from land, and many people were drowned due to high waves and winds on their journey there. At the same time, the majority of the migrants intended to avoid military service and taxation. The island was also vulnerable to invasion by the Japanese pirates (倭寇). For these reasons, Kim In-u, who lived in Samcheok, was appointed as Provincial Commissioner (按撫使) for Ulleungdo to relocate 80 residents there in the 17th year of King Taejong's reign and again in the 7th year of King Sejong's reign (AD 1425). In the 20th year of King Sejong's reign (AD 1438), Nam Hoe was appointed as Third Deputy Commander (護軍) and sent to relocate over 60 settlers, and a navigation ban to the island was issued.[v] However, as fishing near the island was lucrative, it was impossible to completely stop the fishermen in the coastal areas of Gyeongsang and Gangwon Provinces from coming, and therefore, only the settlement of people was restricted. As Ulleungdo was completely empty, Japanese fishermen from Inaba (因幡) and Hoki (伯耆) Provinces, Shimane Prefecture, began to come to fish off the coast of Ulleungdo, which they called Isotakeshima (磯竹島) or Takeshima (竹島) at that time, probably because thick-stemmed bamboo grew there. Then, in the 19th year of King Sukjong's reign [AD 1693, 6th year of Japan's Genroku (元禄)], Korean fishermen from Dongnae, Gyeongsang Province, including An Yong-bok, encountered and clashed with Japanese fishermen from Hoki Province at Ulleungdo. This escalated into a territorial dispute between the two countries, as Japan requested that Korea prevent Korean fishermen from accessing Takeshima as it was Japanese territory, while Korea argued that as Takeshima was the same as Ulleungdo, a Korean territory, Japanese fishermen should be denied voyage to the island. After years of such diplomatic altercations between the two, in the 23rd year of King Sukjong's reign (AD 1697, 10th year of Genroku), Japan's Edo Shogunate (江戸幕府) finally withdrew its wrongful claim and officially confirmed Joseon's sovereignty over Takeshima, thereby banning the passage of Japanese fishermen to the island. This historical event was clearly documented in the Korean materials of *Sukjong Sillok* (肅宗實錄, Annals of King Sukjong's Reign), *Dongmun Hwigo* (同文彙考, Documents on Foreign Relations), and *Tongmungwanji* (通文館志, Records on Foreign Relations with China and Japan) as well as the Japanese records of *Chosen Tsuko Daiki* (朝鮮通交大紀, Chronicles of Diplomatic Relations with Joseon), *Honpou Chosen Oufukusyo* (本邦朝鮮往復書, Records on Diplomatic Relations with Joseon), and *Tsuko Ichiran* (通航一覽, Records on Diplomatic Relations). In the 3rd year of King Heonjong's reign [AD 1837, 8th year of Japan's Tenpo (天保)], Japan executed Hachiemon (八右衛門), a non-resident (*mushuku*, 無宿) from Matsubaraura (松原浦), Hamada (濱田), and Iwaminokuni (石見國) for smuggling in Ulleungdo to keep their promise with Korea. This event was also recorded in *Gaikou Shiko* (外交誌稿, Transcripts on Foreign Relations), *Nihon Zaisei Keizai Shiryo* (日本財政經濟史料, Data for Japanese Financial and Economic History), and "*Tokaido Shuku Shukusonhure* (東海道宿宿村觸, Public Notices of Station Towns along the East Town Road)" which was cited in the paper of Hibata Sekko (樋畑雪湖) published in the *Rekishi Chiri* (歷史地理, Historical Geography), Vol. 55, No. 6. As such, Japan had acknowledged that Takeshima was Korean territory and banned Japanese fishermen from the island by the end of the Edo Shogunate. Japan's confirmation on Ulleungdo means that it also recognized that Dokdo, or Takeshima as the Japanese call it today, was an integral part of Korean territory as it was an ancillary island of Ulleungdo.

6. Development of Ulleungdo and Dokdo

Even after the territorial dispute over Ulleungdo was resolved, Korean authorities still forbade settlement on the island and dispatched the County Magistrate of Pyeonghae (平海郡守) or the County Magistrate of Uljinhyeon

(蔚珍縣令) every two years to patrol whether there were any settlers there. They also collected thick-stemmed bamboo, aromatic trees, and wild ginseng and hunted sea lions. In Japan, however, since the Shogunate was overthrown by the Meiji Restoration, all bans imposed during the Shogunate era were lifted and exploring overseas was encouraged. At this time, Japanese people began to enter Ulleungdo, calling it Matsushima, and illegally logged its dense forests, which had been left untouched for over 1,000 years. Their theft of Ulleungdo's timber led Korea to seriously protest to Japan's Acting Minister of Foreign Affairs (外務卿代理) Ueno Kagenori (上野景範) in the 18th year of King Gojong's reign (AD 1881, 14th year of Meiji).[vi] At the same time, Korean authorities appointed Fourth Deputy Commander (副護軍) Lee Gyu-won as Military Inspector to Ulleungdo (鬱陵島檢察使) to closely inspect its internal and external conditions and then to recruit those who wanted to move to the island as changing its previous repatriation policy.[vii] Once the door to the island that had been tightly closed for hundreds of years was opened with the issuance of the Development Order (開拓令), a great number of people not only from coastal communities in Gangwon and Gyeongsang Provinces but also from Jeolla and Chungcheong Provinces flocked to the island, enabling settlers to reclaim its mountains and valleys in the first year of development. In the following year, the Island Superintendent (島長) of Ulleungdo was appointed, and in the 5th year of Gwangmu (AD 1901), the position was elevated to County Magistrate. According to 85-year-old Hong Jae-hyeon, Choe Heung-uk, and Choe Hak-mok, who migrated to Ulleungdo from Gangreung in the first year of development, Dokdo could be viewed from Ulleungdo when the weather was clear. So soon after the development of Ulleungdo many went there to collect kelp and abalone or catch sea lions, including Hong, who had visited Dokdo over a dozen times. This was also reported in *Chosen Engan Suiroshi* published by the Japanese Navy. In other words, in the 8th year of Gwangmu (AD 1904, 37th year of Meiji), one year before Japan forcibly incorporated Dokdo into its territory, the Japanese warship *Tsushima* conducted a survey of Dokdo and documented that fishermen living on Ulleungdo had built small thatched houses and stayed for over 10 days on Dokdo to hunt sea lions.[viii] This clearly attests to the fact that Dokdo became a part of Korean territory after the development of Ulleungdo, which is why the County Magistrate of Ulleungdo reported on Dokdo to the central government, stating "Dokdo, part of the administrative district of Ulleungdo," in the 10th year of Gwangmu.

7. Japan's Usurpation of Dokdo

While history irrefutably shows that Dokdo, as an ancillary island to Ulleungdo, was a part of Korea, in the 9th year of Gwangmu (AD 1905, 38th year of Meiji), during the Russo-Japanese War, Japan abused the opportunity of Dokdo being uninhabited, thereby referring to it as Takeshima, the old name used for Ulleungdo. On February 2nd of the same year, Japan arbitrarily incorporated the island into Oki Island (隠岐島), Shimane Prefecture,[ix] and used it as a supply base for its Navy.[x] In the 3rd lunar month of the following year, or the 10th year of Gwangmu, over a dozen of Japanese officials, including Governor of Oki (隠岐島司) Higashi Bunsuke (東文輔), traveled to Dokdo and declared that Dokdo was under the jurisdiction of Japan, demanding that Korean fishermen not come to Dokdo. County Magistrate of Ulleungdo Shim Heung-taek, within the context of losing an important ancillary island, which was a famous producer of sea lions, submitted the following report to the provincial and central government:

> Report
> Dokdo, part of the administrative district of Ulleungdo, is located over 100 *li* east from here. On the 4th day of this month, at 7-9 a.m., a steamer docked at the Dodong port of Ulleungdo, and then a party of Japanese officials came to the official residence and said they had come to conduct a field survey on Dokdo as it came under the jurisdiction of Japan. Among them were Higashi Bunsuke, Governor of Oki; Jinzai Yoshitaro

(神田西由太郎), Deputy Director (事務官); Yoshida Heigo (吉田平吾), Director of Tax Supervision (稅務監督局長); Kageyama Iwahachiro (影山岩八郎), Chief of Police Substation (分署長警部); and a police officer, a doctor, an engineer, and 10 other people. They first asked and recorded the number of households, population, land, and production volume, and general affairs, such as the number of officials and expenses. This is why I am submitting this report and ask for your review on this issue. On the 5th day of the 3rd lunar month, 10th year of Gwangmu.

This was reproduced from the copy of the report archived in the local government building of Ulleungdo. It is not clear how it was processed afterward. However, at that time, as the Korean government had already been taken under the control of Japan and the fate of the entire nation hung by a thread, the Korean government did not have the luxury of attending to an uninhabited islet like Dokdo nor did it have the capacity to fight against Japan's claim. This was how Dokdo was forcibly incorporated by Japan, and only the Japanese name of Takeshima appears on nautical maps today.*

8. Dokdo after Japan's Annexation

After Japan arbitrarily took Dokdo from Korea, it forbade Korean fishermen from fishing there. Geographically, however, Dokdo is located a distant 86 nautical miles away from Oki Island and 130 nautical miles from the border of Shimane Prefecture (島根県境市) of Japan, while it is merely 49 nautical miles from Ulleungdo. Therefore, even after the forced incorporation, Ulleungdo residents used the island more than the Japanese. This explains why Dokdo was documented as part of Korea both in *Joseon Engan Suiroshi* and *Kankoku Suisanshi* (韓国水産誌, Korean Fisheries Guide), published by the

* at the time of the article was written.

Japanese government and the Japanese Residency-General of Korea, respectively. The latter was compiled and published by Japanese officials working in Korea, including Ihara Fumikazu (庵原文一), Chief of the Fishery Division of the Ministry of Agriculture and Commerce of the Korean government, after a field survey on all Korean islands and islets and the recording of their locations, resources, and other information in the 2nd year of Yunghui (AD 1908), three years after Japan's incorporation of Dokdo. The book included Takeshima (Liancourt Rocks), or Dokdo, in "Chapter 7 Articles of Hydrographic Notices, Part 1 Geography," vol. 1, which recognized it as an ancillary island of Korea. In 1933 [8th year of Showa (昭和)], along with *Honshu Engan Suiroshi* (本州沿海水路誌, Hydrographic Map of Japan's Honshu), the Japanese Navy published *Joseon Engan Suiroshi*, which also described Ulleungdo and Dokdo in "Chapter 3 East Coast of Joseon," meaning they both belonged to Korea. As *Kankoku Suisanshi* is also available in the National Library, anyone can borrow it. However, as *Honshu Engan Suiroshi* was developed exclusively for the Japanese Navy, it is not accessible for ordinary people. I accidentally found the book in the office of the captain of the *Taejeon*, belonging to the Pohang base of the Korean Coast Guard, which significantly contributed to this Dokdo research. Thanks to the help of Lieutenant Junior Jo Jeong-u, Captain of the *Taejeon*, I was able to borrow the book and excerpt the entire part on Takeshima. I believe that this book holds the key to solving the Dokdo issue. Thanks to this book, I am able to clearly state in Section 6 hereof that Ulleungdo fishermen built small thatched houses and stayed for over ten days on Dokdo to hunt sea lions before Japan's forcible incorporation, which attests to the fact that it belonged to Korea.[viii] If Dokdo was historically under the jurisdiction of Japan, these two books would not have included it, as they only covered Korean islands and islets. *Honshu Engan Suiroshi*, which I also saw in the captain's office of the *Taejeon*, described only the name of Dokdo in "Section 2 Coast of the Sea of Japan," while *Joseon Engan Suiroshi* included detailed information on its location, topography, and resources. It did so because Dokdo was a part of Korean territory throughout history, and it was most reasonable to view it as a part of Korea from a geographical perspective. These two books of the Japanese government and its Residency-General in Korea are sufficient to substantiate that Dokdo was under the jurisdiction of Korea. Meanwhile, in the article "Relations of Japan and Joseon over Takeshima in Japan's Sea" published in *Rekishi Chiri*, Vol. 55, No. 6, in June 1930 (5th year of Showa), the Japanese scholar Hibata Sekko mentioned, "Takeshima and Ulleungdo belong to Gangwon Province, Joseon, as Joseon's territory, which is located in the eastern-most area of the Sea of Japan," thus confirming that Dokdo was recognized as Korean territory.

9. Conclusion

I believe that the ancient records of Korea and Japan as well as the documents presented in this research have substantiated that Dokdo was a part of Korean territory throughout history. To summarize, the findings are as follows.

(1) Dokdo is identical to the island known as Sambongdo during King Seongjong's reign and came under the jurisdiction of Korea in the 15th century.

(2) When Japan confirmed that Takeshima (Ulleungdo) was Korean territory in King Sukjong's reign, it is deemed that Japan also acknowledged Dokdo, an ancillary island of Ulleungdo, as a part of Korean territory.

(3) According to the elderly Ulleungdo resident Hong Jae-hyeon, as well as *Joseon Engan Suiroshi* published by the Japanese Navy, it is evident that Dokdo belonged to Korea as a place where Ulleungdo fishermen freely visited from the development of Ulleungdo until the 9th year of Gwangmu (AD 1904, 37th year of Meiji).

(4) According to the report of the County Magistrate of Ulleungdo on the 5th day of the 3rd lunar month in the 10th year of Gwangmu, as well as *Teikoku Chimei Jiten* (帝國地名辭典, Dictionary of Japanese Place Names) and other Japanese geography books, it is clearly demonstrated that Japan forcibly

took Dokdo from Korea during the Russo-Japanese War.

(5) As Dokdo inherently belonged to Joseon and it was most reasonable to view it as a part of Korea from a geographical perspective, *Joseon Engan Suiroshi* and *Kankoku Suisanshi* recorded by the Japanese government and Japan's Residency-General in Korea as well as Japanese scholar Hibata Sekko acknowledged Dokdo as an ancillary island of Korea.

(6) The MacArthur Line, which has defined the current fishing area of Japan, passes about 12 nautical miles east of Dokdo and expressly categorizes Dokdo within Korea's fishing zone.

Based on the six reasons above, I firmly believe that we can restore our sovereignty over Dokdo and that Korean foreign affairs authorities will bring a good result to the Korean people over this issue. This concludes my research on Dokdo, which I hope I can return the favor of Chief of Civil Administration, An Jae-hong, who is committed to successfully resolving the issue of Dokdo. For helping me during this research, I would like to extend my gratitude to Administrator An and other officials at the central administration; Gwon Dae-il, Chief of the Local Department of North Gyeongsang Province, who offered much help during the investigation; Captain Jo Jeong-u of the *Taejeon* of the Korean Coast Guard; Seo I-hwan, Governor of Ulleungdo (鬱陵島司) and other Ulleungdo officials and residents; Song Seok-ha, Head of the Chosun Alpine Club; and all the members of the Ulleungdo Academic Research Team.

Notes

i   Nakai Takenoshin, "Ulleungdo," *Rekishi Chiri* 38, no. 3 (September, 10th year of Taisho); Tsuboi Kumezo, "About Takeshima," ibid. 56, no. 1 (5th year of Showa); and Tabohashi Kiyoshi, "Response to the Teachings of Dr. Tsuboi on the Name of Ulleungdo," *Seikyu Gakuso*. no. 4 (May, 6th year of Showa).

ii   Tabohashi Kiyoshi, "Ulleungdo: Its Discovery and Sovereignty," *Seikyu Gakuso*, no. 3 (February, 6th year of Showa).

iii   *Seongjong Sillok* 72, October, 10th year of Seongjong.

iv   *Goryeosa* 4, November, 9th year of Hyeonjong; ibid., July, 10th year of Hyeonjong; ibid., July, 13th year of Hyeonjong.

v   *Taejong Sillok* (太宗實錄, Annals of King Taejong's Reign) 32, September, 16th year of Taejong; ibid. 33, February, 17th year of Taejong; *Sejong Sillok* (世宗實錄, Annals of King Sejong's Reign) 29, August, 7th year of Sejong; *Sejong Sillok* 81, April, 20th year of Sejong; and "Mountains and Streams of Uljin County (Ulleungdo)," *Shinjeung Dongguk Yeoji Seungnam* (新增東國輿地勝覽, Revised and Augmented Geographical Survey of Joseon), July, 20th year of Sejong.

vi   *Ilsoengnok* (日省錄, Collection of Journal Entries), May, 18th year of Gojong; and attachment 1 *Byeongeum* (邊禁) and 2 *Shinsa* (辛巳) in *Dongmun Hwigo* (同文彙考, Documents on Foreign Relations).

vii   *Seungjungwon Ilgi* (承政院日記, Diaries of the Royal Secretariat), June 5, 18th year of Gojong.

viii   "Takeshima in the East Coast of Joseon," *Joseon Engan Suiroshi* 3: "There is little space to build houses. When the warship *Tsushima* conducted a field survey in November of the 37th year of Meiji, small thatched houses existed on the East Island, but they were significantly destroyed due to winds and waves. Every summer, as many as dozens of fishermen visit the island from Ulleungdo to hunt sea lions. They usually build small houses and stay for about 10 days each time."

ix   Ota Tamesaburo (太田為三郎), "Takeshima," *Teikoku Chimei Jiten* 2 (45th year of Meiji: 940-41).

x   Tsuboi Kumezo, "About Takeshima," *Rekishi Chiri* 56, no. 1 (July, 5th year of Showa).

Historical Contemplation of Different Names of Dokdo – the Study of Names; Usando and Takeshima

Lee Byeong-do

Professor Emeritus, Seoul National University

1. Although Dokdo—called Usando in ancient Korea and named Takeshima (竹島) by the Japanese—is currently the object of a national dispute between Korea and Japan, it is indisputable that Dokdo is historically and geographically Korean territory. Also, in my opinion, the origin of its name alone justifies the fact that Dokdo is an ancillary island to Ulleungdo. Since the dispute over Dokdo arose, official documents have been exchanged between Korea and Japan several times and many academic discussions have been held. However, most of these documents and discussions dealt with the subject from a historical, geographical, or legal perspective. To my knowledge, no consideration on a purely academic basis has been given to the origin of the island's name yet. Thus, I decided to take this opportunity to delve into the different names given to Dokdo and clarify the affiliation of Dokdo, while providing data to support or counter pertinent arguments that have generated controversy.

2. Before going into the details, I feel it is necessary to describe Japan's past seizure of Dokdo and its background. It would seem out of context to jump into

to the name issue without explaining this pillaging of Korea. More importantly, it must be remembered at all times that Japan's occupation of Dokdo
was one of the Japanese imperialists' first moves in its conquest of Korea.

Then, when and how did imperialist Japan seize Dokdo? The Russo-
Japanese War, which broke out in February 1904 and came to a close around
August 1905, provided a context for Japan's plot to invade and absorb Korea
into its sphere of influence. Immediately after the outbreak of the war, the
Japanese government forced Korea to sign the Korea-Japan Treaty of 1904 and
took over major locations in Korea for their own military use. In August of the
same year, as the war continued to develop in a manner favorable to Japan,
Japan concluded the Korea-Japan Protocol of August 1904 with Korea, as the
first step towards taking control of all matters concerning foreign relations and
the finances of Korea. This treaty required Korea to consult one financial adviser and one diplomatic adviser designated by the Japanese government to su-
pervise and monitor Korea's financial and diplomatic matters. The diplomatic
adviser then was an American named D. W. Stevens. He was apparently a pro-
Japanese collaborator as he was designated by the Japanese government and
was later shot to death by a Korean in San Francisco. When this adviser system
was first adopted, Yozaburo Nakai—a fisherman from Okinoshima—submitted a petition to the Japanese government requesting the annexation of Korea's
Dokdo into Japanese territory and permission to rent the island. His petition
was submitted to the three Ministries of Home Affairs; Foreign Affairs; and
Agriculture and Commerce. The Japanese government did not instantly grant
this petition. However, in February 1905 when victory in the Russo-Japanese
War was imminent, the government stealthily discussed and agreed to the
annexation of Dokdo into the Shimane Prefecture without even notifying
Korea. In November of the same year, Japan forcefully concluded the second
Korea-Japan Agreement or Eulsa Restriction Treaty, which deprived Korea of
its diplomatic sovereignty and made Korea a protectorate of Japan. Based on
this treaty, Japan established a Residency-General in Seoul and stationed a
Resident-General who took control of every Korean state affair. It was then

that Korea officially lost its freedom and independence and failed to function as a sovereign state. In March 1906, several months after the establishment of the Residency-General, the Japanese government sent a group of public officials from the Shimane Prefecture (scores of them, including one named Kanda) to Ulleungdo to notify County Magistrate of Ulleungdo Sim Heung-taek that they "dropped by Ulleungdo after making an inspection of Dokdo as the island has now become Japanese territory." It was a cunning and brazen plot of Japan to not only clandestinely annex Korea's domain but also to have its local officials blurt out claims about the island under the guise of an inspection after extorting Korea's national freedom and independence.

Although County Magistrate Shim reported this event to the central government in written form, the Korean government at the time could not afford to pay any attention to this tiny island in the East Sea as the entire country was on the verge of falling into the hands of the Japanese. Also, the Korean government was already deprived of its diplomatic sovereignty and placed under the control of Japan, thus stripped of its ability to make any protest. While the Eulsa Treaty of 1905 and the Korea-Japan Annexation Treaty of 1910 may be described as a robbery (for they stole the freedom and independence of Korea through force), the annexation of Dokdo four to five years earlier took the form of a pure act of theft. However it is put, it was indisputably the first important premeditated step of Japan aimed at making Korea a victim of Japanese imperialism.

Now that Korea has regained its sovereignty, after its liberation from Japanese colonial rule, nothing should prevent Korea from recovering its sovereignty and jurisdiction over Dokdo. It is the way it should be. However, the Japanese government is still intoxicated with the illusion of imperialism and continues to claim that Dokdo is its territory. Japan argues that, while Ulleungdo has historically fallen under Korea's jurisdiction, Dokdo (or Takeshima as Japan claims) was an uninhabited island outside of Korea's jurisdiction and it has belonged to Japan since olden times. However, if such a claim were true, why would Japan have gone through the trouble of annexing the island into its territory prior to the invasion of Korea? This question pushes Japan into a corner. Most importantly, thought should be given to whether it stands to reason to claim that Ulleungdo and Dokdo (also Usando or Takeshima as the Japanese assert) each fell under the jurisdiction of two different states considering their geographical proximity and the connection inherent in the origin of their names. First, although Dokdo is located between Ulleungdo and Japan's Okinoshima, the distance between Dokdo and Ulleungdo stands at 49 *li* (about 19 kilometers) whereas the distance between Dokdo and Okinoshima reaches roughly 80 *li* (about 31 kilometers). In short, Ulleungdo and Dokdo share an inseparable destiny as a main island and its ancillary island, or as a mother island and its child island. Since the main (mother) island of Ulleungdo is under Korea's jurisdiction, it is only right that the sister (child) island of Dokdo should also be considered Korea's territory. Conversely, had Ulleungdo been considered Japanese territory, then Dokdo should also have been considered Japanese territory.

    The inseparable relationship between Ulleungdo and Dokdo can be more clearly explained by looking into the many names historically given to the two islands by Korea and Japan and their backgrounds. Thus, I will now deal with the name issue.

3. The name Dokdo became known recently, especially during the Gwangmu era. Traditionally, the island was known in Korea as Usan (written 于山 and 芋 山 in Chinese characters). Usan (于山) was originally an ancient name of Ul-leungdo, which had also been called Ureung (written 芋陵 and 羽陵), Ulleung (written 蔚陵 and 鬱陵), and Mureung (written 武陵 and 茂陵) in accordance with ancient documents. Over time, Usan (both 于山 and 芋山) came to refer to Dokdo only. Then, how did Ulleungdo obtain such names in the first place and how did some of them come to indicate Dokdo? In my opinion, the answer should be sought from the historical background of the mainland. From ancient times, Ulleungdo and Dokdo could be accessed most conveniently from Uljin of Gangwon Province. Uljin was Ujinya (于珍也)-hyeon during

the Goguryeo Dynasty and was changed to Uljin-gun during the Silla Dynasty. This name lasted through the Goryeo Dynasty and Joseon Dynasty to this day. In short, Ujinya—a name from the Goguryeo era that was changed to Uljin afterwards—was the port for ships going to and from Ulleungdo, and the "U" from Ujinya and the "Ul" from Uljin were brought together to create Ulleungdo. In turn it spun off different names including Usan (于山), Ureung (芋陵), Ulleung (蔚陵), and Ulleung (鬱陵). Usan (于山) and Usan (芋山) were again assigned to an island (present-day Dokdo) that had frequent exchanges with Ulleungdo as its sister island. The two islands belonged to Uljin-gun administratively, and Korea's geography book published at that time carries the pertinent articles in the Uljin section.

It was customary back then to name an island after the port it could be most conveniently accessed from or the port it was in closest proximity to. Jejudo, called Tamla (耽羅) in ancient times, serves as a suitable example. Tamla was the name used to refer to Jejudo after the era of the Three Kingdoms. Some historical records refer to it as Tammora (乇牟羅 or 牟羅) and Tamla (乇羅). These names originated from Tamjin (耽津) of Gangjin, Jeollanam-do on the mainland—a port and a major gateway to the island. Gangjin was Domu (道武)-gun during the Baekje Dynasty, and Dongeum (冬音)-hyeon within Domu-gun came to be called Tamjin (耽津 or 乇津) during the Silla Dynasty.

Chimmidarye (忱彌多禮, Tomutare) of Namman (南蠻, meaning "southern barbarians"), found in Yonjukyunenjo of Zinguki of *Nihon Shoki* (日本書紀, The Chronicles of Japan) is also viewed as referring to Tamjin. Therefore, it can be concluded that Domu, Dongeum, Chimmi, and Tam, all of which were the names for one port, came to refer to Jejudo across the sea. The fact that Tamjin served as an important port in exchanges between Jejudo and the mainland is well described in the section of Tamla-hyeon in Volume 2 of *Goryeosa Jiriji* (高麗史地理誌, Geography Section of the History of Goryeo): "…至第十五代孫 高厚高淸昆弟 三人 造舟渡海 至于耽津 盖新羅盛時也." This phrase is followed by "邑號曰耽羅 蓋以來時初泊耽津故也." While it is erroneous to say that the name Tamla first appeared during the Silla period, it provides a historical basis for the fact that the name was derived from Tamjin.

Another good example may be Seungcheonpo on the northern shore of Ganghwado Island. The name Seungcheonpo undoubtedly came from Seung-cheon-bu or Seungcheon-gun of the Goryeo period located across the sea on the mainland, which is present-day Pungdeok-myeon, Gaepung-gun. In addition, a town called Sapyeong-ri used to exist in Sindong-myeon, Siheung-gun of the past on the southern bank of the Han River, and this name originates from the river port earlier called Sapyeongdo. It is also a fun fact that Jang-howon of Icheon-gun, Gyeonggi Province and Janghowon of Eumseong-gun, Chungcheongbuk Province share the same name as the port in between them.

The above examples imply that the name Usan must have moved to Dok-do from Ulleungdo in the wake of frequent exchanges between the two islands and establishes Dokdo's connection to Ulleungdo as its sister island.

4. I have looked into the historical background of the name Usan used by Koreans so far. Now I intend to move on and state my views about the name Takeshima (竹島) used by Japan. Though the Japanese refer to Dokdo as Takeshima today, they originally referred to Ulleungdo as Takeshima or Iso-takeshima (磯竹島). Takeshima is no doubt a shortened form of Isotakeshima, which must be explained in detail here. I mentioned this subject to give tips to Mr. Hwang Sang-gi—a graduate student of law at Seoul National University—as a thesis adviser and evaluator for his thesis entitled "Study of the Dokdo Issue" in 1954 when I served as the dean of the Graduate School of Seoul National University. I also briefly dealt with this subject in my paper entitled "Contemplation on the Name Goguryeo," published in a *SNU Dissertation Collection* (Volume 3 of *Humanities and Social Sciences*). However, I would like to state my opinion in depth here. While conducting research for his thesis, the abovementioned Mr. Hwang discovered some ancient Japanese-made maps housed at SNU's library, including *Chosen Seihyo Zenzu* (朝鮮世表全圖, Standard Map of Joseon) published by *Naniwa Shoshi* (浪華書肆) in 1789 and *Chosen Hachidonozu* (朝鮮八道之圖, Map of the Eight Provinces of

Joseon) made by Shihei Hayashi in 1806. In one of those maps, Ulleungdo is marked as both Ulleungdo and Cheonsanguk (千, read as "cheon," is similar in shape to 于, read as "u"), with a drawing of a mountain added next to those names and a word in Chinese characters 弓嵩 (read as "gungsung") inside the drawing. Next to this drawing is the word Isotake written in Japanese characters. These words were also marked on *Map of the Three Neighboring Countries of Great Japan* (大日本接壤三國之圖) of an unknown period published by *Naniwa Shorin* (浪花書林). I could not help but slap my knee in astonishment when I came across this map. I instantly recognized 弓嵩 written exactly as it is used in Korea and conjectured that Isotake was a liberal translation of 弓嵩. Assuredly, 弓嵩 must have come from an ancient document or map. The Japanese mapmaker must have inquired about this term to a person from Ulleungdo and loosely translated it as Isotake.

Then, what does 弓嵩 or Isotake stand for? It refers to Seonginbong Peak (present-day Jungbong Peak) located in the center of Ulleungdo. 弓 (read as "goong") is a Chinese character borrowed to phonetically represent the Hangeul word *gom* (meaning "bear"), while 嵩 (read as "soong") was borrowed to represent the Hangeul word *suri* or *sul*, meaning "high mountain or peak." Therefore, 弓嵩 is equivalent to *gomsuri*. Gom is found to have been phonetically represented by 弓 also in the Gojoseon section of Volume 1 of *Samguk Yusa* (三國遺事, Memorabilia of the Three Kingdoms): "弓忽山 又名 今彌達." 今彌 (read as "geummi") is a phonetic representation of *gomi*, which is the same as *gom*. Therefore, 弓忽山 (read as "gungholsan") converted to pure Hangeul form is *gomgolsan* and 今彌達 (read as "geummidal") converted to pure Hangeul form is *gomidal*, both of which are equivalent in meaning. Other ancient place names containing 弓 include 弓漢 (read as "gunghan"), 弓谷 (read as "gunggok"), 弓村 (read as "gungchon"), 弓山 (read as "gungsan"), 弓島 (read as "gungdo"), and many more. 弓 is assuredly used as a phonetic representation of *gom* in all these cases, and needless to say *gom* was an animal considered divine in ancient times. 嵩 is found to have been phonetically represented as *suri* or *sul* in the fact that 松岳 (read as "songak")—a mountain located in Gaeseong—was also marked as 崧山 (read as "sungsan"), 嵩山 (read as "sungsan"), and 神嵩 (read as "sinsung"). The Chinese character 松 (read as "song") in the mountain's original name is also a mere phonetic representation of the Hangeul terms *suri*, *sul*, and *sol*, and 崧山 (read as "sungsan") and 嵩山 (read as "sungsan") both are equivalent in pronunciation and meaning. In the Sungsanmyo section of Volume 17 of *Goryeo Dogyeong* (高麗圖經, Records of Observations in Goryeo), the phrase "其神本曰 '高山'… 後封其山爲崧 以祠奉 其神也" is found. *Goryeojeon* (高麗傳, Section of Goryeo) of *Songsa* (宋史, History of Song) also says "開成(城)府依大山 … 其山曰神嵩." More specifically, 高山 (read as "gosan"), which is the name of an ancient god, and 崧山 (read as "sungsan") and 神嵩 (read as "sinsung"), both of which are mountain names, are all phonetic representations of *suri* and *sul* (or *sol*). In particular, 神嵩 is the same as 弓嵩 (phonetically representing "gomsuri"). Seonginbong (or Sinseongbong) was also derived from 弓嵩 (phonetically representing "gomsuri").

As for Isotake, the Japanese of a later generation changed its Chinese-character representation to 磯竹 (also read as "isotake") from 弓嵩 and began to refer to the entire Ulleungdo as Isotakeshima or Takeshima. However, this phonetic representation deviated far from the original. Isotake was originally the Japanese translation of 弓嵩; *iso* can either mean bravery or 50, which symbolizes "many". *Take* clearly stands for "mountain (山)" instead of "bamboo (竹)." In short, Isotake means "high, valiant mountain" and should be viewed as a translation of 弓嵩. *Inshu Shicho Gakki* (隱州視聽合記, A Collection of Observational Records of Inshu), penned by Toyonobu Saito in the 7th year of Kanbun (寬文) or the year 1667, reads "戌亥(西北)間 行二日一夜 有松島" and 又一日程 有竹島." It also includes "俗言磯竹島 多竹魚海鹿 按神言所謂五 十猛歟" in a note on 竹島. 松島 refers to present-day Dokdo, while 竹島 refers to present-day Ulleungdo. 海鹿 means 海驢 (meaning "seal"), while 五十猛 is Isotake, which is the name of an ancient Japanese god and thus a highly subjective interpretation of Isotake by the author. It is noteworthy that the author did not take the meaning of Isotake as it is notated (磯竹) but viewed it as being associated with divinity. Though Isotake was a translation of 弓嵩

(phonetically representing "gomsuri"), the later generations of Japan misunderstood it and notated it as 磯竹. Thus, they came to refer to the island using the Chinese characters 磯竹島 or 竹島, believing this name stands for the island's abundance of bamboo trees (竹). It is unclear exactly when the Japanese began to use this erroneous name, but it presumably dates quite far back since this name appears in Volume 2 of *Jibong Yuseol* (芝峰類說, Topical Discourses by Jibong) written by Yi Su-gwang (1563-1628).

5. The origin of the name 松島 is somewhat unclear, but two views are considered the most plausible: 松 (read as "song") may have been borrowed from Chinese to represent *suri* (also *sul* or *sol*) of *gomsuri* (弓嵩) or brought up to form a symmetry with 竹島 (an erroneous name for Ulleungdo), its mother island. Either suffices to testify to a close association between Ulleungdo and Dokdo. 竹島, as explained above, is originally a name used by the Japanese to refer to Ulleungdo, and it was clearly derived from an incorrect translation of Ulleungdo's name used by the Korean natives of Ulleungdo. Even if we concede to the point of assuming that the names 竹島 and 松島 were created entirely by the Japanese, the inclusion of 松 and 竹—the two characters that often form a set in the cultures that use Chinese characters—in the names of the islands prove the close geographical relationship between the two islands. Moreover, the names of the two islands were switched in later days (竹島 came to refer to 松島 and vice versa). This fact alone demonstrates that the two islands are bound together by a common destiny. As such, if the main island of Ulleungdo falls under Korea's jurisdiction, then it only stands to reason that its sister island Dokdo should be considered Korean territory. I would accept the idea that the same principle should apply if Ulleungdo were Japan's. What is stated in this paper thoroughly proves that these two islands cannot be separated in terms of sovereignty and cannot be governed by two different countries.

<Published in the Journal of Buddhist History in 1963>

About the author

The author was born in Gyeonggi Province and majored in history and sociology in the Literature Department of Waseda University in Tokyo, Japan. He is a doctor of literature, an honorary professor at Seoul National University, and the president of The National Academy of Sciences, Republic of Korea.

Dokdo as Illustrated on Maps

Choi Seo-myeon
Director, International Korea Research Institute

Although many academic papers on Dokdo have been released in Korea, I have not yet come across a book about this issue in separate volumes. On the contrary, Japan has seen the publication of three books, in addition to an array of academic papers. Two among those were written by researchers specializing in territorial issues; *Historical-Geographical Study of Takeshima* (竹島の歴史地理的研究) written by Kenzo Kawakami and published in 1966, and *Takeshima Shiko* (竹島史稿, History of Takeshima) written by Ryoichi Ookuma and published in 1968. The remaining book, *Shimaneken Takeshima No Kenkyu* (島根縣竹島の研究, Study of Takeshima by the Shimane Prefecture) was published in 1965 and was written by a historian Seizaburo Tamura from the Shimane Prefecture, an area that has been closely associated with Dokdo throughout history.

These three books conclude that Dokdo is a part of Japanese territory and provide maps as evidence. However, Korea has yet to create a discourse on Dokdo's position supported by maps, although many renowned scholars have dealt with Dokdo from diverse perspectives in a series of papers. Korea needs to provide evidential maps and pertinent explanations to refute Japan's claims and produce a historically straight, fair conclusion. Korea must address the unfinished task of proving its sovereignty over Dokdo through maps. This study was conducted to help complete this task by taking a look at Dokdo as illustrated on Korean maps; Dokdo as illustrated on Japanese maps; and Dokdo as illustrated on Western maps.

Before going into further details, it is necessary to point out why maps are important in clarifying the Dokdo issue. One of the major reasons is that both Korea and Japan have marked the island as their territory on their national boundary maps, which must be sorted out. Maps made by Western countries and Dokdo's positioning on them are also crucial because they were created largely beyond the influence of Korea or Japan. It is important to compare how Dokdo appears on maps produced from a third party's perspective and on the maps made by Korea and Japan and to explore the implications of such findings.

Dokdo as Illustrated on Korean Maps

It is hard to trace when ancient maps marked with Dokdo first came into being in Korea because the date of their publication was rarely specified. At present, *Sinjeung Dongguk Yeoji Seungnam* (新增東國輿地勝覽, Revised and Augmented Survey of the Geography of Korea) is one of the few easily accessible ancient atlases marked with Dokdo and a publication date. This atlas was released in 1530 (the 25th year of King Seongjong's reign). Based on the order to create an atlas in the first year of King Sejong's reign, information was collected and developed into *Sinchan Paldo Jiriji* (新撰八道地理志, Newly Compiled Geography Book of the Eight Provinces of Joseon) by Maeng Sa-seong and *Sejong Sillok Jiriji* (世宗實錄地理志, Geography Section of the Annals of King Sejong's Reign), which were updated and revised into *Dongguk Yeoji Seungnam* (東國輿地勝覽, Survey of the Geography of Korea) published in the

12th year of King Seongjong's reign. More accurate updates and improvements were made afterwards and compiled into *Sinjeung Dongguk Yeoji Seungnam* by the government to deliver the latest geographical information about Korea. Attached to this book was *Paldo Chongdo* (八道總圖, Complete Map of the Eight Provinces of Korea), which depicts both Ulleungdo and Dokdo and refers to Dokdo as Usando (于山島). Therefore, *Paldo Chongdo* may arguably be Korea's very first map that specifies its publication date and notes the location of Dokdo.

This map depicts Usando as an island slightly smaller than Ulleungdo and places it between Ulleungdo and mainland Joseon. The location of the island is an unmistakable error if it was intended to refer to Dokdo. It should have been marked to the right of Ulleungdo, not between Ulleungdo and the mainland. Japanese scholars view this map as evidence that proves Usando refers to Jukseo (竹嶼)—a small ancillary island to the east of Ulleungdo—and thus is irrelevant to Dokdo.

However, in my opinion, this claim only sheds light on their lack of ability to discern accurate information from an ancient map. It should be noted that maps of the ancient world were created in a manner that mirrors what people believed at the time, instead of scientific measurements and surveys. Focus should be placed on the fact that it was technically impossible in the 1530s to accurately mark the location of an island two full days away from the mainland by sea. Given the realities of cartographic history, one cannot expect maps made during these times to show pinpoint locations.

However, Korean maps afterwards show gradual improvements in accuracy regarding the location of Dokdo and prove that this island referred to as Usando at that time was neither Ulleungdo nor a rocky ancillary island of Ulleungdo as asserted by Japanese scholars.

Hanguk Gojido (韓國古地圖, Ancient Maps of Korea), published in 1977 by the Korea Library Science Research Society, introduces collections of ancient maps housed by the Korea University Library, the National Library of Korea, Seoul National University's Kyujanggak Archives, the Soongjeon University (present-day Soongsil University) Museum, the Yeungnam University Library, the Sung Am Archives of Classical Literature, and Kansong Library. On nine maps among these, Dokdo is located between Ulleungdo and the mainland of Korea, while three refer to Dokdo as Usando located to the east of Ulleungdo. Unfortunately, *Hanguk Gojido* was not made with the Dokdo issue in mind and therefore carries the photos of only three maps that mark the location of Dokdo.

In addition to the three maps appearing in *Hanguk Gojido* in photos, many more maps are found to have marked Dokdo to the east of Ulleungdo. As many as ten such maps are housed at the Korea Research Institute in Tokyo.

The changed location of Usando in ancient Korean maps from a point between Ulleungdo and Korea's mainland to a point to the east of Ulleungdo holds great significance. The fact that Usando was sometimes marked to the north and the south of Ulleungdo before it was finally assigned to the sea to the east of Ulleungdo is a testament to the fact that the island called Usando was not Jukseo, a small ancillary island to the east of Ulleungdo, but an independent island. *Hwanyeongji* (寰瀛誌, Geography Book about Joseon, China, and Japan), an atlas published in 1762, strongly supports this fact. This atlas depicts Usando as being to the southeast of Ulleungdo, with the former appearing larger than the latter. In conclusion, ancient Korean maps were created based on the recognition that Usando, comparable to Ulleungdo in size, existed at a location to the east of Ulleungdo and that the island should not be omitted from any map of Korean territory.

Dokdo as Illustrated on Japanese Maps

The first Japanese-made map to clearly mark Dokdo was *Nihon Yochi Rotei Zenzu* (日本輿地路程全圖, Complete Map of Japanese Lands and Roads) created by Sekisui Nagakubo in 1773. This map stands apart in that it took as many as 20 years to be completed and it was the first Japanese map to employ lines of longitude and latitude. Nagakubo published another map entitled *Nihon Rotei Yochizu* (日本路程輿地圖, Map of Japanese Roads and Lands) in 1778, in which he marked Dokdo and Ulleungdo and referred to them as Matsushima (松島) and Takeshima (竹島) respectively. Nagakubo's map is a colored block print. However, while Japan's mainland was fully colored, Dokdo and Ullelungdo were not. Also, a phrase, "見高麗猶雲州望隱洲," was added to Ulleungdo. This phrase means that Ulleungdo provides a view of Korea's mainland just as Izumo, Japan's westernmost border town, provides a view of the Oki Islands. If I may put it more specifically, it is saying that Japan's outermost archipelago, the Oki Islands, can be seen on the westernmost edge of its mainland and that, in a similar manner, Korea's mainland can be seen when standing on the edge of Korea's outermost island of Ulleungdo.

In 1804, *Sangoku Tsuran Zusetsu* (三國通覽圖說, An Illustrated Description of the Three Countries) by Shihei Hayashi was published. As is widely known, the French version of this book, translated by Klaproth of Germany in 1832, made great contributions to the expansion of the West's knowledge of the East Asian world. Among the five maps included in this book, two show an island marked at a location around Dokdo or Ulleungdo. In short, three islands were illustrated between Japan's Oki Islands and Korea's mainland. This is puzzling as only two islands (Dokdo and Ulleungdo) exist between the Oki Islands and Korea's mainland. As is explained in the introduction written by the author, *Sangoku Tsuran Zusetsu* is not a map strictly speaking; it is a type of a military map handbook aimed at alerting people to the urgency of Japan's national defense issues. It was written to wake up the nation and its people to the danger of a foreign invasion and urge on proactive measures following Russia's attack on Hokkaido.

As such, Hayashi colored only Honshu, Shikoku, Kyushu, Tsushima Island, and the Oki Islands in blue and colored in most of Hokkaido with a different color. Also, the Ogasawara Islands were colored in red because this part was not finalized as Japanese territory at the time, while Ryukyukoku (present-day Okinawa) was colored in brown. Korea and its islands were colored in yellow. As this map was intended to illustrate how vulnerable Japan was to foreign invasions, it was probably very conscious of Japan's territorial limits. The fact that this map colored all three islands between the Oki Islands and Korea's mainland in yellow—the color of Korea's mainland—proves that the westernmost border of Japan at the time was the Oki Islands. Although it marked the names of the islands in Japanese style (Takeshima and Matsushima), it recognized them as Korean territory and even made notes on them as "the territory of Joseon" (Dokdo, or Matsushima, is not recognized as a formal island name here).

In 1804, Morishige Kondo, who made significant contributions to the advancement of maps defining Japan's boundary, published *Henyo Bunkai Zuko* (邊要分界圖考, Book of Maps of Japan's Border Areas) marked with Ulleungdo. This map also states that Ulleungdo and Dokdo are Korean territory, thus proving that Dokdo belongs to Korea.

Thus far, I have introduced and analyzed some of Japan's historically significant maps that have been published up until the early 19th century and, in particular, those that depict Dokdo and/or Ulleungdo. At this point, I would like to focus on Kageyasu Takahashi, who has pointed to some problems found in Western maps, although I will elaborate on this subject in greater detail later in the section about Western maps. Takahashi was a public official of the Shogunate government who produced *Nippon Henkai Ryakuzu* (日本邊界略圖, Simplified Map of Japan's Boundary) along with a global map in 1809 based on Western maps imported through Nagasaki. This map illustrated Dokdo and Ulleungdo as being situated very close to Korea's mainland. Also, this map marks Ulleungdo as 苑陵島 (Ulleungdo) and the East Sea as 朝鮮海 (the Sea of Joseon).

One of the maps that hold great significance in the history of Japanese maps is the complete map of Japan created based on the surveys led by Tadataka Ino from 1800 to 1816, which has come to be considered the vanguard of modern maps. This map placed a heavy focus on using a 1,150 point longitude and latitude system obtained by the observation of celestial bodies during the surveying stage, in which the surface of the earth was recognized as being a part of a sphere. This map, published in 1821 under the title *Dai Nihon Enkai Yochi Zenzu* (大日本沿海輿地圖, Map of Japan's Coastal Areas), does not illustrate Dokdo. Also, none of the 214 cadastral maps, currently housed at Naikaku Bunko (內閣文庫, Library of Ancient Documents of the Japanese Cabinet), illustrate Dokdo. The fact that the surveyed maps of this complete map of Japan, which Japan flaunts as one of its modern scientific achievements, does not illustrate Dokdo refutes head-on Japan's claim that Dokdo has historically been Japanese territory.

Furthermore, neither the map of Sanbobu (參謀部, Japanese General Staff Office in Korea)—published in 1876 as an extension of the Japanese government's effort to illustrate Japan and its neighboring countries in minute detail—nor the map of the Ministry of Culture and Education—published in 1877—illustrates Dokdo. As can be seen here, the maps made by Japan itself have come to more clearly demonstrate that Dokdo does not belong to Japan, as they did not depict Dokdo with any regularity despite continued cartographic improvements made far in advance of ancient times when the existence of Ulleungdo and Dokdo was only vaguely indicated.

Lastly, Dokdo cannot be considered Japanese territory as the island did not appear on the local maps of Japan. Contrastively, Dokdo has been marked on some of the maps of Gangwon Province and Gyeongsang Province of Joseon. However, in the case of Japan, Dokdo is not even included on the local maps of the Shimane Prefecture—a region that is the closest to Dokdo from mainland Japan and had control over the Oki Islands and Dokdo, as asserted by Japan. This testifies to the fact that Dokdo and Ulleungdo were marked on Japanese maps only for the purpose of defining the border of Japan and thus the maps of local regions, which did not need to define the national border, had no reason to include these islands.

Dokdo as Illustrated on the Maps of Countries Other than Korea and Japan

I will simply refer to the maps described under this section as foreign-made maps hereinafter. The first foreign-made Korean map (or Western-made Korean map to be more specific) that clearly marks Ulleungdo and Dokdo is D'Anville's Korean map. This map illustrated Fan Ling Tao and Tchian Chan Tao at positions near 37°N in the East Sea of Korea, clearly stating that Dokdo belongs to Korea. Fan Ling Tao refers to Ulleungdo. The character 戀 of 戀陵 島 (Ulleungdo's representation in Chinese characters) was mistakenly recognized as 欒 while making a copy and thus the Chinese pronunciation of 欒陵 島 was romanized into Fan Ling Tao.

Some of the Japanese-made maps as well as Korean-made maps are found to have replaced this 戀 with 苑, 杰, or 离 and 于 of 于山島 with 夭 or 千. Tchian Chan Tao is a romanized form of the Chinese pronunciation of 千山 島 from a map that used this representation instead of 于山島.

The original copy of this map is housed at Bibliothèque Nationale, Paris as part of its D'Anville Collection. It is drawn on two pieces of Chinese paper measuring 530 millimeters by 785 millimeters. This map served as the prototype for the 1735, 1737, and 1779 maps of Royaume de Corée.

All these are based on the achievements of the Catholic priest Régis who published *Observations Geographiques sur le Royaume de Corée* (Geographical Contemplation of the Joseon Kingdom) in 1717. The D'Anville Collection has seven more Korean maps that are undoubtedly the product of thorough studies of the Straits of Korea and Korean islands. The creation of D'Anville's maps can be said to have been fueled by the Qing Dynasty's effort to complete *The Complete Map of Qing* (皇輿全覽圖) and map the boundaries of Qing with the help of Catholic missionaries.

Most Western-made maps that illustrate Korea and Dokdo are based on these D'Anville maps and data obtained from imported maps of Japan and China.

The first foreign-made map that illustrated the islands in the East Sea of Korea by making actual surveys was the map of La Pérouse. This map refers to Ulleungdo as Dagelet. La Pérouse discovered an island 80 kilometers off the southeastern coast of Korea on May 27, 1787, which was not yet marked on nautical charts, while travelling across Asia by royal command. He named this island Dagelet. Two years later in 1789, James Colnett—a British explorer and navigator—discovered Ulleungdo and named it Argonaut after his ship.

In 1849, a French whaling ship named the *Liancourt* came across an island and sent a report to France without knowing that it was a new discovery. This became the first discovery of Dokdo by a Western ship.

Around this time, one incident occurred that created great confusion regarding the position of Ulleungdo on Western-made maps. La Pérouse misreported the coordinates of Ulleungdo as 37°25'N and 129°25'E when they are in effect 37°9'30"N and 131°55'E, and thus the *Argonaut* had to measure Ulleungdo's position on its own. What's more, the *Argonaut* was experiencing some problems with some of the ship's fittings. As a result, it recorded an incorrect position for the island. This is how Ulleungdo came to be illustrated in two positions in the East Sea, which affected the making of Japanese maps up until 1876.

In 1854, a Russian fleet under the command of Admiral Putiatin docked in the port of Geomundo for the first time ever and made surveys of Ulleungdo and Dokdo during its journeys to and from Japan to urge the country to put an end to its isolationist policies. Most Japanese books say that Admiral Putiatin's flagship the *Palada* was in charge of the surveys. However, that is a mistake resulting from having neglected to check the original records of Admiral Putiatin; it was the *Olivutsa*, a ship also under the command of Putiatin, which conducted the surveys of Dokdo and Ulleungdo.

The *Olivutsa*'s surveys led to the conclusion that Argonaut Island must be Ulleungdo and that the incorrect position of Argonaut Island should be discarded, thereby putting an end to the confusion that had lasted for years. This is how the fictional island of Argonaut disappeared from Western maps.

Dokdo was named the Manalai and Olivutsa Rocks after their ships. However, as information could not be disseminated as rapidly as today, the UK's *Hornet* that was navigating the surrounding waters of Dokdo came across the island and named it the Hornet Rocks in 1855.

Today's world maps mark Ulleungdo as Dagelet and Dokdo as the Liancourt Rocks for the sake of the history of maritime affairs and in honor of the discoverers. Maps of the UK and Russia are no exception. The two most notable Western maps that depict Ulleungdo and Dokdo are a set of two maps attached to *Nippon* published by Siebold in 1840. This set consists of one map of Japan's outlying territories created based on Japanese-made maps purchased in Japan and one map of Korea. The map of Korea illustrates Ulleungdo and Dokdo as being a part of Korean territory. On the contrary, the map of Japan's outlying territories depicts two islands besides the Oki Islands in the waters near the borderline between the two countries: Dagelet with no Dokdo nearby and the fictional island of Argonaut. Siebold refers to Argonaut as Takeshima (竹島), the Japanese name for Ulleungdo, and Dagelet as Matsushima (松島), the Japanese name for Dokdo. Siebold's maps are thought to have brought great disadvantages to Japan. Dokdo had been referred to as Matsushima by the Japanese, but as Siebold referred to Ulleungdo as Matsushima and referred to Argonaut as Takeshima, the world maps were affected accordingly and Dokdo was deleted. The disappearance of Dokdo is believed by some Japanese scholars to have compromised Japan's claim over Dokdo as its territory. Siebold, who is considered to have contributed greatly to advancing the modernization of Japan, is often ruthlessly criticized as far as his maps are concerned. What is referred to as "Siebold's error" never goes unmentioned in papers concerning Japan's history of maps and in particular the maps that depict Dokdo. However, the erroneous naming was not Siebold's fault. It can be seen in the maps, which were taken to Europe by Siebold from Japan and are now exhibited at the National Museum of Antiquities in Leiden, the Netherlands and other museums, as well as by the maps that were originally included in the map collection possessed by Siebold. Based on these maps and the

Japanese-made maps of Korea, Siebold naturally inferred that the two islands located between the Oki Islands and Korea's mainland belonged to Korea. It is nothing but an unjust and unfair act to lay the blame on Siebold without taking such facts into account. If Japanese scholars and territorial researchers wish to continue to lay the blame on Siebold, then they must come up with feasible explanations as to why the maps made by the Japanese (including those commissioned by the Japanese government) based on Japanese-created data had continuously excluded the two islands from Japanese territory until 1877.

The position of Dokdo on Western maps testifies to the fact that Ulleungdo and Dokdo cannot be considered Japanese territory.

Lastly, I would like to once again emphasize that the abovementioned Korean maps, Japanese maps, and maps created in countries other than Korea and Japan all alike clearly indicate Dokdo belongs to Korea.

The Japanese appear to be mixing up facts about Dokdo frequently to this day. One of the examples is the map of Takejiro Akioka, who is a much respected geographer in Japan and the author of *Nihon Chizushi* (日本地圖史, History of Japanese Maps). He discussed Dokdo and Ulleungdo in the East Sea in his paper entitled "Matsushima and Takeshima located to the Southwest of the Sea of Japan" published in 1950 in the 27th issue of *Shakai Chiri* (社會地理, Social Geography). He then modified what he stated in this paper in *Nihon Chizushi* published in 1955. Such willingness to recognize and revise errors by a scholar should always be praised and admired. However, it also cannot be denied that his error derived from his failure to carefully study the original documents and to screen unfounded reports (such as the report about the discovery of Ulleungdo and Argonaut by Broughton who had never actually travelled to Ulleungdo) due to his excessive desire to validate Japan's claim of sovereignty over Dokdo.

I believe a combination of unbiased examinations of maps marked with Dokdo and a thorough examination of the original documents will provide momentum in settling the sovereignty issue of Dokdo.

Japan's Annexation of "Ryanko Island" and Shim Heung-taek's Report to the Korean Government

Song Byeong-kie

Professor Emeritus, Dankook University

Japan's Annexation of "Ryanko Island"

Japan's annexation of Dokdo occurred five years after the Korean government reaffirmed its sovereignty over the same island (Seokdo/Dokdo) through "Imperial Decree No. 41, 4th Year of Gwangmu (October 1900), On the Renaming of Ulleungdo to Uldo and the Promotion of the Post of Island Chief to County Magistrate." This was when the Russo-Japanese War was at its height, shortly before the famous Battle of Tsushima. On February 22, 1905 (38th year of Meiji), the Shimane Prefecture of Japan issued its Prefecture Public Notice No. 40, declaring the annexation of Ryanko Island (Dokdo) to its jurisdiction.

To understand the background to this decision to annex Dokdo to Japan, announced through Shimane Prefecture Public Notice No. 40, it is necessary to mention Nakai Yozaburo, a fisherman residing in Shimane, as it was a petition filed by him that set off the entire affair. Yozaburo, who went on a fishing trip to Ryanko Island on two occasions, once in May 1903 and once in August

1904, thought highly of the lucrative potential of hunting sea lions inhabiting this rocky island.

Nakai Yozaburo, therefore, decided to rent the island and went to Tokyo to find out how he could obtain a lease on the island. The first in the series of government officials he met was Maki Bokushin, the chief of the Fisheries Bureau of the Ministry of Agriculture and Commerce. The latter told him that it was not certain that Ryanko Island was a Korean possession. When Nakai addressed his inquiry to Kimotsuki Kaneyuki, the director of the Hydrographic Department of the Japanese Navy, the latter said that Ryanko Island was a terra nullius, in other words, unoccupied territory, belonging to no one. Based on this information, Nakai Yozaburo filed his petition for the annexation of Ryanko Island (Dokdo) and a grant of permission to rent it, with the Japanese Ministry of the Interior, Ministry of Foreign Affairs, and Ministry of Agriculture and Commerce.

The Interior Ministry official who received Nakai's petition, however, refused to consider it, stating that annexing Ryanko Island at this juncture would arouse suspicions about Japanese ambitions over Korea. This reluctance to assist Nakai Yozaburo with his petition probably also had to do with the fact that the Ministry of the Interior, not long before, had recognized Matsushima (Ryanko Island) as a Korean possession (1877), a view which was supported by the Dajokan (Grand Council of State) as well. This Interior Ministry official's opinion was later overridden by Yamaza Enjiro, the chief of the Political Bureau of the Ministry of Foreign Affairs, who argued that the annexation of Ryanko Island was more urgently needed than ever, given that Japan was at war and the considerations of the Ministry of the Interior were not necessary from a diplomatic perspective.

The Japanese Ministry of the Interior at last accepted Nakai Yozaburo's petition for the annexation of Ryanko Island on September 29 of the same year (1904). A little more than three months later, on January 10, 1905, the Ministry of the Interior submitted to the Japanese cabinet a proposal entitled "The Case of an Uninhabited Island," asking for the annexation of Ryanko

Island to Japan, renaming the island "Takeshima" and placing it under the jurisdiction of the Oki Islands administration of Shimane Prefecture. The proposal was approved on January 28. The Shimane Prefecture was instructed on February 15 (Order No. 87) to publicize the cabinet's decision through a prefectural notice; hence, Shimane Prefecture Public Notice No. 40.

The memorandum of the Japanese cabinet's resolution is highly significant in relation to the process of the annexation of Ryanko Island. According to this memorandum, the decision to annex Ryanko Island was based on the fact that the uninhabited island, situated at 85 *li* northwest of the Oki Islands shows no signs of occupation by another country, and that Nakai Yozaburo moved to the island in 1903 and had been engaged in fishing there since that time a fact that was deemed to constitute evidence of occupation under international law. The resolution also approved changing the name of the island to Takeshima and placing it under the jurisdiction of the governor of Oki Islands in Shimane Prefecture, as proposed by the Ministry of the Interior.

The premise of the Japanese Cabinet's decision to annex Ryanko Island, namely, that this island was a *terra nullius*, was completely erroneous. Ryanko Island, in other words, Dokdo had long been perceived in Korea as a dependent island of Ulleungdo, hence a part of Korean territory, This perception had been acknowledged by the Tokugawa Shogunate through the Tsushima governor's letter of 1699 and by the Meiji Government (Dajokan) through the directive of the *Udaijin* (Minister of the Right) in 1877. This perception was, moreover, reconfirmed through "Imperial Decree No. 41, 4th Year of Gwang-mu, On the Renaming of Ulleungdo to Uldo and the Promotion of the Post of Island Chief to County Magistrate," enacted and proclaimed in October 1900 (33rd year of Meiji). Article 2 of this decree, as has been discussed earlier, includes Seokdo (Dokseom, Dolseom or Dokdo) within the jurisdiction of the newly-established County of Uldo. The Japanese cabinet's decision was, therefore, founded on a patently mistaken premise.

Furthermore, the so-called evidence of occupation, cited in the memorandum of the Japanese cabinet's resolution, in other words, the evidence that

Nakai Yozaburo had resided and fished on Ryanko Island ever since 1903 (36th year of Meiji) was a counterfactual claim. During this period, Nakai was illegally residing on the Korean island of Ulleungdo and sailed twice, in 1903 and 1904, to Dokdo for a brief stay during the fishing season, which in no way constitutes evidence of occupation of any sort.

In regard to this decision of the Japanese cabinet it is also important to note that there were hardly any precedents in Japan, indicating that Dokdo was ever perceived there as being part of its national territory. The best proof to this effect is the fact that at the time of this decision of annexation, the island was known under its Western name "Ryanko Island (Liancourt Rocks)," and was only renamed "Takeshima" for the purpose of annexing it to Japan. Hence, prior to February 1905, the Japanese authorities not only never regarded this island as Japanese territory, but also and more importantly, were well aware that it was a Joseon possession. *Inshu Shicho Gakki* (A Collection of Observational Records of Inshu, 1667) by Saito Hosen, the oldest surviving Japanese work containing a reference to Dokdo, is evidence that supports this point.

When the Tokugawa Shogunate decided to ban Japanese navigation to Takeshima (1696, 9th year of Genroku), in the context of the Joseon-Japan territorial dispute in the late seventeenth century—the Ulleungdo Dispute—Matsushima, the dependent island of Takeshima (Ulleungdo), was implied in the scope of the application of this ban; hence, also recognized as a Joseon possession. The Tokugawa Shogunate stood by this decision throughout the years of its existence. The Meiji government, which later succeeded to the Tokugawa regime, was also well aware of the fact that both Ulleungdo and Dokdo had been Joseon's territorial islands since the early years of the dynasty.

During Japan's early modernization period as well, the Meiji government respected the Shogunate's decision that not only Ulleungdo but also Dokdo were Joseon's territory. This is illustrated by the compilation of maps carried out as groundwork to establish a modern land management system.

The Dajokan compiled Japan's geography from 1872 to 1873 and published the results from 1874 consecutively and completed the seventy-seven books in eight volumes of the "*Nihon Chishi Teiyo* (Summary of Japanese Geography)." Book 50 of Volume 4, "Oki" (published in 1875) describes 179 islands as its independent islands. Neither Takeshima (Ulleungdo) nor Matsushima (Dokdo), however, was included among the 179 islands with the two islands being marked separately. In other words, the Japanese government perceived the two islands as being outside Japanese sovereignty.

The Meiji government published maps from the late 1870s. The first maps produced were the *Dainihon Zenzu* (The Whole Map of the Great Japan, 1877), published by the General Staff of the Army, and the *Nihon Teikoku Zenzu* (1877) by the Japanese Ministry of Education. After that, six to seven maps including *Dai Nihonfuken Bunkatsuzu* (Map of Prefectural Divisions of Great Japan, 1876) by the Department of Geography in the Ministry of Interior and *Dainihonkoku Zenzu* (Complete Map of Japan) were produced. One thing these public maps all have in common is that they all depict Takeshima (Ulleungdo) and Matsushima (Dokdo) as being outside of Japan's sovereignty and as belonging to Joseon. This can be linked to the reproduction of *Kanpan Jissoku Nihon Chizu* (State-Published Map of Japan from Actual Survey) during the late years of the Meiji government, in which Takeshima and Matsushima were depicted as being outside Japanese sovereignty.

What appears to have been even more influential, however, was the declaration by the *Udaijin* (Minister of the Right) of the Dajokan that Takeshima and Matsushima did not belong to Japan.

The Ministry of the Interior investigated and reviewed the diplomatic documents exchanged between Korea and Japan during the Ulleungdo Dispute and concluded that "Takeshima and another island," namely, Takeshima and Matsushima, were not related to Japan. The Dajokan accepted this perception and issued its directive that "Takeshima and another island (Matsushima) are not related to Japan." Thus declaring in an indirect way that the two islands were Korean territory.

The records show that the Ministry of Foreign Affairs and the Navy perceived Ryanko Island (Dokdo) as being Korean territory. The Ministry of Foreign Affairs forwarded an inquiry dated November 29, 1881 to the Ministry of the Interior regarding the status-quo of Ulleungdo. The response to the inquiry included a directive by the Dajokan declaring that Takeshima (Ulleungdo) and Matsushima (Dokdo) were outside Japan's sovereignty. The Ministry of Foreign Affairs, however, did not raise any objection to the response, even though the repatriation of the Japanese illegally residing on Ulleungdo emerged as a pending issue between Joseon and Japan. Until the annexation of Dokdo in 1905, it never handled the sovereignty of Takeshima and Matsushima separately. In other words, the Ministry of Foreign Affairs consistently perceived Dokdo as Korean territory.

In the meantime, the Liancourt Rocks (Dokdo) were included along with Matsushima (Ulleungdo) in reflections on the results of the *Amagi* survey in Russian and Korean coastal waters in September 1880 in *Kanei Suiroshi* (The Sealanes of the World) published by the Navy Hydrographic Office (1883) and in the 1894 and 1899 version of *Chosen Suiroshi* (Korea's Sealanes) by the Japanese Hydrographic Department (formerly Hydrographic Office). On the other hand, *Nihon Suiroshi* (Japanese Sealanes), which was consecutively published from 1892 covering only Japanese territory, does not contain the description of the Liancourt Rocks. Takeshima (Liancourt Rocks), however, was added in the west coast section of the mainland in Chapter 3 of the first revised edition of Volume 4 of the *Nihon Suiroshi* published in 1907 after the annexation of Ryanko Island. It contains the comment at the end of page 6 that Dokdo had been incorporated into the Shimane Prefecture in the 38th year of Meiji (1905).

This means that the Japanese Navy originally perceived Liancourt Rock as being Korean territory. This indicates that not only the Navy but also the *Amagi* survey team perceived Ryanko Island as Korean territory in its survey of Dokdo. Accordingly, the Navy Hydrographic Office acknowledged in its "Chosen Tokaiganzu" (Map of the Eastern Coast of Korea, first edition, 1876) that Dokdo was Korean territory and confirmed the fact through the on-the-spot survey (1880) by the *Amagi*. This confirmation was subsequently reaffirmed through the publication of *Chosen Suiroshi* (1894, 1899).

Meanwhile, Nakai Yozaburo, the petitioner who had provided the original stimulus for the annexation of Ryanko Island (Dokdo), personally never had any doubts about the island being a Korean possession. Knowing that Dokdo belonged to Korean territory, he needed to go through his own government in order to try to rent the island, which was why he headed for Tokyo in 1904, when the fishing season was over, to meet Maki Bokushin, the head of the Fisheries Bureau of the Japanese Ministry of Agriculture and Commerce. It was only through the instigation of Maki Bokushin, Kimotsuki Kaneyuki, Director of the Hydrographic Department of the Japanese Navy, and Yamaza Enjiro, Director of the Political Bureau of the Japanese Ministry of Foreign Affairs, that he subsequently filed a petition for the annexation of Ryanko Island (Dokdo) with the Japanese government.

Nakai Yozaburo, in other words, provided a great pretext for the Japanese government to set off a process to make an unwarranted claim on Dokdo and declare it annexed to its territory. Nakai certainly was counting on a tacit promise that he would receive exclusive fishing rights to this island. The most important role in this whole affair, however, was played by such Japanese officials as Maki Bokushin, head of the Fisheries Bureau of the Japanese Ministry of Agriculture and Commerce, Kimotsuki Kaneyuki, Director of the Hydrographic Department of the Japanese Navy and Yamaza Enjiro, Director of the Political Bureau of the Japanese Ministry of Foreign Affairs. New light undoubtedly needs to be shed on their crucial roles in Dokdo's annexation by Japan at the beginning of the twentieth century.

The navigation ban issued in the late seventeenth century by the Tokugawa Shogunate had the effect of gradually erasing Takeshima (Ulleungdo) and Matsushima (Dokdo from Japanese memory. In the mid-nineteenth century (the late Tokugawa period to the early Meiji period), a name change occurred, and Ulleungdo was thereafter referred to as "Matsushima," and Dokdo as "Ryanko Island." The Japanese government of the Meiji period, after having declared that Ryanko Island was Korean, nevertheless, went ahead and annexed this island, renaming it "Takeshima" in the process. This annexation carried out in an underhanded manner, to say the least, was prompted by the need to use Dokdo as a strategic base during the Battle of Tsushima between the Russian and Japanese naval fleets that Japan was anticipating at that time.

The annexation of Ryanko Island also failed to meet procedural requirements that would normally be expected of this type of state action relating to notification and publication. The Japanese government, for instance, did not publish its decision to annex Ryanko Island in the government gazette. The notification process was perfunctory at a local level as well. Shimane Prefecture Public Notice No. 40 was posted outside the prefectural government building and published in one or two local papers. Although this may have been consistent with the order of the Ministry of the Interior (No. 87) to publicize the annexation of Ryanko Island within the prefectural jurisdiction, it hardly qualifies as "due notification," given that the decision could adversely affect the interests of another country. Hence, the Japanese government's claim that its annexation of Dokdo had been notified to the international community is extremely hard to accept.

The Japanese government obviously feared Korean protests. But another possible explanation why Japan hushed up its annexation of Ryanko Island was that it wanted to avoid provoking mistrust among the Western powers who had thrown their support behind Japan in the Russo-Japanese War. The most important reason why the annexation of Ryanko Island took place behind such a veil of secrecy, however, must be that Japan was planning to use Dokdo as a strategic base in the Battle of Tsushima (May 1905). This high-stakes battle was to determine not only the outcome of the Russo-Japanese War, but also the entire prospects of Japan, as a rising regional power. The time-frame of the annexation of Ryanko Island, for instance, closely coincided with that of a series of strategic actions taken by the Japanese fleet commander ahead of the Battle of Tsushima. The remark by Yamaza Enjiro, Director of the Political Bureau of the Japanese Ministry of Foreign Affairs, arguing for the need to use Ryanko Island as a strategic base, also lends support to this view. Further evidence includes the survey conducted on Dokdo and Ulleungdo in November 1904, shortly before the annexation of the former, in preparation for the building of observation posts connected by submarine cable. Although the results of the feasibility study proved positive, the Japanese decided to postpone construction work until the following spring. But the Battle of Tsushima broke out before the Japanese could complete these installations. The plan for the watchtower and submarine cable installation project was finalized in June 1905, with construction starting from July 1905. By August, in other words, before the conclusion of the Treaty of Portsmouth (September 1905), Japanese observation posts (four guards at Dokdo Observation Post and nine at Ulleungdo Observation Post) were already in operation.

In fact, under the Korea-Japan Protocol, forced upon the Korean government in February 1904, Japan had the right to use Dokdo for military purposes (Article 4). The annexation, therefore, was unnecessary, if Japan's goal was just to use Dokdo to support its war effort. There were even less reasons to take such formal steps, if Dokdo were indeed a terra nullius, as the Japanese claimed. Hence, what pushed the Japanese to take these steps could also be due to the thought Dokdo could be lost should the Battle of Tsushima (May 1905) end with Russia's victory, and wanted to stake a claim on this island before this could happen.

Shim Heung-taek's Report to the Joseon Government

In the spring of the year immediately following the conclusion of the Russo-Japanese War (March 26, 1906, 39th year of Meiji), the Shimane Prefecture sent a large survey team of forty-five members, led by a prefecture official named Jinzai Yoshitaro, to Ryanko Island (Dokdo). Among the members of this expedition were Higashi Bunsuke, the Governor of the Oki Islands, Nakai Yozaburo, the fisherman who had petitioned for the annexation of Ryanko Island, and Okuhara Hekiun, who later drafted the report on this survey project (titled *Takeshima Oyobi Utsuryoto* (Takeshima and Ulleungdo)). The Shimane survey team cast anchor at Dokdo on March 27 and successively inspected Dongdo (East Island) and Seodo (West Island).

On March 28, the Shimane expedition disembarked at Ulleungdo, and Jinzai Yoshitaro and others paid a visit to Uldo County Magistrate Shim Heung-taek at the county administration building. The Shimane team informed County Magistrate Shim of the annexation of Dokdo by Japan. This encounter, although not mentioned in *Takeshima Oyobi Utsuryoto* or in its appendix *Takeshima Toko Nisshi*, was discussed both in Shim Heung-taek's report to Yi Myeong-rae, the Acting Governor of Gangwon-do (Gangwon Province), and Yi Myeong-rae's report to the government, relaying Shim's report. Even if only to a county magistrate, Japan at last notified Korea of its annexation of Ryanko Island one year and two months after the prefectural notice had been issued in Shimane. This was in sharp contrast to how Japan had proceeded with its 1876 annexation of the Ogasawara Islands. At that time Japan had several times contacted Great Britain and the United States, two countries that had potential interests in the islands, to confer with them. When the latter showed no objection to Japan's annexation of the Ogasawara Islands. At that time Japan had several times contacted Great Britain and the United States, two countries that had potential interests in the islands, to confer with them. When the latter showed no objection to Japan's annexation of the Ogasawara Islands, it notified twelve Western countries of its decision for annexation.

Japan maintained the utmost secrecy in its annexation of Ryanko Island. Secrecy and stealth were also characteristics of Shimane Prefecture Governor Matsunaga Takekichi's tour of Takeshima (Ryanko Island/Dokdo) in August 1905. Matsunaga and his staff, who were supposed to travel onboard Oki Maru II, made a last minute change of plan and instead boarded the navy ship Kyoto Maru. As for the Shimane expedition, led by Jinzai, not only did it comprise an equal number of officials and resident representatives, but also and more importantly, it acted in the open. The team traveled aboard Oki Maru II, and paid an official call on County Magistrate Shim at the county administration office, announcing Japan's annexation of Dokdo.

This certainly was related to the timing of Jinzai's expedition. When the latter was sent to Dokdo and Ulleungdo, the Treaty of Portsmouth (September 1905) had already been signed, putting an official end to the Russo-Japanese War. In other words, Japan's "special interests" on the Korean peninsula were no longer contested by any of the regional or Western powers. By November of the same year, Japan forced upon the Korean government a treaty under which the latter surrendered its diplomatic rights to the former and accepted the installation of a Japan's "Resident General" (the Second Korea-Japan Protocol also known as the "Eulsa Restriction Treaty"). One month later, in December, all Korean diplomats stationed overseas were summoned back home, and in January of the following year (1906), the Korean government was completely stripped of its diplomatic rights, as the Ministry of Foreign Affairs was dissolved, and its duties transferred to the Foreign Affairs Office under the Uijeongbu (State Council of the Empire of Korea). With the opening of the Residency General in February of the same year, Korea came fully under Japanese control, and Japan, therefore, could announce its annexation of Ryanko Island with impunity to Korea or anyone else. It no longer had anything to fear.

Rattled by the news that Dokdo had been annexed to Japan, Uldo County Magistrate Shim Heung-taek reported the news to the acting governor of Gangwon-do without delay. Although Shim Heung-take's original report, dated March 5, 1906 (lunar calendar) is no longer extant, a counterpart was discovered in Ulleungdo's county administration archives by the late Professor Sin Seok-ho in August 1947. The content of this report is also quoted in its entirety in the report by Yi Myeong-rae, the Acting Governor of Gangwon-do, to the Uijeongbu Chamjeong Minister (equivalent to today's Deputy Prime Minister), dated April 29, 1906 (10th year of Gwangmu).

According to these two surviving reports, Oki Maru II, carrying the Shimane prefecture expedition team, arrived at Jeodong Port on Ulleungdo in the morning of the March 4 (lunar calendar). At dawn on the following day, Oki Maru II changed anchorage and entered Dodong Port. This is consistent with the report in *Takeshima Toko Nisshi* in the appendix of *Takeshima Oyobi Utsuryoto* (Takeshima and Ulleungdo) that the expedition disembarked from the island around 9:00 am. In these two reports "Officer Jinzai Yoshitaro (事務官神西由太郎)" is also recorded as "Jinzai Zentaro (神西田太郎)," of which the former is an abbreviation of "Shimane Prefectural Officer Jinzai Yoshitaro (島根縣事務官神西由太郎)", and the latter a misprint of "Jinzai Yoshitaro (神西由太郎)." The "tax office chief" is a reference to the chief of the Matsue Tax Office, and the "police chief" a reference to the head of the Urako District Police Department. Finally, the "council" refers to a member of the prefectural council. The two Korean documents report that a delegation composed of some twenty members, including assistants, came to the county office; a figure only slightly above the number reported in "Takeshima Toko Nisshi," which mentions "Jinzai Yoshitaro and a dozen people." Shim Heung-taek's report, therefore, appears to be accurate overall.

The highlights of Shim Heung-taek's report, according to its counterpart found in Ulleungdo and Yi Myeong-rae's account of it, were (1) that Dokdo, an island under the jurisdiction of Uldo County, was located about 100 *nautical miles* from Ulleungdo, in the open sea; (2) that on the 4th day, 3rd month (March 28), some twenty Japanese officials, including Oki Islands Governor Higashi Bunsuke and Shimane Prefecture official Jinzai Yoshitaro, came to the county office and announced that Dokdo had been annexed to Japan; and (3) that these people wanted information about the island's population and amount of farmland and its productivity, as well as the staff size and expenditures of the county office and its primary responsibilities.

Dokdo, mentioned in Shim Heung-taek's report as an island within the jurisdiction of Uldo County, is the same island as the one referred to as "Seokdo" in Imperial Decree No. 41, 4th year of Gwangmu. "Seokdo" derives from the name "Dokseom" or "Dolseom," used among coastal residents of Jeollanam-do who had regularly sailed to Ulleungdo or the locals of Ulleungdo, to refer to Dokdo. "Seokdo," therefore, is a Sino-Korean transcription of "Dokseom," created in part by transliterating the syllable *dok* using the Sino-Korean character 獨 (*dok*). The character 獨 was, besides, used quite frequently when transliterating the sound *dok* in the vernacular place names of Jeollanam-do, as well as those of Jejudo. For example, Dokseom in Muan, Jeollanam-do, and Dokgae in Jejudo are transliterated as "獨島 (Dokdo)" and "獨浦 (Dokpo)," respectively. *Gunkan Niitaka Kodo Nisshi*, the logbook of the Japanese warship Niitaka, for instance, reports, in its September 25, 1904 entry, that the Liancourt Rocks (Ryanko Island) were referred to as "Dokdo" by the Korean residents of Ulleungdo.

The date of Uldo County Magistrate Shim's report to the Acting Governor of Gangwon-do, although not specified in the latter's report to the Uijeongbu, is stated in the counterpart of this report, found in Ulleungdo. This date is "Byeongo day, 3rd month of 10th year of Gwangmu," which corresponds to March 29, 1906. In other words, Magistrate Shim made his report to the governor of Gangwon-do, his direct superior, on the day immediately following March 28, 1904, when he received the visit by the Shimane delegation. Realizing the urgent nature of the matter, Yi Myeong-rae, as soon as he received Shim's report, drafted his own report to the Uijeongbu, citing the content of Shim's report without modification (dated April 29). The time lag of about one month separating Shim Heung-taek's report from that of Yi Myeong-rae was probably caused by the transportation conditions at that time, which made communication between the mainland and Ulleungdo quite a slow process.

The report by Yi Myeong-rae, the Acting Governor of Gangwon-do and County Magistrate of Chuncheon-gun, was received by the Uijeongbu on May 7, 1906 (Incoming Communication No. 325). The Uijeongbu Chief (*Chamjeong Daesin*) replied to Yi Myeong-rae through Order No. 3, dated May 20, which read: "The report has been perused, and the claim over Dokdo is unfounded. Report back with further details on the situation at the island

and Japanese activities." This order constitutes a formal objection to the Japanese annexation of Dokdo (Ryanko Island), issued by the highest official of the Uijeongbu, reaffirming that Seokdo was a possession of the Korean Empire. The Deputy Prime Minister (*Chamjeong Daesin*) at that time was Park Je-sun.

Another important detail to note with regard to Shim Heung-taek's report is that the Magistrate of Uldo County, according to the May 1, 1906 issue of *Daehan Maeil Sinbo* (The Korea Daily News) sent another report to the Ministry of the Interior, also providing an account of the visit by the Shimane delegation, Given the date of the press article (May 1) and the poor transportation conditions between the mainland and Ulleungdo at the time, this report, which basically had the same content as the one Shim Heung-taek had submitted to the Acting Governor of Gangwon-do, could also have been sent around March 29. What is likely to have happened is that County Magistrate Shim thought he could accelerate the process and more quickly alert the government in Seoul to the Japanese annexation of Dokdo by sending another report directly to the Ministry of the Interior, at the same time as sending one to his direct superior.

In this report sent to the Ministry of the Interior, Magistrate Shim stated that he had received a visit by a group of Japanese officials who had announced to him that Dokdo, an island within the county's jurisdiction, had been annexed to Japan, and who, further, had inquired about the extent of the county's jurisdiction, its population and farmland area. The Ministry of the Interior, according to the report by *Daehan Maeil Sinbo*, responded to this report by stating that it was one thing to request information about a county, visited in the course of a trip, but quite another thing to make a territorial claim over an island in that county's jurisdiction, and that it was mystified by this report and the outlandish facts related within it. The response of the Ministry of the Interior, therefore, was essentially no different from that of the Uijeongbu. The Ministry of the Interior, thus, also objected to the Japanese annexation of Dokdo and made it clear that the latter was an island in Korean possession.

Meanwhile, Deputy Prime Minister (*Uijeongbu Chamjeong Daesin*) Park Je-sun, as mentioned earlier, instructed the governor of Gangwon-do, through Order No. 3, dated May 25, to re-ascertain the facts reported by Shim Heung-taek by conducting an inquiry into the current status of Dokdo and to find out what exactly the Japanese had done. The Interior Ministry's response to Shim Heung-taek's report is likely to have contained similar instructions, although there is no direct evidence. No follow-up report on this affair, however, either by the governor of Gangwon-do or the magistrate of Uldo County, has ever been found.

It is possible that these orders from the Korean government never reached the governor of Gangwon-do or the magistrate of Uldo County, or that they did reach the latter, but their follow-up reports never got to their destinations. By being forced to sign the Korea-Japan Protocol (February 1904), shortly after the outbreak of the Russo-Japanese War, the Korean government never reached the governor of Gangwon-do or the magistrate of Uldo County, or that they did reach the latter, but their follow-up reports never got to their destinations. By being forced to sign the Korea-Japan Protocol (February 1904), shortly after the outbreak of the Russo-Japanese War, the Korean government ceded to the Japanese its control over all postal and telecommunications services. Japan, therefore, had the means to block or seize any official communications deemed to potentially undermine its interests.

Another possible scenario is that the follow-up reports by the governor of Gangwon-do and (or) the magistrate of Uldo County were received by the Korean government, but later vanished from its archives. In the post-Russo-Japanese War years, the Japanese had de facto control of the Korean government. It was not at all beyond their means to have a document that they saw as being undesirable from the point of view of Japanese interests removed or destroyed, having one of their own officials or a Korean official carry out the deed. Besides, there are a few other cases of missing government documents in which the prime suspects behind the documents' absence are the Japanese. An Yong-bok's testimony to the Border Defense Council and the missing entries of *Sukjong Sillok* (Annals of King Sukjong's Reign), between the 1st month, 22nd year of Sukjong (1696) and the 12th month, 24th year of Sukjong (1698), the period during which the Ulleungdo Dispute (Takeshima Ikken) was at its height, are cases in point.

Usando of Uldo County

The Korean government, after learning that Japan had annexed Dokdo through the reports of Acting Governor of Gangwon-do Yi Myeong-rae and Shim Heung-Taek, County Magistrate of Uldo County appears to have made no protest. By that time the government had not means at its disposal to make official protests vis-à-vis a foreign state. The government, whose ability to externally represent the Korean state had been increasingly sabotaged by the Japanese during the Russo-Japanese War, was completely divested of control over its foreign relations with the signing of the Eulsa Restriction Treaty (November 1905). The Foreign Ministry was shut down two months after the conclusion of the treaty, in January 1906, with all diplomatic rights surrendered to the Japanese. The opening of the Japanese Residency General in February of the same year reduced Korea to the state of a de facto occupied nation. In such a situation, the Korean government, even if it wanted to lodge an official protest against the Japanese annexation of Dokdo, simply had no means to do so. The only option remaining was to have a Japanese official stationed in Korea contact the Foreign Ministry of Japan; in other words, to forlornly hope that the Japanese would help the Korean government save itself from Japan's machinations.

Much had also changed with the onset of the Russo-Japanese War. The stationing of Japanese policemen in Ulleungdo and Japanese residing illegally on the island were issues on which the Korean government continued to place diplomatic pressure on Japan up until the Russo-Japanese War. With the outbreak of this war, however, a deafening silence on the part of the Korean government ensued with regard to these issues. The Russo-Japanese War was a game-changer for Japan, and the odds were becoming increasingly stacked against Korea, which also faced the imminent prospect of being annexed to Japan. In a situation where the entire country was on the brink of being annexed to Japan, the government could hardly afford to worry about Dokdo— or even Ulleungdo.

The Korean government's silence over the Japanese annexation of Dokdo, however, does not mean that it accepted or tolerated this action. The fact that the Japanese decision to annex Dokdo did not in any way change the Korean perception of this island as being part of its sovereign territory is made clear, for instance, by government publications such as the *Jeungbo Munheon Bigo* (Revised and Enlarged Edition of a Reference Compilation of Documents on Korea). In the article on Uljin in *Yeojigo* of *Jeungbo Munheon Bigo*, an updated body of historical government records and documents, published on Emperor Gojong's order, the following description of Usando (Dokdo) may be found:

"Usando and Ulleungdo … are two islands, one of which is called "Usan." Today, they belong to Uldo County."

"Today," here, refers to 1908, the year of the *Jeungbo Munheon Bigo*'s publication; hence, the passage states that Usando and Ulleungdo, as of 1908, were part of Uldo County. Usando (Dokdo), in other words, Seokdo, was placed under the jurisdiction of Uldo County through "Imperial Decree No. 41, 4th Year of Gwangmu, On the Renaming of Ulleungdo to Uldo and the Promotion of the Post of Island Chief to County Magistrate," as has been mentioned repeatedly. Korea was not in a position to protest against the annexation of Dokdo by Japan, but it is a well-known and established fact that Dokdo is Korean territory, not Japanese."

Reference

Ikeuchi Hiroshi, "Chosen Koraicho ni Okeru Tojoshin no Kaiko (Eastern Jurchen Pirates during the Joseon and Goryeo Dynasties)," in *Man-Sen Chiri Rekishi Kenkyu Hokoku* (Geographical and Historical Research Report on Manchuria and Joseon) 8, 1921, pp. 216-217.

Goryeosa, "Sega," Byeongo day, 8th month, Taejo 13.

Sejong Sillok, "Jiriji," Uljin County, Gangwon-do; Sin Gyeong-jun, *Ganggyego*, (Ulleungdo); *Dongguk Munheon Bigo, Yeojigo* 13, Gwanbang 3, Donghae Uljin; *Mangi Yoram*, "*Gunjeongpyeon*" 4, Haebang, Donghae.

Takeshima no Kakitsuke; Tsukamoto Takahashi, "Takeshima Kankei Kyu Tottorihan Bunsho Oyobi Ezu," *Reference* 411 (1985), pp. 80-81; Yi Hun, "Joseong Hugi-Ui Dokdo Yeongsok Sibi (The Territorial Dispute Over Dokdo During the Late Joseon Period)," in *Dokdo-wa Daemado* (Dokdo and Tsushima), Seoul: Jiseong-ui Saem, 1996, pp. 39-40; Naito Seichu, op cit., pp. 84-86; Park Byoung-sup, op. cit., pp. 50-51.

Yi Byeong-do, "Dokdo Myeongching-e Daehan Sa-jeok Gochal – Usan Jukdo Myeongchinggo (The Historical Names of "Dokdo": Usando and Jasando)," in *Chomyeong Ginyeom Bulgyosa Nonchong* (A Collection of Papers on the History of Buddhism Commemorating the Work of Cho Myeong-gi), 1963; Song Byeong-kie, "Gojong-ui Ulleungdo Dokdo Gyeongyeon (The Administration of Ulleungdo and Dokdo During the Reign of Gojong)," *Dokdo Yeongu*, Society for Modern Korean History Sources, 1985, pp. 189.

Hori Kazuo, "1905 nen Nihon no Takeshima Ryodo Hennyu," *Chosenshi Kenkyukai Rombunshu* 24 (1987), pp. 103-104; Naito Seichu Park Byoung-sup, *Takeshima=Dokuto Ronso*, Tokyo: Shinkansha, 2007, p. 89.

Ikeuchi Satoshi, *Taikun Gaiko to Bui* (Imperial Diplomacy and Military Might), Nagoya: Nagoya Daigaku Suppankai, 2006, pp. 205-259.

Tabohashi Kiyoshi, op. cit., "Utsuryoto Sono Hakken to Ryoyu (Discovery of Ulleungdo and the Question of Its Ownership)," *Seikyu Gakuso*, no. 3, 1931, pp. 20-21; Kawakami Kenzo, *Takeshima no Rekishi Chirigakuteki Kenkyu*, Tokyo: Kokoshoin, 1966, p. 159; Ikeuchi Satoshi, op. cit., pp. 320-321. *Takehima Kiji*, which is considered to be a basic primary source for the study of the Ulleungdo Jaenggye, is not an exception in this view; *Takehsima Kiji* (1726), entry of 5th month, 11st year of Genroku and 19th day, 10th month, 12th year of Genroku.

Nihon Gaiko Bunsho, vol. 2 and 3, Document no. 574, and vol. 3, Document no. 87; Sin Yong-ha, op. cit., pp. 156-164.

Hori Kazuo, op. cit., p. 105.

Hori Kazuo, op. cit., p. 118.

Jeungbo Munheon Bigo I, "Jeungbo Munheon Bigo Byeomrye."

Japan Knows the Truth

Survey of Oki by the Japanese Navy Hydrographic Office and Its Perception of Dokdo

Han Cheol-ho

Professor, Dongguk University

1. Introduction

Because Dokdo is clearly and inherently Korean territory both historically and geographically, and also in terms of international law, there should be no reason for a territorial dispute to exist over Dokdo in the first place. In spite of this fact, Japan has shown no remorse over its land grab of Dokdo from Korea in February 1905. Japan forcibly annexed Dokdo based on the logic that the island was a *terra nullius* and by taking advantage of its superior military power and the favorable international political climate at the time. Rather than trying to redeem the past, Japan has instead redoubled its efforts to thrust Dokdo back into the internationally spotlight as a disputed territory. This year, for the first time, a member of the Japanese government's cabinet attended a so-called "Takeshima Day" event, and the Japanese Ministry of Foreign Affairs has continued, as in the previous years, to publish its *Diplomatic Bluebook* noting Japan's territorial claims to Dokdo. Also, the Japanese Ministry of Education, Culture, Sports, Science and Technology approved publication of a textbook for high school social studies, history, and geography depicting Dokdo as part of Japan.

Under these circumstances, urgent work remains to be done to expose the fallaciousness of the Japanese arguments and to highlight the legitimacy of Korea's claims by refining existing evidence and further developing arguments that objectively validate Korea's rightful sovereignty over the island. Based on newly discovered data, this paper seeks to establish that, prior to Japan's forced annexation of Dokdo in 1905, the Japanese Hydrographic Office (水路部)[1] had consistently perceived Dokdo as Korean territory. It is an established fact that the Hydrographic Office, which was charged with surveying sea routes and coasts, had the most accurate knowledge of an island's territorial status, and thus it would appear to be a fitting representative of the Japanese government's official position with regards to Dokdo.

The issue of how the Japanese Navy's Hydrographic Office perceived Dokdo was raised for the first time not by academia but at the government level in memoranda exchanged twice between the Korean and Japanese governments in 1953 and 1954, respectively, concerning Dokdo. In these memoranda, Japan discussed *the World Sea Directory* (寰瀛水路誌; *Kan'ei Suiroshi*) (1866) in an attempt to explain that there had been some confusion over the geographic name of Dokdo in Japan. In doing so, however, it failed to mention the fact that Dokdo was recorded as "Liancourt Rocks" in the chapter titled "East Coast of Joseon."[2] Thus, it publicly disclosed the existence of an important historical data source, which provided further evidence that Dokdo was in fact Korean territory. However, at the time, the Korean govern-

---

1   The Hydrographic Office of Japan changed names several times, to *suirokyoku* (水路局) of the Navy Ministry in October 1871; *suiroryō* (水路寮) directly under the Minister of the Japanese Navy in April 1872; *suirokyoku* of the Navy in September 1876; *suirobu* (水路部) of the Navy in April 1886; and *suirobu* (水路部) since June 1886. This paper generally refers to it as the Hydrographic Office.

2   Treaty Bureau of the Japanese Foreign Ministry, *Sovereignty over Takeshima*, Treaty Bureau, 1953, pp. 30-32.

ment failed to recognize the significance of this fact, and in consequence did not engage in any further discussion or study of that document. Instead, it merely referred Japan to the part titled "East Coast of Joseon" in *Sea Directory off the Coast of Joseon* (朝鮮沿岸水路誌) (1933), Volume 3, which recorded in precise detail the location and terrain of Dokdo under the section "Ulleungdo and Takeshima," and argued on that basis that even during Japan's forceful occupation of Korea, Japan recognized Dokdo as an island associated with Ulleungdo in Korea.[3]

In response to this argument, the Japanese government countered that "a sea directory (水路誌; *suiroshi*) is published for the convenience of the user, and as such has no bearing on an island's territoriality." It went on to say that, "Takeshima is an island that is occasionally relevant when navigating in the vicinity of Ulleungdo, and it is noted along the port of Ulleungdo for no other reason than that." They argued further that Takeshima was also mentioned under the section "Oki Islands & Takeshima" (隠岐島及竹島) in *Sea Directory off the Coasts of Honshu, Japan* (日本本洲沿岸水路誌) because it was also relevant to navigation in the vicinity of Oki islands, "clearly showing that the Hydrographic Office did not consider Takeshima as an island associated with Ulleungdo."[4] In response, the Korean government pointed out that in *Sea Directory off the Coast of Joseon*, Takeshima's location and terrain were recorded in precise detail, whereas the *Sea Directory off the Coasts of Honshu, Japan* merely mentioned the name of Takeshima, an indication that Dokdo was not considered to inherently belong to Japan. The Korean government's argument was that the striking difference in the way Dokdo was listed in this additional mention of Dokdo merely confirms once again that the Japanese Hydrographic Office viewed Dokdo as Korean territory associated with Ko-

---

3   International Law Bureau of the Korean Foreign Ministry, *Overview of the Dokdo Issue*, Ministry of Foreign Affairs, 2012, p. 102.

4   Information & Culture Bureau, "On the proposal made to the Korean Government regarding the submission of the Takeshima issue to the International Court of Justice," *Monthly Report on Overseas Research*, Nov. 1954, pp. 68-69

rea's island of Ulleungdo.[5]

Even though the aforementioned discussion between the two countries was limited *Sea Directory off the Coast of Joseon* published in 1933, sea directory (水路誌; *suiroshi*) published by the Japanese Navy's Hydrographic Office subsequently emerged as a focal point in the dispute over the territorial status of Dokdo, and it is noteworthy that the two countries' basic positions on the relative significance of these sea directories continues to this day. The Japanese government continues to maintain its position that sea directories have no bearing on an island's territoriality, whereas the Korean government presents these directories as decisive evidence that the Japanese government perceived Dokdo as Korean territory as these documents represented the official view of the Japanese government's Hydrographic Office. On the other hand, Yamabe (山邊健太郎) assessed that, because *Sea Directory off the Coast of Joseon* predated Japan's forcible annexation of Dokdo, the directory's notation of Dokdo as an island associated with Ulleungdo is definitely evidence more favorable to the Korean position, though he did not make an issue of the nature of sea directories.[6]

Hori (堀和生) was one of the first in Japanese academia to seriously criticize the Japanese government's position that sea directories of the time are completely irrelevant to the issue of Dokdo's territorial status. He argued as follows, based on the assumption that because a sea chart only shows geographical perception, more weight should be given to its corresponding sea directory, which serves as an interpretation of that chart, in determining the territorial status of an island in the middle of that chart. While acknowledging that *the World Sea Directory* is a global sea directory not intended for use

5   International Law Bureau of the Korean Foreign Ministry, *Overview of the Dokdo Issue*, pp. 109-110, p. 129.

6   Yamabe Kentarō, "A historical study of the Takeshima issue," *Korea Review* 7-2, 1965, pp. 7-8, p. 13. See Han Cheol-ho, "Issues and tasks related to the study of the Japanese policy and perception of Dokdo Island in the Meiji Period," *The Journal for the Studies of Korean History* 28, 2007, pp. 342-344.

in determining the territoriality of an island such as Dokdo, he argued that Dokdo (Liancourt) and Ulleungdo are excluded from the *Japan Sea Directory* (日本水路誌; *Nihon Suiroshi*) (1897), the scope of which is clearly limited to the territorial land and waters of Japan, while the two islands are featured in the *Korea (Joseon) Sea Directory* (朝鮮水路誌; *Chōsen Suiroshi*) (1894, 1899). As such, he concluded that, around 1900, at least the Hydrographic Office, and with all likelihood the other relevant agencies of the Japanese government as well, undoubtedly perceived both Dokdo (=Takeshima) and Ulleungdo as Korean territory.[7]

Since then, extensive research has been conducted on other publications of the Japanese Navy's Hydrographic Office, such as *Hydrographic Magazine* (水路雜誌) and various sea charts. The findings can be summarized as follows: 1) it is clear that sea directories were published by state territory or state jurisdiction, based on the fact that the 1897 edition of *Japan Sea Directory* listed Taiwan (臺灣) after it was acquired by Japan in the Russo-Japanese War, and the fact that *Joseon Sea Directory* eased to be published after Japan "annexed" Joseon and was instead included in *Japan Sea Directory* starting in 1911; 2) Dokdo and Ulleungdo were consistently featured under the section "East Coast of Joseon" of *the World Sea Directory* (1883, 1886) and *Joseon Sea Directory* (1894, 1899, 1907); 3) *Japan Sea Directory* did not include Dokdo and Ulleungdo in its 1897 edition; rather, it was only in its 1907 edition that the two islands were included for the first time, under "Northwest Coasts of Honshu (Main Island)" (本州北西岸) in the third volume, along with a note that they had been annexed into Shimane Prefecture (島根縣); 4) as the head of the Japanese Hydrographic Office and the person responsible for editing *Joseon Sea Directory* and *Japan Sea Directory* and for writing the preface to both, Kimotsuki Kaneyuki (肝付兼行) knew better than anyone that Dokdo was Korean territory; however, it was he who talked fisherman Nakai Yozaburo

7   Hori Kazuo, "Japan's annexation of Takeshima in 1905," *Collection of dissertations of the Society for Study of Korean History* 24, 1987, pp. 105-107.

(井養三郎) into submitting the "Petition for Annexation of Ryanko Island (Dokdo) and Permission to Lease the Island" to the Japanese government.

These facts clearly show that not only the Hydrographic Office but also the Japanese government as a whole considered Dokdo as an island associated with Ulleungdo and hence a part of Korean territory, at least until 1905. Furthermore, even if it were to be conceded, as the Japanese government argues, that sea directories are irrelevant to an island's territorial status, and that the Hydrographic Office was never intended to be an institution responsible for determining the borders of countries, it has been definitely proven that sea directories did represent the official perception and position of the Hydrographic Office and by implication of the Japanese government as a whole as well, and thus are decisive evidence that can be used in determining the territorial status of Dokdo.[8]

However, previous research has failed to meticulously analyze the survey records of the Hydrographic Office contained in *Hydrographic Magazine* and other sources, which were used as base data for publishing sea directories. It has also been limited by its failure to holistically consider the implications of various maps, including sea directories, for determining perceptions of an island's territoriality contained in them. In addition, the focus placed on examining the content on Dokdo and Ulleungdo in sea directories resulted in

---

8   Some key studies on Japanese sea directories include Shin Yong-ha, A *Historical Study of Dokdo as a Territory of Korea*, Jisik Saneop-sa, 1996; Song Byung-gi, *Historical Examination of Ulleungdo and Dokdo*, Yeoksa Gong-gan, 2010; Naitō Seitsu, *The History of Japan-Korea Relations over Takeshima (Ulleungdo)*, Taga-shuppan, 2000 [Naitō Seitsu, translated by Kwon O-yeop and Kwon Jeong, *Dokdo and Jukdo*, J&C, 2005]; Naitō Seitsu & and Park Byoung-sup, *Dokdo=Takeshima Dispute—Thinking from Historical Documents—*, Shinkansha, 2007 [Naitō Seitsu and Park Byoung-sup, *The Dokdo-Takeshima Controversy: A Study based on Historical Documents*, Bogo-sa, 2008]; Yu Mi-rim, Choi Eun-suk, *Trends in Perception of Ulleungdo and Dokdo, Perception of Dokdo and Ulleungdo in Modern Maps of Japan*, Korea Maritime Development Institute, 2010; Hosaka Yuji et al., "Westerners' Exploration of the East Sea and Dokdo inside Sea Directories," *Journal of Japanese Culture* 46, 2010; and Song Hwi-young, "Japan's Perception of Ulleungdo and Dokdo as reflected in the Sea Directories of Modern Japan," *Daegu History Studies* 106, 2012.

relatively insufficient weight to be given to the Japanese government's perception of Oki as it relates to Dokdo. In particular, previous research has paid little attention to the fact that Kimotsuki, who was deeply involved in Japan's forcible annexation of Dokdo, personally surveyed and studied Oki and recorded its exact geographic location; it also failed to meticulously analyze how Oki was perceived and recorded in sea directories that Kimotsuki was directly or indirectly involved in publishing.

Therefore, this paper will proactively utilize findings of existing research as well as newly identified sea directories to reveal how the Japanese Navy's Hydrographic Office perceived Oki and Dokdo. The intent of this study is to show that the Hydrographic Office, after directly surveying Oki, consistently excluded Dokdo from the territorial jurisdiction of Oki, while recognizing it as being within Korean territory elsewhere. To this end, this paper will first examine reports by Kimotsuki and others with regards to the Hydrographic Office's survey of Japan's northwest coast, as well as associated charts such as those of "Oki Islands" (隠岐列島) and "All Islands of Oki" (隠岐全島), which reveal the Hydrographic Office e's perception of Dokdo in relation to Oki. This will be followed by an overall summary of the Hydrographic Office's perception of Oki and Dokdo as revealed in *the World Sea Directory*, *Joseon Sea Directory*, and *Japan Sea Directory*.

2. The Japanese Hydrographic Office's Survey of Oki in the Northwest Coast, Charts Development, and Perception of Dokdo

1) The 1879 Survey of Oki by Kimotsuki Kaneyuki on the *Mōshun*

The first time the Japanese Hydrographic Office surveyed the Oki Islands was in April, 1879. Initially, the Hydrographic Office had been given the task of surveying the coasts of Sanin (山陰) and Hokuriku (北陸), with officials of the Hydrographic Office on board the *Daini Teibō* (第二丁卯), a survey ship under the administration of the Hydrographic Office. However, when the *Daini Teibō* reached Shimonoseki (下關) after departure for survey, it was ordered to participate in military action against Joseon along with the warships *Unyo* (雲揚) and *Kasuga* (春日). The ship stopped surveying and changed course, arrived in Busan on June 12 and stayed there until July 1. This was because Japan had decided to pursue gunboat diplomacy by dispatching the *Unyo* and other ships in late May in order to find a pretext for forcing Joseon to open its ports. Three months later, the *Unyo* again sailed to Joseon on the pretext of surveying, and finally on September 20, deliberately instigated the "*Unyo* Incident." This resulted in the *Kasuga* and the *Daini Teibō* being repeatedly dispatched to Joseon to protect Japanese nationals there.[9]

Following the return of the *Daini Teibō* to its survey mission in November of 1875, discussion was initiated in January of 1876 on whether or not to survey the northwest coast of Japan between Nagato (長門) and Noto (能登), which were the original targets of the survey. However, this survey was cancelled due to opinions held by Nakamuta Kuranosuke (中牟田倉之助) and others that conditions were not favorable. Ultimately, in February, the *Daini Teibō* was reorganized to being a regular ship. In light of the new Treaty of Amity signed with Joseon and the on-going gradual development of the coastal area of the East Sea ("the Sea of Japan"), Yanagi Narayoshi (柳楢悅), the head of the Hydrographic Office, saw it as an urgent priority in January 1877 to have two survey teams on a survey ship, with one team going to the northwest coast, and the other sailing on further to survey the approximately 660 *li* from Busan, along the southern coast of Joseon, and then up its west coast to the Aprok River (a.k.a. Yalu), and simultaneously select and survey four to five key ports. He thus submitted a survey plan and a detailed budget

---

9   [Japanese Navy Ministry] Published by the Hydrographic office, *History of the Hydrographic Office: Meiji years 2-18,* Hydrographic Office, 1916, pp. 122, 126, 138; Yokoyama Yoshinori, "Surveys of the coastal waters of Japan in the 19th century," compiled by Kuroda Hideo et al., *A political and cultural history of maps and paintings,* University of Tokyo Press, 2001, p. 321.

proposal, but his request was not accepted.[10]

Subsequently, Japan focused on the surveying of Joseon's coasts, while domestically most of its naval power was mobilized to suppress the *Satsuma* Rebellion. For this reason, the task of surveying Japan's coasts remained largely on hold.[11] "Because of the increasing demands placed on the military and the limited number of naval ships available, no opportunity availed for execution, but finally in 1879, demands upon the military gradually subsided and the number of warships not in use saw a relative increase, resulting in more favorable conditions for the survey of the northwest coast."[12]

Following the arrival of the warship *Mōshun* (孟春艦) to replace the *Takaomaru* (高雄丸) in March of 1879, the Hydrographic Office began a survey of the harbors along the northwest coast of Japan's main island (本州; Honshu), which had previously been a top priority.[13] Five people, including Navy Lieutenant Kimotsuki Kaneyuki, Ensigns Kanaki Juichiro (金木十一郎), Kobayashi Harumi (小林春三), and Arikawa Sadashiro (有川貞白), and Second Lieutenant on Probation Arahata Iwajiro (荒畑岩次郎), meticulously surveyed the northwest coast including Oki for approximately seven months, from April 20 to November 20, on board the *Mōshun*. They departed Tokyo on April 20 and surveyed the port of Saigo (西郷港) in May, the port of Ogi (小木) of Sado (佐渡) in June, Nanaohoku Bay (七尾北湾) and the Port of Husiki (伏木港) of Noto (能登) in July, Obama Bay (小浜湾) of Wakasa (若狭) and Miyazu Port (宮津港) of Tango (丹後) in August, and Yuya Bay (油谷湾) of Nagato (長門) in October, and then returned to Tokyo. In the meantime,

---

10   *History of the Japanese Hydrographic Office*, 138, pp. 144-145, pp. 180-181.

11   Yokoyama, pp. 321-322.

12   Kimotsuki Kaneyuki, "Brief Records of Sea Lanes on the Northwest Coast of Japan 1," *Hydrographic Magazine* 38, 1883, pp. 3-5.

13   丙 31, "notice of the warship *Mōshun* under the control of the Hydrographic *Office*" March 3-27, Meiji 12, National Institute for Defense Studies of the Ministry of Defense, Retrieval Code Kaigunshyou(海軍省)-Koubungenshyo(公文原書)-M12-34-277.

Kimotsuki and others measured the longitudinal difference between Niigata
(新潟) and Tokyo in June and between Shimonoseki and Tokyo in October.[14]

The 1879 survey of the northwest coast including Oki carries ground-
breaking significance in the history of Japanese hydrographic surveys, so much
so that Kimotsuki, who was responsible for the survey, remarked that "the
navigation of the *Mōshun* last year [1879] can be said to be the beginning of
imperial navigation following Meiji. Therefore, the parts of the coasts that
were subject to our surveys were definitely not insignificant."[15] Of particular
significance within the scope of the *Mōshun*'s survey, as noted by individuals
such as Kimotsuki, are the Oki Islands and their surroundings, which are
closely related to Dokdo. The survey of these islands is worthy of note in two
respects. The first is that the *Mōshun* survey's delineation of the boundaries of
the Oki Islands (or All Islands of Oki) provides a definite and important basis
for establishing the territorial status of Dokdo. The second is that the person
responsible for the Oki survey was Kimotsuki, who played an important role
in Japan's forcible annexation of Dokdo in 1905.

As is widely known, Kimotsuki was the best authority on coastal and hydrographic surveying in Meiji-era Japan, and for that reason was more familiar
with the territorial status of various islands than anyone else. Of note, it was
no other than Kimotsuki himself who convinced fisherman Nakai to submit

---

14   履入 600, "Report to the Hydrographic *Office* on the departure of Kimotsuki and four others on board the *Mōshun*," April 19-21 of Meiji 12, National Institute for Defense Studies of
the Ministry of Defense Retrieval Code 海軍省-公文類纂-M12-13-421; 往入 2205, "Report
to the Hydrographic *Office* on the surveys of Sanin and Hokuriku by the *Mōshun*, and seven
other cases," July 7 – December 2 of Meiji 12, National Institute for Defense Studies of the
Ministry of Defense Retrieval Code 海軍省-公文類纂-M12-63-471; 秘入 1098, "Report to the
Hydrographic *Office* regarding the order for Kimotsuki and four others to return, and two other
cases," November 12-21 of Meiji 12, National Institute for Defense Studies of the Ministry of
Defense Retrieval Code 海軍省-公文類纂-M12-52-460; compiled by the Hydrographic *Office*
of the Maritime Safety Agency, *Hydrographic History of Japan: 1871-1971*, Japan Hydrographic
Association, 1971, p. 34.

15   Kimotsuki, "Brief Records of Sea Lanes on the Northwest Coast of Japan 1," p. 2.

the so-called "Petition for Annexation of Ryanko Island (Dokdo) and Permission to Lease the Island" to the Japanese government before Japan forcibly placed Dokdo under the jurisdiction of the governor of Oki in the Shimane Prefecture on February 22, 1905. Nakai had perceived Dokdo as Korean territory and was going to request a permit for monopoly rights on the hunting of sea lions in Dokdo to the Korean government. Kimotsuki, however, advised and persuaded Nakai that Dokdo should be annexed by Japan, on grounds that there was no clear evidence that Dokdo belonged to anyone, it was closer to Japan than to Korea by 10 *li*, and there was no evidence that Koreans had ever governed the island while the Japanese were already administering it. Kimotsuki's logic to occupy Dokdo as *terra nullius* is still used to this day and serves as the basis for Japan's claims of sovereignty over Dokdo.

Then, how did Kimotsuki, who was one of the three main players involved in Japan's forcible annexation of Dokdo, along with Yamaza Ejiro (山座円次郎), head of the Political Affairs Bureau at the Foreign Affairs Ministry, and Maki Naomasa (牧朴眞), head of the Fisheries Bureau at the Ministry of Agriculture and Commerce, assess and perceive Oki's boundaries after his direct involvement in the survey of Oki? Reports of Kimotsuki's surveys of the northwest coast were published in *Hydrographic Magazine* under such titles as "Brief Records of Navigation of Oki" (隠岐回航畧記), and "Brief Records of Sea Lanes on the Northwest Coast of Japan 1-3" (日本北西岸水路畧記 1~3). In one of these reports, Kimotsuki wrote as follows regarding the territorial boundaries of Japan's northwest coast including Oki:

> Japan's northwest coast is the coast extending east from Kanmon Straits (下關海峽) to Tsugaru Strait (津輕海峽), and in navigational terms is called Kitamae (北前). Although it is called the north-facing coast, the reason is unclear. Westerners call it the west coast of Japan. As it is a coast that faces west, such an appellation cannot be said to be inappropriate. However, in actuality, it has [a ratio of] 6 north and 4 west, so it would

be appropriate to call it the northwest coast.[16]

The length of the entire coast begins at 33° 57' North and ends at 41° 16' North, and starts at 133° 48' East and ends at 140° 22' East. Thus, it begins from the western end of the Kanmon Straits, extends northeast, and ends at the southern corner of the western end of the Tsugaru Strait. Its length is approximately 1,000 *li* (translator's note: approximately 4,000 km), extending over four circuits (道; dō) of San'yo (山陽), Sanin, Hokuriku, and Higashiyama (東山), and bordering 16 provinces including Nagato, Iwami (石見), Izumo (出雲), Houki (伯耆), Inaba (因幡), Tajima (但馬)… and Mutsu (陸奥). The two provinces of Oki and Sado extend east and west like a bowstring, and touch the Sea of Japan facing the faraway coasts of Joseon and Manchuria. The distance from the northwest corner of Nagato is less than 100 *li* and can be crossed with a small boat. In short, this coast forms the southwest coastline of the Sea of Japan… Where the islands extend out like a bow are five big islands, that is, Oki Islands, Sado-shima, and Mishima (見島) is at Nagato, Aoshima (粟生島) at Echigo (越後), and Tobishima (飛島) at Ugo (羽後).[17]

To summarize, the northwest coast extends almost 1,000 *li* east from the Shimonoseki Strait to the Tsugaru Strait, spanning San'yo and three other provinces, bordering 16 provinces such as Nagato and Izumo, and including the two provinces of Oki and Sado. Oki is the next largest of the five main islands after Sadogashima (佐渡島). As one proceeds west, one approaches Joseon, and from the northwestern corner of Nagato, the distance between the two countries is less than 100 *li* and can be crossed easily. It is inferred that such a geographic location was one of the main factors in the northwest coast being selected as a priority area to survey. Of particular note is the fact that the

---

16   Kimotsuki, "Brief Records of Sea Lanes on the Northwest Coast of Japan 1," p. 1.

17   Kimotsuki, "Brief Records of Sea Lanes on the Northwest Coast of Japan 1," pp. 5-8.

boundary of the northwest coast in its entirety is defined as being from 33° 57' North to 41° 16' North, and from 133° 48' East to 140° 22' East. However, the "133°" mentioned here, let alone the "48'," is certainly an erroneous recording, as it should have been 130°. This is supported by the fact that the northern coast of Nagato, the westernmost part of the northwest coast, was described as having "an area spanning from 33° 56' North to 34° 47' North, and 130° 47' East to 131° 42' East."[18] It can also be easily confirmed by the longitude and the latitude measurements of the coast as recorded in the "Northwest Coast of Japan, from Nagato to Hoki" (日本北西岸 自長門至伯耆) in *Hydrographic Magazine*. Given these longitude and latitude, the point to be made here is that, if Kimotsuki and others at the Japanese Hydrographic Office viewed Dokdo as Japanese territory, they would not have neglected to include it within the boundaries of the northwest coast.

Kimotsuki noted the limitations of the survey report of the northwest coast as follows: "Fortunately, the weather was good, and there were many clear days, which allowed us to make progress in our survey and carry out a large amount of investigation. So, during the above navigation, records were put down for each and every location surveyed, and whatever could be improved based on records of the West were translated and reflected, resulting in a comprehensive overview of the sea lanes of the northwestern coast. These records were based on a single trip of six months along the 1,000 *li* coast, so it is needless to say that many things were missed."[19] While the above statement suggests that the northwest coast was not surveyed in greater detail and depth due to limited time, it does not imply that coasts, islands, and harbors

---

18   Kimotsuki Kaneyuki, "Brief Records of Sea Lanes on the Northwest Coast of Japan 2," *Hydrographic Magazine* 39, 1883, Chart (Map) in the front, pp. 1-2. It is conjectured that corrections made to "Brief Records of Sea Lanes on the Northwest Coast of Japan 1" were listed on the first page of "Brief Records of Sea Lanes on the Northwest Coast of Japan 2" and "Brief Records of Sea Lanes on the Northwest Coast of Japan 3" because the first manuscript had contained quite a number of typos.

19   Kimotsuki, "Brief Records of Sea Lanes on the Northwest Coast of Japan 1," pp. 3-5.

within the boundaries of the area were omitted or excluded from the survey. Kimotsuki himself wrote that he recorded the entire sea lanes of the north-west coast, going so far as to translate westerners' records to make up for any shortcomings.

Charts (Map) 1
"Northwest Coast of Japan, from Nagato to Hoki" (日本北西岸 自長門至伯耆)

Kimotsuki wrote as follows with regards to Oki's location and its bound-aries:

The province of Oki is at the southwestern corner of Hokkokukai (北國海) [in other countries, it is conventionally called the Sea of Japan], and is located approximately 25 *li* (translator's note: approximately 100km) due north from the shores of Izumo. The province consists of one major island and three minor islands, and 179 small islands [these small islands are grouped together and called the small islands of Oki]. The shape is long from north east to south west, and short from east south to west north. The longitude and latitude begins at 35º 57' North and extends to 36º 18' North, and from 132º East to 133º 23' East. Westerners named these islands the Oki Islands (隠岐列島). The four districts of the province are largely organized into two groups. That is, the two districts of Chibu (知夫) and Ama (海士) are called "Dozen" (島前), and the two districts of Suki (周吉) and Ōchi (隠地) are called "Dogo" (島後) [*Dozen* and *Dogo* are the local dialects.].[20]

Noteworthy in the above quote is the clear delineation of the boundaries of Oki. Following an accurate survey, Kimotsuki recorded that 179 islands belonged to Oki, and that its location was between 35º 57' North and 36º 18' North, and between 132º East and 133º 23' East. This fact alone clearly reveals that Kimotsuki did not include Dokdo, located at 37º 14' North and between 131º 51 East and 131º 52' East, within the boundaries of Oki. Had he perceived Dokdo to be one of the 179 small islands that belonged to Oki, he would have included it within Oki's northern limit and expanded its latitude and longitude measurements accordingly. However, Kimotsuki understood more accurately than anyone that Dokdo was Korean territory, not Japanese; thus, he not only excluded Dokdo from the scope of his survey but also did not write anything about it in the "Brief Records of Navigation of Oki." The fact that Dokdo was included neither in the scope of the northwest coast of Honshu nor in that of the Oki Islands is also further attested to in the "Northwest Coast of Japan, from Nagato to Hoki," which is a part of the Chart(map) of the northwest coast drawn up by Kimotsuki.[21]

---

20 Kimotsuki Kaneyuki, "Brief Records of Navigation of Oki," *Hydrographic Magazine* 19, 1883, pp. 1-2.

21 Kimotsuki Kaneyuki, "Northwest Coast of Japan, from Nagato to Hoki," "Brief Records of Sea Lanes on the Northwest Coast of Japan 2," p. 1.

2) The *Tsukuba*'s Second and Third Navigations of Seas Surrounding Japan in 1879 and 1883

The warship *Tsukuba* (筑波艦) departed Tokyo on September 26, 1879 and carried out the second navigation of the seas surrounding Japan, by circumnavigating the Japanese coast in a counter-clockwise direction, arriving in Tokyo on November 23.[22] During the 57-day journey, the ship sailed for approximately 29 days and was in port for approximately 28 days, covering an overall distance of 2,722.4 *li* at an average speed of 3.85 *li* per hour. Hokkaido (北海道), Ogasawara-shoto (小笠原諸島; Ogasawara Islands), and Ryukyu (琉球) were excluded from this journey. Though Ryukyu was incorporated into Okinawa Prefecture (沖縄縣) following the abolishment of feudal domains and the establishment of *prefectures* (Haihan-chiken; 廃藩置県) on March 27, 1879, it was likely excluded owing to increased tensions with the Qing (China) as a result of protests from the latter about the annexation.[23]

This journey lasted only 57 days, focusing on a survey of the overall sea lanes and observation of weather, including strength and direction of winds, and ocean currents, rather than making a detailed study of the entire Japanese

---

22   It is unclear when the first navigation of the *Tsukuba* of the seas surrounding Japan took place. However, it was most likely around April 1875, given the existence of records kept by three British instructors (including Austin) who were hired by the Japanese Navy Ministry and were on board the *Tsukuba* in April 1875. See 外入 88, "Return of port license by instructor Austin and two others, application to the Navy Military School," February of Meiji 10, National Institute for Defense Studies of the Ministry of Defense Retrieval Code 海軍省-公文類纂-M10-23-243; 外出 95, "Return of port license by Austin and two other British nationals to Foreign Ministry," February 19 of Meiji 10,National Institute for Defense Studies of the Ministry of Defense Retrieval Code 海軍省-公文原書-M10-16-51; "Return of port license by Austin and two other British nationals to Foreign Ministry," February of Meiji 10, National Institute for Defense Studies of the Ministry of Defense Retrieval Code 海軍省-公文備考-M10-26-61; and "Navy Military School, return of port license by instructors," February of Meiji 10, National Institute for Defense Studies of the Ministry of Defense Retrieval Code 海軍省-公文備考-M10-26-61.

23   Kashiwabara Nagashige, "Report of Navigation of Seas Surrounding Japan," *Hydrographic Magazine* 33, 1883, pp. 1, 15, and 19.

coastline. The *Tsukuba* departed Hakodate (函館) on October 16, and continued to sail north of Oki without stopping until it reached Ikitsukishima (生月島) in Hirado (平戸), Hizen (肥前), Nagasaki Prefecture (長崎県) on the 27th. The situation at the time is described as follows in the ship's log:

> From 37° 25' North, 134° 16' East, the direction of the wind changed, becoming a westerly wind. The strength decreased, going from light to none. Daybreak was in 8 hours, and a strong wind came from the south. The weather is evenly divided between cloudy and clear. Approaching near 36° 30' North and 132° North, a bow-like cloud, strong winds and showers came from the southwest. Then, the nature of the wind changed, becoming a strong west-northwest wind. At around 15 o'clock, the strength decreased gradually to no wind. Two hours later, it turned into a strong west-southwest wind. This changed to west, and near 36° North, 131° 20' East, the wind again became northwesterly. With the decrease in the strength, northerly became northeasterly, and to easterly, and ended with a strong east-southeasterly wind.[24]

In short, since Oki is located between 35° 57' North and 36° 18' North, and between 132° East and 133° 23' East, one can see that they passed north of it and recorded the weather and the wind conditions. They did not write about Oki or its surroundings.

However, the "Chart Showing the Course of the *Tsukuba*'s Second Navigation of Seas Surrounding Japan" (筑波艦第二回日本環海航跡之圖), attached at the end of the "Report of Navigation of Seas Surrounding Japan" (大日本環海航行記) written by Navy Lieutenant Colonel Kashiwabara Nagashige (柏原長繁) under the command of Navy Commander Aiura Norimichi (相浦紀道), captain of the *Tsukuba*, demands our attention. This chart marked the actual surveyed route in indigo and the estimated route in red. It depicts the

---

24   Kashiwabara, pp. 10-11.

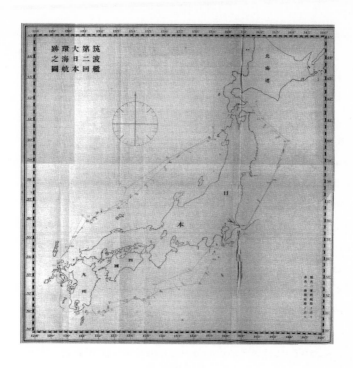

Charts (Map) 2

"Map Showing the Course of the *Tsukuba*'s Second Navigation of Seas
Surrounding Japan" (筑波艦第二回日本環海航跡之圖)

Japanese territory between 30º North and 45º North and between 128º East
and 146º East. Parts of northern Hokkaido, Ogasawara-shoto, and Ryukyu,
not within the scope of the map, are not included. Of particular note is that
the Korean territory to the north and south of Tsushima (對馬島) are not
drawn at all. And the obvious result is that neither Ulleungdo nor Dokdo, an
island associated with Ulleungdo located at 37º 14' North and between 131º
51' East and 131º 52' East, is drawn. Thus, this map is an important source
proving that the Japanese Navy, including the Hydrographic Office, perceived
and understood that Dokdo was Korean territory, not Japanese.[25]

---

25   Kashiwabara, last page.

The crew of the *Tsukuba* made the third navigation of Japan's surrounding seas in 1883. Unlike the second time, they departed Tokyo on February 26, circumnavigated the Japanese coast in a clockwise direction, and arrived in Tokyo on May 21. Ogasawara-shoto and Ryukyu, which had been excluded previously, were included this time. Thus, from Tokyo, the *Tsukuba* sailed through Ogasawara-shoto, turned around at Naha Port (那覇 港) in Ryukyu, sailed past Kyushu, the northwest coast, and the Tsugaru Strait, and returned to Tokyo. Consequently, the area from Tokyo to southern Kyushu, which was navigated during the second trip, was inevitably excluded from the journey. The fact that Ryukyu is not recorded as Okinawa (沖縄) seems to indicate the condition at the time that its territorial status was still unresolved. What is noteworthy about the *Tsukuba*'s third navigation of Japan's surrounding seas is that it sailed around the entirety of what was Japanese territory at the time, except for Hokkaido.

The third journey covered a greater area than the second, taking 85 days, but still did not go beyond observing the route, wind directions, and sea currents. The *Tsukuba* departed Obata Port (小畑港) at 1:45 a.m. on April 17, and arrived on the North side of Oki on the morning of April 18 on its way to Miyazu Port. The situation at the time was recorded as follows.

The wind changed from east-southeast to south-leaning east, and became light. Arriving at 36° 28' North, 133° 8' East, and reviewing the tidal current, it flows 22 *li* towards the East, to 37° 41' North. The temperature is 60 degrees, the barometer on average is 30 *chon* 23, and thermometer shows 62 degrees.[26]

Much like in its second navigation, the *Tsukuba* did not stop at Oki but

---

26   Toho Kakuyuki, "Records of *Tsukuba*'s Navigation of Seas Surrounding Japan," *Hydrographic Magazine* 74, 1883, p. 40.

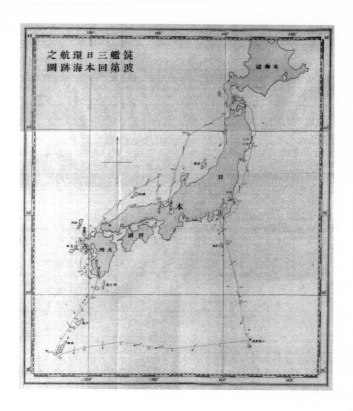

Charts (Map) 3

"Map Showing the Course of *Tsukuba*'s Third Navigation of Seas Surrounding Japan"
(筑波艦第三回日本環海航跡之圖)

navigated north of it; as such, no records of Oki or its surroundings remain
from the third journey.

Also, in the final part of the "Records of the *Tsukuba*'s Navigation of
Seas Surrounding Japan" (筑波艦日本環海周航記事) developed at this time,
the "Map Showing the Course of the *Tsukuba*'s Third Navigation of Seas Surrounding Japan" (筑波艦第三回日本環海航跡之圖) is attached, with the entire
navigation route marked. Drawn on this map is the Japanese territory between
25° North and 45° North and between 126° East and 147° East. The Ogasawara Islands and Ryukyu are shown because they were planned as part of

the trip, unlike the second time. Only some parts of northern Hokkaido are excluded. Again, Korean territory to the north and south of Tsushima, as well as Ulleungdo and Dokdo, are not drawn on the map, an indication that this map only showed areas that were within Japan's territory at the time.[27] Based on these findings, the "Map Showing the Course of the *Tsukuba's* Third Navigation of Seas Surrounding Japan" suggests, much like the "Map Showing the Course of the *Tsukuba's* Second Navigation of Seas Surrounding Japan," that the Japanese Navy perceived Dokdo as territory of Joseon. This finding is quite significant, given that this map acknowledges and reflects Kimotsuki's survey results of Oki, i.e. that Dokdo did not belong to Oki.

3) 1884 Survey and Study of Oki by Kato Shigenari (加藤重成) on the *Raiden* (雷電艦)

Following the 1879 survey of Oki led by Kimotsuki, Kato Shigenari carried out another survey of Oki in 1884. The Japanese coastal survey projects underwent some significant changes during the years between the two surveys, and Kimotsuki and Kato were at the heart of these changes. After becoming the head of the survey branch at the Hydrographic Office, Kimotsuki issued the "Order for Hydrographic Survey" (水路測令) and published a compiled edition of the "Instructions for the Compilation of Hydrographic Maps, Instructions for Sea Surface Measurements, Instructions for Dealing with Longitudinal Lines (水路誌編輯 心得, 驗潮心得, 經線儀取扱心得)," improving survey technology and significantly enhancing the reputation of sea charts in general.

In November of the same year, Yanagi, the head of the Hydrographic Office, established the "12-Year Plan for Survey of All of Japan's Coasts" in order to hasten the day when Japan would conduct its own survey of coastlines as

---

27   Toho, last page.

soon as possible and possess sea charts for every corner of Japanese territory. Kimotsuki, the head of the survey branch, was charged to develop the survey plan. The Navy approved the plan on May 13, 1882, and the survey began in earnest in July. Two separate teams, led by Kimotsuki and Kato, respectively, conducted the survey, with the two leaders alternating as the heads of teams 1 and 2.[28]

During this process, plans were made in January 1884 to survey Tosa (土佐), Hyuganada (日向灘), and other parts of Oki from Japan's Southern Sea, Western Sea, and Sanin, as previous surveys of these areas had been inadequate. Among these, the Oki Islands, situated at the "key gateway to the Northwest" of Japan, had many good ports that were important for coastal defense, but also were the best refuge from the fluctuating winds and tides even in ordinary times. These facts were given consideration. While on board the *Mōshun* during the 1879 survey of Oki's northwest coast, Kimotsuki had recognized the importance of these ports but only surveyed the port of Saigo due to time constraints. Therefore, he saw it necessary to survey the facing coasts of Izumo and Hoki (伯耆) as well. It was further proposed that a ship was needed because of the volatile seas and weather, and that the survey would commence in early March. As a result, instructions were issued in March to inform the Navy base that the *Raiden* would be mobilized for the survey, the time of continued navigation would be limited to 24 hours, and the relevant regional governments should be requested to cooperate with and facilitate the survey.[29]

The *Raiden* needed dock repairs before sailing, but was behind in the queue, so orders were sent to the shipyard to give it special priority. The repairs were still delayed, so Kimotsuki and his team were forced to sail towards the southern sea on board a mail ship. Subsequently, on April 20, 1884, a month

---

28   *History of the Japanese Hydrographic Office*, p. 406; *Hydrographic History of Japan*, pp. 38-42.

29   *History of the Japanese Hydrographic Office*, pp. 407-409.

behind the initial scheduled departure date, Lieutenant Kato, Sub-Lieutenant Kobayashi, Ensigns Tanaka and Arabata, Probationary Officer Ito, and three seamen boarded the *Raiden* and set sail for the northwest coast. Since the *Raiden* was leased for a detailed survey of Ritou (離島), an island far from land, Kato and his team not only surveyed Oki but also the coast facing it in the Izumo region, from Tayusaki (手結埼) to *Mikuriyasaki* (御來屋埼), in detail in August. In September, they surveyed the latitude and the longitude between Tokyo and Sakaiminato (境港). Because the survey of Japan's Southern Sea, Western Sea, and Sanin were considered so important, Yanagi, the head of the Hydrographic Office, personally inspected the survey locations from May to June. He boarded the *Raiden* on May 10 at Kyumoziura (旧門司) and oversaw the progress of the survey at Yuya Bay (油谷灣), Esaki Bay (江崎灣), Mihogaseki (三保ケ関), and Sakaiminato (境港). He arrived at Nishi Port (西郷港) in Oki on the 20th, where, over the course of two days, he inspected the surveys of the Oki coastline by Kato and his team. He also looked at the area around Kitsuki (杵築浦) on Onshu (雲州) on the 22nd and returned to Tokyo on June 26.[30]

The results of the survey by Kato, which were carried out with so much devotion that the head of the Hydrographic Office himself inspected it, are summarized in "Digest of 17 Years of Hydrographic Offices" (十七年事業總攬). In it, it is stated that the purpose of surveying Oki, Izumo and Hoki was to clearly define the mid-part of the northern coast of Nakatsuchi (中土), as well as to enhance Japan's ability to navigate the waters and defend the coast. In detail, the area of Oki surveyed was 578 in square *li*; 494 square *li* in ocean surface area (with the sea depth measured); 5,186 locations where depths were measured; 184 *li* of coastal depth measured; 77 days of tide measurements; and 103 days of surveying. This was, in every respect, superior to the survey

---

30   "Getting on board the *Raiden* on May 27 to Sanin," National Institute for Defense Studies of the Ministry of Defense, Retrieval Code 海軍省-受号通覧- M17-17-40, Navy Ministry Major General Yanagi Narayoshi, May 27-June 6, Meiji 17; *History of the Japanese Hydrographic Office*, pp. 414-416, p. 427; *Hydrographic History of Japan*, p. 40.

done of the area from Izumo's Taigasaki to Hoki's Mikuriyasaki, which measured 411 square *li* in the area surveyed; 269 square *li* in ocean surface (with the sea depth measured); 2,001 locations where depths were measured; 158 *li* of coastal depth measured; 68 days of tide measurements; and 90 days of surveying. It can be conjectured from this fact that Kato focused more on surveying the coasts of Oki than those of Izumo and Hoki.

Of particular note, the longitude and latitude of the measured boundaries of the entirety of Oki are listed as "from 35° 55' North to 36° 27' North, and from 132° 44' East to 133° 31' East." Though slightly different from Kimotsuki's 1879 survey, which observed areas from 35° 57' North to 36° 18' North, and from 132° East to 133° 23' East, the new measurements were deemed to be more accurate. Of course, what the two have in common is that Dokdo, located at 37° 14' North and between 131° 51 East and 52' East, is not included within the boundaries of Oki. The fact that both Kimotsuki and Kato, the best authorities of the era in terms of coastal surveys and longitude-latitude measurements, made a meticulous survey of the entirety of Oki, yet excluded Dokdo from its boundaries, demonstrates that both of them accurately perceived or acknowledged Dokdo as Korean territory.[31]

Kato's survey results, along with the previous results of Kimotsuki's survey, led to the development of charts(maps) of the northwestern coast, including Oki. First, based on Kimotsuki's 1879 survey, the Hydrographic Office published "Oki Province, Saigo Port" (隠岐国西郷港) (No. 107) on February 13, 1880, and "Oki Islands (Division Map), Saigo Port" (隠岐列島(分圖)西郷港) (No. 124) in December 1880. Next, based on Kato's 1884 survey, the Hydrographic Office published "Kasaura, a Coast North of Honshu" (笠浦日本·中土北岸) (No. 161) in May 1885; "Harbors South of Dogo, the Oki Archipelago on the Northern Coast of Japan's Honshu (島後南部諸港灣 日

---

31   "Digest of 17 Years of Hydrographic *Office*," Annex on the Origin and Development of the Hydrographic *Office*, Meiji 17, no. 15 (December), *History of the Japanese Hydrographic Office*, pp. 354-355.

本·中土北岸·隠岐列島)" (No. 174), "Dogo Fukuura" (島後福浦) (No. 175), "Kagaura" (加賀浦) (No. 176) in July 1885; and "Miho Bay" (美保灣) (No. 180) in October 1885. These charts(maps) were published in revised editions in April and December of 1886 with some minor changes.[32] Yanagi reported the publication of these charts(maps) to Navy Minister Enomoto Takeaki (榎本武揚)[33] and also forwarded them to the Staff Headquarters of the Navy Ministry.[34]

Subsequently, the Hydrographic Office consolidated these maps and published "Oki Islands off the Northwest Coast of Honshu, Japan" (隠岐列島 日本·本洲北西岸) (No. 124) in January 1893, which was an improvement upon "Oki Islands (Division Map), Saigo Port." In February of the following year, it published a significantly revised edition of "Oki Islands off the Northwest Coast of Honshu, Japan," which included the depth measurements of coastal waters near Oki. This is confirmed by the notation on these maps that they were "compiled" using the surveys of 1879 and 1884. Next, in January

---

32   Published by the Hydrographic *Office*, *List of Sailing Directions* (海圖水路誌), *January of Meiji 22*, Japanese Navy Ministry Hydrographic *Office*, Mar. 1889; *Hydrographic History of Japan*, p. 78. Also see the notes on the maps owned by the National Archives and the National Diet Library of Japan.

33   往入 181, "Map of Oki Islands reported by the Hydrographic *Office* upon its Publication)," January 24 of Meiji 14, National Institute for Defense Studies of the Ministry of Defense, Retrieval Code 海軍省-公文類纂-M14-18-592; 往入 181, "Report by the Hydrographic Office on the completion of the Oki Islands Map," January 24 of Meiji 14, National Institute for Defense Studies of the Ministry of Defense, Retrieval Code 海軍省-公文原書-M14-4-426; 水 4124, "Regarding the completion of Oki Islands map, including that of Fukuura," September 25 of Meiji 18, National Institute for Defense Studies of the Ministry of Defense, Retrieval Code 海軍省-受号通覧-M18-19-72.

34   参水 1590, *Journal of the General Staff*, November 4 of Meiji 18, National Institute for Defense Studies of the Ministry of Defense, Retrieval Code 参謀本部-大日記-M18-6-46; 参水 1608, *Journal of the General Staff*, November 11 of Meiji 18, National Institute for Defense Studies of the Ministry of Defense, Retrieval Code 参謀本部-大日記-M18-6-46; "Map of Harbors in the South of Oki Islands newly published by the Hydrographic *Office*," April 23-27 of Meiji 19, National Institute for Defense Studies of the Ministry of Defense, Retrieval Code 海軍省-公文雑輯-M19-23-23, Chief of Staff Taruhito Shinnō.

1904, the Hydrographic Office published "Oki Islands, Japan N. W Coast of Honshu" (隱岐全島 日本·本洲北西岸), which were "organized" based on the surveys conducted from 1879 to 1901. This shows that the surveys led by Kimotsuki and Kato significantly influenced the development and publication of the maps of Oki Islands and those of all Islands of Oki even up to 1904. Of course, none of these maps show Dokdo. These maps, developed based on multiple surveys by the Hydrographic Office including those led by Kimotsuki and Kato, wholly reflect the perception that Dokdo was Korean territory, not an island of Oki. Through the publication and distribution of those maps, this perception would obviously have extended beyond the Hydrographic Office to the relevant agencies and ministries within the Japanese government, and further, to the Japanese people, and to foreign governments and agencies that acquired and used those maps.

3. Japan's Perception of Oki and Dokdo as Reflected in the Sea Directory Published by the Japanese Hydrographic Office

The Japanese Hydrographic Office not only used the results of its Oki surveys to develop maps (sea charts), they also used them as the most basic and important data to publish sea directories (水路誌; *suiroshi*). A ship cannot navigate or anchor safely by merely depending on a sea chart, as the latter does not accurately show navigation routes, harbors, coasts, or weather on the sea. Recognizing the absolute need to produce sea directories that provide such information in a detailed and holistic way, the Hydrographic Office made every effort possible to compile and publish sea directories not only of Japan, but of other countries around the world. As is widely known, the Hydrographic Office had published *The World Sea Directory* since 1881. They ceased to do so in 1889, instead beginning to publish country-specific sea directories.

In April 1883, the Hydrographic Office published the second volume of *The World Sea Directory*, in which it described Dokdo and Ulleungdo for the first time under chapter 5, "East Coast of Joseon." Dokdo is described under "Liancourt Rocks," and Ulleungdo follows under "Ulleungdo, known as Matsushima [Western Name "Dagelet"]," respectively.[35] Under "Liancourt Rocks," the first part narrates the discovery by the French ship *Liancourt* in 1849, later investigations by Russia and Britain, and the notes of Charles Forsyth, captain of the British ship *Hornet*, on the longitude, latitude, and the conditions on Dokdo; the latter part notes the distance between Dongdo and Seodo islands, their coastal contours, depth measurements, locations and conditions for navigation.[36]

Subsequently, in March 1886, the Hydrographic Office published *The World Sea Directory*, Volume 1, Part I, which dealt with the southern and western coasts of Japan, and in June 1885, and *The World Sea Directory*, Volume 1 Part II, which dealt with the northern and western coasts of Japan, respectively. With this, the "*Japan Sea Directory*" section of *The World Sea Directory* was completed. Both the "Index Map of Published Sea Charts" (刊行海圖索引圖) following the "Legends" in Volume 1, Part I, and the same map that follows the table of contents in Volume 1, Part II show the entire territory of Japan, but notably, Dokdo is excluded.

In the sub-heading "All Islands of Oki," which is described under chapter 6 on "Northern Coast of Nakatsuchi" (中土北岸), Volume 1, Part II of *The World Sea Directory*, the first part states as follows:

---

35 The second volume of *The World Sea Directory* published in April 1883 has been considerably referenced with respect to Dokdo. However, it is questionable whether such references were made based on an actual reading of the Sea Directories, since many of them are inaccurate; for example, the information that Dokdo (Liancourt Rocks) is included in the "General situation of the state of Joseon" or in chapter "East Coast of Joseon," and was mentioned for the first time in the second edition of the second volume of *The World Sea Directory* (1886) is incorrect. Shin, p. 175; Yu & Choi, p. 137; Hyun Dae-song, "*The World Sea Directory*" *Dokdo Dictionary*, Korea Maritime Institute, 2011, p. 364; Song, p. 252.

36 Japanese Navy Hydrographic Office, *The World Sea Directory*, Volume 2, Japanese Navy Hydrographic Office, 1883, pp. 257-258.

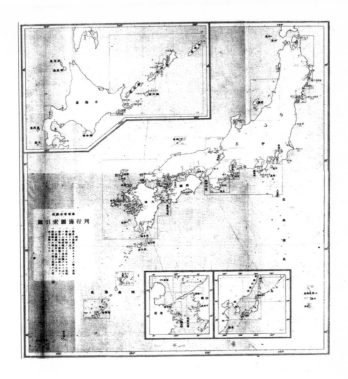

Charts(Map) 4
"Index Map of Published Sea Charts" (刊行海圖索引圖)
(*the World Sea Directory* Volume 1, Part I & II)

Oki Province is at the **southwestern** corner of the **Sea of Japan**, located
approximately 25 *li* due north from the coast of Izumo (出雲). It forms
one state with one large island and three small islands, and 179 small
islets belong to it. [These islets are collectively called the small islets of
Oki.] The shape is long from northeast to southwest, and short from
southeast to **northwest**. The area begins from 35° 57' North and ends
at 36° 18' North, and begins at 132° East and ends at 133° 23' East.
The four districts of the state are largely organized into two groups. That
is, the two districts of Chibu and Ama are called "Dozen", and the two
districts of Suki and Ōchi are called "Dogo." [*Dozen* and *dogo* are local

dialects.] (Bold by the author)[37]

Except for the parts printed in bold, the content above is nearly identical to "Brief Records of Navigation of Oki" that Kimotsuki wrote following his 1879 survey of Oki. That is, the "Hokkokukai [in other countries, it is conventionally called the Sea of Japan]" was changed to "the Sea of Japan," and the sentence "Westerners named this the Oki Islands," which came after the longitude and latitude coordinates, was deleted. Another minor change involved the wording of the cardinal directions.[38] Except for the rewording of phrases or a few additions, the remainder is identical to the content in "Brief Records of Navigation of Oki." In short, Kimotsuki's "Brief Records of Navigation of Oki" was written almost verbatim in the "All Islands of Oki" portion of *The World Sea Directory*.

In fact, Kimotsuki himself revealed that he had taken part in the publication of *The World Sea Directory*, at the same time that he was writing "Brief Records of Sea Lanes on the Northwest Coast of Japan" (日本北西岸水路略記) after finishing "Brief Records of Navigation of Oki." He related the following:

In 1879, Kaneyuki conducted surveys of the coasts of Hokurikudō (北陸道) and Sanindou (山陰道) according to orders given him. Based on the surveys, he wrote "Brief Records of Navigation of Oki" and "Brief Records of Sea Lanes of Noto" (能登水路略記). Subsequently, he proceeded to write five chapters of "Brief Records of Sea Lanes on the Northwest Coast of Japan." The first and the second chapters were written, and recently, the third chapter, that is, this manuscript, was finished. Upon orders to work on the publication of the domestic portion of *The World Sea Directory*, he included the uncompleted chapters 4 and 5 in this journal

---

37 Japanese Navy Hydrographic Office, *The World Sea Directory*, Volume 1, Part II, Japanese Navy Hydrographic Office, 1886, pp. 53-54.

38 See the text corresponding to footnote 20).

[of *The World Sea Directory*]. This concludes this post script.[39]

Moreover, according to the editor's comments by Chief Editor Ishikawa Yonosuke (石川洋之助), head of the cartography department of the Hydrographic Office, all of chapter 6 "Northern Coast of Nakatsuchi" was, in his words, "based on Kaneyuki Kimotsuki's 1879 writing," and additionally, that parts of that chapter referring to the coasts of Izumo and "All Islands of Oki" were further revised based on Kato's 1884 writings.[40]

In other words, the information on "All Islands of Oki" in *The World Sea Directory* was drafted by Kimotsuki and Kato, the best surveyors at the time who were directly involved in the surveys of Oki. More accurately, Kato's survey results were included in Kimotsuki's "Brief Records of Navigation of Oki," which was then reviewed and revised by Ishikawa and his team at the Hydrographic Office before being approved by the head of that organization, Yanagi, for publication. This indicates that following two separate surveys of Oki, the perception or knowledge of Kimotsuki and Kato, who accurately confirmed that Dokdo was part of Korean territory, and not Japan's, was becoming firmly established as the official view of the Japanese Hydrographic Office, and furthermore of the Japanese government.

The Hydrographic Office continued to maintain its official view that Dokdo was Korean territory in the second edition of *The World Sea Directory* Volume 2, published in December 1886, nine months after the publication of the first volume. The description of the "Liancourt Rocks" included in the chapter "East Coast of Joseon" remained the same as the first volume, albeit with some modifications in the wording. Again, following the content on Dokdo was the section on "Ulleungdo, known as Matsushima [Western Name "Dagelet"]." Admittedly, *The World Sea Directory* is a guide to the wa-

---

39   Kimotsuki Kaneyuki, "Post Script," "Brief Records of Sea Lanes on the Northwest Coast of Japan 3," *Hydrographic Magazine* 40, 1883, pp. 53-54.

40   Ishikawa Yōnosuke, "Hensyuengi (編輯縁起)," *The World Sea Directory*, Volume 1 Lower, p. 1.

terways of the world, and as such cannot be regarded a means to determine the territorial status of an island. Yet, it is still an important criteria for assessing the perception of the Japanese Navy Ministry, including the Hydrographic Office, as to which country held dominion over Dokdo and Ulleungdo, by observing where in that very guide the two islands are featured. As such, the consistent inclusion of Dokdo and Ulleungdo under the chapter titled "East Coast of Joseon" in *The World Sea Directory* indicates that Japan not only viewed Dokdo as an island associated with Ulleungdo but also considered the two islands as part of Korean territory.[41]

This perception of Dokdo and Ulleungdo held by the Japanese Hydrographic Office and the Navy Ministry continued to be reflected in Japan's country-specific sea directories, even after publication of *The World Sea Directory* was discontinued. As it is well known, in the first edition of *Joseon Sea Directory*, published by the Hydrographic Office in November 1894 (separately from *Japan Sea Directory* and in the second edition of the same guide published in February 1899, the information under "Liancourt Rocks" in chapter 4 "East Coast of Joseon" is practically the same, albeit with some modifications to the wording. Just as *The World Sea Directory*, they provide records of "Ulleungdo, known as Matsushima" after the section on Dokdo. Even the second edition of *Joseon Sea Directory*, published in March 1907 after Japan forcibly annexed Dokdo, includes "Takeshima" and Ulleungdo under "Sea of Japan and East Coast of Joseon."

The fourth volume of *Japan Sea Directory*, which the Japanese Hydrographic Office published in May 1897, still did not list Dokdo as part of the "Oki Islands" in chapter 3 "Northwest Coast of Honshu." The first time that Dokdo was mentioned in *Japan Sea Directory* was in the first edition of the guide's fourth volume published in June 1907, three months after the second edition of *Joseon Sea Directory* was published. There, in chapter 3 "Northwest Coast of Honshu," "Takeshima [Liancourt Rocks]" was listed under "Oki Is-

41   Shin, p. 175; Song, pp. 252-254, p. 265.

lands" along with information that it had been "annexed to Shimane Prefecture in the 38th year of the Meiji (1905)." However, the sixth volume of *Japan Sea Directory* published by the Japanese Hydrographic Office in June 1911, a year after Japan colonized Korea in August 1910, included a compilation of the "sea lanes of the entire coast of Joseon," which again featured Ulleungdo and "Takeshima [Liancourt Rocks]" under chapter 2 "East Coast of Joseon." These facts indicate that even after its forcible annexation of Dokdo and the subsequent colonization of Korea, Japan still viewed Dokdo and Ulleungdo as a pair, i. e. Dokdo as an island associated with Ulleungdo.[42] The same can be affirmed in "Index Map of Published Sea Directories" (刊行水路誌索引圖) published by the Japanese Hydrographic Office in April 1908.[43]

Lastly, it is noteworthy that the preface to *Joseon Sea Directory*, published in November 1894, as well as the prefaces to *Joseon Sea Directory* 2nd Edition and *Japan Sea Directory* Volume 4, published in 1905 before Japan annexed Dokdo, were written by Kimotsuki, head of the Japanese Hydrographic Office.[44] As the chief editor, he wrote the prefaces to these guides, which established Dokdo and Ulleungdo as islands belonging to the "East Coast of Joseon," and not Oki. Furthermore, as shown above, Kimotsuki also published "Brief Records of Navigation of Oki" in *Hydrographic Magazine*, which, as a result of the first official survey of Oki, shows longitude and latitude coordinates of Oki that exclude Dokdo from its scope. The same information, to the letter, is also included in *The World Sea Directory*. Thus, it can be ascertained that, as the highest authority for coastal and sea-lane surveying in Japan at the time, Kimotsuki understood more accurately than anyone that Dokdo was Korean territory.

42   See papers mentioned in footnotes 7) and 8).

43   Hydrographic Office [Published], "Index Map of Published Sea Directories," Navy Ministry Hydrographic Bureau, 1908.

44   "朝鮮水路誌序," Hydrographic Office, *Joseon Sea Directory* all editions, Hydrographic Office, 1894, pp. 1-3; *Joseon Sea Directory* 2nd Edition, 1899, pp. 1-2; *Japan Sea Directory* Volume 4, 1897, pp. 1-2; Yu & Choi, pp. 140-141.

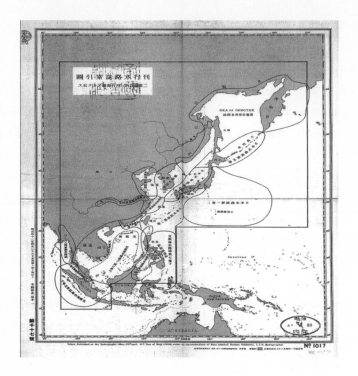

Charts(Map) 5
Index Map of Published Sea Directories (刊行水路誌索引圖) (1908)

Nonetheless, immediately before Japan forcibly annexed Dokdo and placed it under the jurisdiction of the governor of Oki in Shimane Prefecture, fisherman Nakai, who believed that Dokdo was Korean territory, had planned to ask the Korean government to lease the entire island to him to hunt sea lions. However, it was none other than Kimotsuki who convinced Nakai otherwise. Kimotsuki informed him that Dokdo should be annexed to Japan on the grounds that there was no proof that it belonged to anyone, it was closer to Japan than to Korea by 10 *li*, and there was no evidence that Koreans had ever governed the island while Japan was already administering it. Consequently, instead of submitting a permit request to the Korean government, Nakai submitted a "Petition for Annexation of Ryanko Island (Dokdo) and Permission

to Lease the Island" to the Japanese government. It is a well-known fact that,
based on that petition, the Japanese government forcibly annexed Dokdo as
its territory by invoking the theory of occupation of *terra nullius* on February
22, 1905.

The theory of occupation of *terra nullius* used by Kimotsuki along with
Enjiro Yamaza, head of the Political Affairs Bureau at the Foreign Affairs Ministry, and Maki, head of the Fisheries Bureau at the Ministry of Agriculture
and Commerce, to instigate Nakai to petition was illogical and unconscionable sophistry, not to mention a distortion of the truth. Even Kimotsuki's
argument that Dokdo was closer to Takobana (多古鼻), *Izumo* of Japan by 10
li than to Jukbyeon in Korea was, in all likelihood, a desperate claim to intentionally conceal the fact that Ulleungdo, which Kimotsuki had consistently
recognized as Korean territory, was closer to Dokdo than to Oki. In his position as chief of the Japanese Hydrographic Office for approximately 16 years,
Kimotsuki knew better than anyone about the territoriality and dominion of
islands, including Dokdo and Oki, their locations and relevant distances.

4. Conclusion

This paper sheds light on the fallaciousness of Japan's logic regarding its claim
that Dokdo is Japanese territory by using newly identified documents including "Brief Records of Navigation of Oki" to show that the Japanese Hydrographic Office, up until Japan's land-grab of Dokdo, had viewed the island
as Korean territory. As the institution with the most accurate understanding
of the territoriality and jurisdiction of Dokdo and other islands, the Japanese
Hydrographic Office reflects the official position of Japan regarding Dokdo.
In conclusion, a summary of the findings is given as follows.

First, Kimotsuki Kaneyuki, the person responsible for the 1879 survey of
Japan's northwest coast, including the Oki Islands, made it clear in his report
entitled "Brief Records of Navigation of Oki" that the scope of Oki spanned

from 35° 57' North to 36° 18' North, and from 132° East to 133° 23' East, revealing that Dokdo was not part of that scope. Had he considered Dokdo to be one of the 179 small islands belonging to Oki, he would have included it at the northernmost end of that area and extended the scope of the longitude and latitude coordinates of Oki. However, Dokdo was neither in the scope of the Oki survey nor was it ever mentioned in "Brief Records of Navigation of Oki," because Kimotsuki viewed Dokdo as a part of Korean territory, and not Japan's. Kimotsuki's perception is again apparent in the map attached to that report "Northwest Coast of Japan, from Nagato to Hoki," showing part of Japan's northwest coast.

Second, Dokdo was featured neither on "Map Showing the Course of the *Tsukuba*'s Second Navigation of Seas Surrounding Japan" nor on "Map Showing the Course of the *Tsukuba*'s Third Navigation of Seas Surrounding Japan," which shows the entire navigation route of *Tsukuba* during its second and third navigation of seas surrounding Japan in 1879 and 1883, respectively. The first map depicts Japanese territory lying between 30° North and 45° North and between 128° East and 146° East, and the second map Japanese territory between 25° North and 45° North and between 126° East and 147° East. This is supported from the fact that part of northern Hokkaido, Ogasawara-saito, and Ryukyu are excluded from the first map, and part of northern Hokkaido is excluded from the second map, as they are beyond the scope of the given coordinates; also, no part of the Korean territory to the north and south of Tsushima is included in these maps, despite being within the scope of the coordinates. The fact that both Ulleungdo and its associated island Dokdo are excluded from these maps provides circumstantial evidence that the Japanese Navy, including the Hydrographic Office, understood and viewed Dokdo as a part of Korea, and not Japan. The implications are significant in the sense that the maps are reflective of Kimotsuki's Oki survey results, which excluded Dokdo from Oki.

Third, Kato Shigenari who surveyed the Oki Islands in 1884 also measured and reported the longitude and latitude of Oki to be from 35° 55'

North to 36° 27' North, and from 132° 44' East to 133° 31' East, an indication that he also viewed Dokdo as not being a part of Oki. At the time, the Japanese Hydrographic Office was ambitiously surveying the coasts of Japan under the "12-Year Plan for Survey of All of Japan's Coasts" of 1882 in order to establish sea charts for each and every corner of Japanese territory. In charge of the actual surveys were Kimotsuki and Kato. Thus, the fact that both Kimotsuki and subsequently Kato, who were the top authorities in the fields of coastal surveying and longitude-latitude measurements in Japan, excluded Dokdo from the scope of Oki Islands following a meticulous survey of the latter is a clear indication that they accurately recognized Dokdo as being part of Korean territory.

Fourth, the results of Oki surveys by Kimotsuki and Kato had a considerably significant influence on the production and publication of the maps known as "Oki Islands" or "All Islands of Oki" until 1904, immediately before Japan's land-grab of Dokdo from Korea. Needless to say, none of these maps show Dokdo, again a reflection of the views held by Kimotsuki, Kato, and others at the Hydrographic Office following Oki surveys that Dokdo was not a part of Oki but a part of Korea. Through the publication and distribution of those maps, this perception would obviously have extended beyond the Hydrographic Office to the relevant agencies and ministries within the Japanese government, and further, to the Japanese people, and to foreign governments and agencies, that acquired and used those maps.

Fifth, it is worth noting that the information on "All Islands of Oki," mentioned for the first time in chapter 6 "Northern Coast of Nakatsuchi," in *The World Sea Directory* Volume 1, Part II (1886) was, albeit with minor rewording of phrases or additions, identical to the information found in Kimotsuki's "Brief Records of Navigation of Oki." In other words, the content of "Brief Records of Navigation of Oki," which excluded Dokdo and Ulleungdo following Kimotsuki's first survey of the longitude and latitude of Oki, was taken almost verbatim from the chapter on "All Islands of Oki" in *The World Sea Directory*. As such, the fact that the information on "All Islands of Oki" in

The World Sea Directory was drafted by adding Kato's survey results to Kimotsuki's "Brief Records of Navigation of Oki," and then underwent the review and revision by other responsible persons at the Hydrographic Office before it was approved by head of the Hydrographic Office Yanagi for publication, plus the fact that this information subsequently served as the basis for publishing *Joseon Sea Directory* and *Japan Sea Directory* up until Japan forcefully annexed Dokdo in 1905, indicate that the perception or knowledge of Kimotsuki and others, who confirmed that Dokdo is part of Korean territory, was becoming firmly established as the official view of the Japanese Hydrographic Office, and furthermore, of the Japanese government. The same can be affirmed in "Index Map of Published Sea Directories" published by the Japanese Hydrographic Office in April 1908.

Finally, it should be noted that the prefaces to *Joseon Sea Directory* and all *Japan Directory* published before February 1905 were written by none other than Kimotsuki, the head of the Japanese Hydrographic Office who played an important role in Japan's land-grab of Dokdo. Kimotsuki was the chief editor of these sea directories, which all established Dokdo and Ulleungdo as belonging to the "East Coast of Joseon." He was also the highest authority for coastal and sea-lane surveying at the time in possession of the most accurate understanding of the jurisdiction and dominion of islands. Thus, Kimotsuki undeniably understood more accurately than anyone that Dokdo was Korean territory. Nonetheless, together with Yamaza, head of the Political Affairs Bureau at the Foreign Affairs Ministry, and Maki, head of the Fisheries Bureau at the Ministry of Agriculture and Commerce, Kimotsuki talked fisherman Nakai into cancelling his plan to request a seal-hunting permit from the Korean government and instead, convinced him to submit to the Japanese government a "Petition for Annexation of Ryanko Island (Dokdo) and Permission to Lease the Island." The logic that Kimotsuki used to instigate Nakai—that Dokdo should be annexed to Japan as *terra nullius* on the grounds there was no clear evidence of Dokdo's territorial status, it was closer to Japan than to Korea, there was no evidence that Koreans had ever governed the island, and finally, that the Japanese were already administering it—is clearly forced logic and unconscionable sophistry, as well as a distortion of the truth.

<Paper submitted on May 2; Evaluation completed on May 24>

Keywords

Dokdo, Oki (隱岐), Kimotsuki Kaneyuki (肝付兼行), Kato Shigenari (加藤重成), Hydrographic Office, "Brief Records of Navigation of Oki" (隱岐回航畧記), sea directory (*suiroshi*)

References

Kimotsuki Kaneyuki, "Brief Records of Navigation of Oki" (隱岐回航畧記), *Hydrographic Magazine* 19, 1883.

Kimotsuki Kaneyuki, "Brief Records of Sea Lanes on the Northwest Coast of Japan 1" (日本北西岸水路畧記 1), *Hydrographic Magazine* 38, 1883.

Kimotsuki Kaneyuki, "Brief Records of Sea Lanes on the Northwest Coast of Japan 2" (日本北西岸水路畧記 2), *Hydrographic Magazine* 39, 1883.

Kimotsuki Kaneyuki, "Brief Records of Sea Lanes on the Northwest Coast of Japan 3" (日本北西岸水路畧記 3), *Hydrographic Magazine* 40, 1883.

Kashiwabara Nagashige, "Report of Navigation of Seas Surrounding Japan" (大日本環海航行記), *Hydrographic Magazine* 33, 1883.

Toho Kakuyuki, "Records of the *Tsukuba*'s Navigation of Seas Surrounding Japan" (筑波艦日本環海周航記事), *Hydrographic Magazine* 74, 1883.

Japanese Navy Hydrographic Office, *The World Sea Directory* (寰瀛水路誌), Volume 1 Part I, Japanese Navy Hydrographic Office, 1886.

Japanese Hydrographic Office, *Joseon Sea Directory* (朝鮮水路誌), all editions, Japanese Hydrographic Office, 1894.

Japanese Hydrographic Office, *Joseon Sea Directory* (朝鮮水路誌), 2nd Edition, Hydrographic Office, 1899.

Japanese Hydrographic Office, *Japan Directory* (日本水路誌), Volume 4, Hydrographic Office, 1897.

Japanese Hydrographic Office [Published], "Index Map of Published Sea Directories" (刊行水路誌索引圖), Navy Hydrographic Office, 1908.

Naitō Seitsu, translated by Kwon O-yeop and Kwon Jeong, *Dokdo and Jukdo*, J&C, 2005 [Naitō Seitsu, *The History of Japan-Korea Relations over Takeshima (Ulleungdo)*, Taga-shuppan, 2000].

Naitō Seitsu and Park Byoung-sup, *The Dokdo-Takeshima Controversy: A Study based on Historical Documents*, Bogo-sa, 2008 [Naitō Seitsu & and Park Byoung-sup, *Dokdo=Takeshima Dispute – Thinking from Historical Documents—*, Shinkansha, 2007].

Hosaka Yuji et al., "Westerners' Exploration of the East Sea and Dokdo inside Sea Directories," *Journal of Japanese Culture* 46, 2010.

Song Byung-gi, *Historical Examination of Ulleungdo and Dokdo*, Yeoksa Gong-gan, 2010.

Song Hwi-young, "Japan's Perception of Ulleungdo and Dokdo as reflected in the Sea Directories of Modern Japan," *Daegu History Studies* 106, 2012.

Shin Yong-ha, *A Historical Study of Dokdo as a Territory of Korea*, Jisik Saneop-sa, 1996;

Yu Mi-rim and Choi Eun-suk, *Perception of Dokdo and Ulleungdo in Modern Maps of Japan*, Korea Maritime Development Institute, 2010.

Han Cheol-ho, "Issues and tasks related to the study of the Japanese policy and perception of Dokdo Island in the Meiji Period," *The Journal for the Studies of Korean History* 28, 2007.

[Japanese Navy Ministry] Published by the Hydrographic Office, *History of the Hydrographic Office: Meiji years 2-18*, Hydrographic Office, 1916.

Hori Kazuo, "Japan's annexation of Takeshima in 1905," *Collection of dissertations of the Society for Study of Korean History* 24, 1987, pp. 105-107.

Published by the Hydrographic Office of the Maritime Safety Agency, *Hydrographic History of Japan: 1871-1971*, Japan Hydrographic Association, 1971.

Yokoyama Yoshinori, "Surveys of the coastal waters of Japan in the 19th century," compiled by Kuroda Hideo et al., *A political and cultural history of maps and paintings*, University of Tokyo Press, 2001.

The Declaration of Ulleungdo and Usando (Dokdo) as Foreign Possessions by Japanese Dajokan Minister

Song Byeong-kie

Professor Emeritus, Dankook University

The Directive by the Japanese Dajokan Minister

Even after the Japanese government had imposed a ban prohibiting fishing trips to Takeshima (Ulleungdo, 1696), not everyone in Japan was aware of the fact that Matsushima (Dokdo) was an island of Joseon.

Some considered it to be an island under the jurisdiction of Oki Province (Kitamoto Tsuan, *Takeshima Zusetsu* (Explanation of Takeshima with Maps), Horeki era (1751-1763)), or the outer extremity of the West Sea of Japan (Yada Takamasa, *Chosei Takeshimaki* (An Account of the Long Living Takeshima), 1801). Some authors were even unaware that Ulleungdo was a Joseon island (Matsuura Takeshiro, *Take Jimma Zasshi*, 1854), These are mostly private publications, however, that are hardly reflections of the Japanese government's view on the matter. In important Japanese works contemporary to the Joseon state-sponsored publications such as *Ganggyego* (Study of National Boundary), *Dongguk Munheon Bigo* (Reference Compilation of Documents of Korea) and the "Gunjeong-pyeon" of *Mangi Yoram* (Manual of State Affairs for the Monarch) and other major maps form this period, Matsushima (Dokdo) is marked as a Joseon island.

Kaisei Nihon Yochi Rotei Zenzu (Complete Revised Map of Japanese Lands and Roads) (1773), the first Japanese map using geographical coordinates by Nagakubo Sekisui, considered the greatest cartographer in the period leading to the early Meiji years, and *Kaisei Nihon Yochi Rotei Zenzu* (1779), the revised version of the latter, are cases in point. In both of these maps, all Japanese-controlled territories are colored in ink, and Takeshima (Ulleungdo) and Matsushima (Dokdo), along with the Korean peninsula are left uncolored. Longitudinal and latitudinal lines also stop before Takeshima and Matsushima. Near Ulleungdo and Matsushima, there is a comment that says. "Goryeo can be seen [from the two islands], just as Inshu can be seen form Unshu" echoing a similar remark found in *Inshu Shicho Gakki* (A Collection of Observational Records of Inshu). It was, therefore, unequivocal that Matsushima, in Nagakubo Sekisui's mind, was a Joseon island.

In *Sankoku Setsujo no Zu*, a map included in *Sankoku Tsuran Zusetsu* (1985), Ulleungdo and Dokdo are also depicted accurately in terms of their geographical locations and sizes, consistent with their actual sizes relative to each other. The two islands are colored yellow, just like mainland Joseon, in contrast to Japan and islands in its possession, which are colored in green. No ambiguity whatsoever can exist as to the fact that Dokdo was an island belonging to Joseon. Even more noteworthy is the commentary placed next to Dokdo, which reads: "Joseon's possession." This commentary appears to be a reminder of the outcome of the Ulleungdo Dispute, the dispute ever Ulleungdo and Dokdo that had concluded with the recognition that the two islands were in Joseon's possession.

Meanwhile, in *Dainihon Enkai Yochi Zenzu* (1821) by Ino Tadataka, and early nineteenth century map of Japan, considered one of the greatest accomplishments in Japanese cartography, Takeshima (Ulleungdo) and Matsushima (Dokdo) are omitted. The two islands were excluded for the very simple reason that had no business being on this map that was exclusively dedicated to Japan and the territory under its control. This map, also the result of a state-sponsored cartographic project, suggests that the Tokugawa Shogunate continued to uphold its earlier position concerning the territorial status of Ulleungdo and Dokdo-expressed through the navigation ban issued in the late seventeenth century-that they were Joseon islands.

With the restoration of imperial rule on the December 9, 1867 (lunar calendar), a new government was launched in Japan under Emperor Meiji. In the last month of 1869, in the context of a plan to establish a direct diplomatic relationship with Joseon, the Foreign Ministry of the newly-formed Meiji administration dispatched Sada Hakubo, Moriyama Shigeru and Saito Sakae to Tsushima and Busan (Japan House) on an intelligence mission to gather information about the status of the two countries' relations. The intelligence officers returned in the April (lunar calendar) the following year (1870) and submitted a ten-item report entitled "Chosenkoku Kosaishimatsu Naitansho."

The ten topics were topics that had been pre-approved by the Dajokan, before Sada and the others had departed on their mission. The part of this report with direct relevance to Joseon's sovereignty over Ulleungdo and Dokdo is the last of the ten items, called "How Takeshima and Matsushima Came to Belong to Joseon." What this states is that the new Meiji government (more specifically, the Japanese Foreign Ministry and Dajokan) form its early years was already aware of the fact that Ulleungdo and Dokdo had been recognized formally as Joseon territory. 9)

Also worthy of note is *Kanpan Jissoku Nihon Chizu* (State-Published Map of Japan from Actual Survey, 1867), a map commissioned by the Bakufu and produced in the mid-nineteenth century (late Tokugawa period). Just as in the coastal maps of Japan by Ino Tadataka, Takeshima and Matsushima are absent from this map, indicating that the two islands were not considered by its author to be part of Japanese-controlled territory. *Kanpan Jissoku Nihon Chizu* was re-published in 1870, by the Meiji government (Kasei Gakko), a fact significant insofar as it attests to the continuous perception through to the Meiji period that the two islands were foreign possessions lying outside

Japanese jurisdiction.

During the early years of the Meiji era, a geographical publication project was carried out by the Dajokan's Department of Geography. The geographical description of Japan, completed during the one-year period between 1872 and 1873, was published in progressive installments (77 volumes in 8 books), between 1874 and 1879. In the section on the Oki islands, in Volume 50, Book 4 of this work, entitled *Nihon Chishi Teiyo*, 179 islands are cited as being dependent islands to the archipelago, and this list did not include Takeshima and Matsushima which were, however, mentioned elsewhere in the text. This, therefore, is further evidence that the two islands were consistently perceived in Japan, as foreign territories. Other government-published maps, which appeared after *Kanpan Jissoku Nihon Chizu* also expressed this same position with regard to the territorial status of Takeshima and Matsushima. This remained true at least until 1905 when Japan annexed Ryanko Island.

The Meiji administration soon had the opportunity to officially state its position on the territorial status of Ulleungdo and Dokdo. This pronouncement by the Dajokan was occasioned by an inquiry form the Ministry of the Interior. The Japanese Ministry of the Interior, in the process of carrying out a national land registration project, was faced with the need to determine the territorial status of the two islands and requested the Dajokan's input on the issue.

In October 1876, the Geographical Office (Chiriryo) of the Japanese Interior Ministry sent a request for information on Takeshima to Shimane Prefecture, in conjunction with this land registration project. The prefectural authority of Shimane conducted an investigation on the fishing activities by the Oya and Murakawa families at Takeshima during the seventeenth century, and submitted the results to the Interior Ministry in a report entitled "Inquiry about the Land Registration of Takeshima and Another Island in the Sea of Japan," along with a document named "A Brief History" and a map of the two islands, found in the possession of the Oya family. Here, "Another Island" designates Matsushima (Usando: Jasando), as the following passage in the document named "A Brief History" makes abundantly clear: "…here is another island in proximity to [Takeshima] known as 'Matsushima'…"

After receiving this report from Shimane Prefecture, the Japanese Interior Ministry conducted its own investigation into the Ulleungdo Dispute and reached the conclusion that the two islands belonged to Joseon. Given the "serious nature of this issue, concerning territory," however, the Japanese Interior Ministry decided to submit the case to the Dajokan for deliberation. The "Inquiry about the Land Registration of Takeshima and Another Island in the Sea of Japan" was thus sent to the Dajokan on March 17, 1877.

Four separate supporting documents were enclosed with this inquiry to the Dajokan. The first document explained the background to the former government's decision in the 1st month, 1696 (Genroku 9) to ban Japanese fishing trips to Takeshima, thereby recognizing that the island was part of Joseon's territory. The second supporting document was the letter from the So clan of Tsushima that Pyong Jin-hyon had brought with him and handed over to the Joseon education officer and interpreter (*hundo byeolcha*) in the 10th month of the same year, announcing the Bakufu's imposition of a ban on navigation to Takeshima and expressing regret over An Yong-bok's attempt to directly petition the Bakufu. The third document enclosed with the inquiry petition the letter by Yi Seon-bu, Joseon's Deputy Minister for Ceremonies and Protocol, dated March, 1698 (Sukjong 24: Genroku 11), addressed to Tsushima regent So Yoshizane, in which he stated that his government welcomed the Edo authority's decision to ban Japanese fishing trips to Takeshima and stressed that Takeshima and Ulleungdo were one and the same islands. This letter also responded to the complaint about An Yong-bok, stating that he and his companions were mere castaways. The fourth document was the letter by So Yoshizane, dated 3rd month, 1699 (Genroku 12), informing Joseon's Ministry of Ceremonies and Protocol (Deputy Minister Yi Seon-bu) that its last letter had been transmitted to the Edo Shogunate. Attached to this document was also the verbal note from Tsushima, drawing attention to Tsushima's contributions in bringing the dispute over Takeshima to an outcome that favorable to

Joseon. Finally, a summary map of Takeshima, provided by Shimane Prefecture, entitled "Isotakeshima Ryakuzu," was also included in the documentation submitted to the Dajokan. This map, which could be considered the fifth supporting document, shows Matsushima next to Takeshima, indicating the understanding that the former was a dependent island of Ulleungdo, hence, also an island in Joseon's possession.

The Dajokan, at the end of its deliberation on the case presented by the Interior Ministry, upheld the latter's opinion and issued a ruling stating that the exchange of documents between Japan and Joseon that had occurred after Joseon people had landed on Ulleungdo in 1692 (Genroku 5) had led to the acknowledgement that the two islands were unrelated to Japan:

With regard to Takeshima and another island that was made the object of an inquiry, let it be known that the two islands are unrelated to our country (Japan).

On March 29, 1877, the Dajokan, after receiving the approval of the *Udaijin* (Minister of the Right) Iwakura Tomomi, communicated this ruling to the Japanese Ministry of the Interior, which in turn notified Shimane Prefecture on April 9.

By declaring the Takeshima (Ulleungdo) and Matsushima (Dokdo) were unrelated to Japan, in response to an inquiry by the Ministry of the Interior about the territorial status of Matsushima, the Dajokan, the highest authority of the Meiji-era Japanese government, officially recognized that the two islands were in Joseon's possession. The Meiji government, therefore, which succeeded the Tokugawa Bakufu, upheld its predecessor's position concerning Joseon's territorial rights to Ulleungdo and Dokdo.

We can also find records indicating that the Japanese Ministry of Foreign Affairs and the Navy recognized Ryanko Island (Usando/Dokdo) as being Joseon's territory in the 1880s. On November 29, 1881, the Japanese Foreign Ministry received and inquiry from the Interior Ministry concerning Ulleungdo. The inquiry included a series of supporting documents such as the Dajokan's directive declaring Takeshima (Ulleungdo) and Matsushima

(Dokdo) to be territories lying outside Japanese jurisdiction. Although this inquiry came at a time when the Foreign Ministry was under pressure from Joseon, which had demanded that all Japanese be evacuated from Ulleungdo, it expressed no objection to the fact that the two islands belonged to Joseon. This was because the Japanese Foreign Ministry, from the early of the Meiji administration, had been aware of the fact that Takeshima (Ulleungdo) and Matsushima (Dokdo) were Joseon possessions. The Foreign Ministry, furthermore, never indicated a difference of opinion concerning the territorial status of Takeshima and Matsushima, at least not until Japan's annexation of Dokdo (Matsushima) in 1905.10) The evidence, therefore, suggests that the Japanese Foreign Ministry consistently saw Matsushima as being a dependent island of Takeshima.

Meanwhile, the results of the *Amagi* survey in September 1880 were reflected in Volume 2 of *Kanei Suiroshi* published by the Navy Hydrographic Office (1883), and the 1894 and 1899 editions of Chosen Suiroshi by the Hydrographic Department (formerly Hydrographic Office). Both of these hydrographic maps feature the Liancourt Rocks (Ryanko Island/Dokdo) alongside Matsushima (Ulleungdo). On the other hand, the Liancourt Rocks are omitted in *Nihon Suiroshi*, a series of coastal charts, covering only areas within the Japanese sea borders, which was published in successive installments, starting form 1892, this omission is significant insofar as these coastal charts are a quite exhaustive representation of Japanese possessions, featuring territories that had been recently annexed through the Treaty of Shimonoseki (1895), such as Taiwan and Penghu Island, and even Simusyu Island, the northernmost member of the Kuril Archipelago.

These examples make it patently clear that for the Japanese Navy, Ryanko Island (Dokdo) was a Joseon possession, and not a Japanese possession. Given that all of these sea charts were based on the survey of Matsushima (Ulleungdo) by Amagi, it also proves that this was the opinion of the *Amagi* survey team, concerning the territorial status of Ryanko Island. In sum, the fact that Dokdo was a Joseon island, recognized in Chosen Tokaigan Zu (the first edition appeared in 1876), was later re-confirmed by the Amagi survey (September, 1880) and the two successive editions of Chosen Suiroshi (1894 and 1899) that followed it.

That the *Amagi* survey team perceived Ryanko Island to be a Joseon possession from the outset is made clear by the reports of Kitazawa Masanobu, which were based on both the results of literature research and this hydrographic survey. Matsushima, Kitazawa Masanobu stated in the conclusion of his report, lay outside Japanese territorial jurisdiction and should be understood as including Ulleungdo's dependent island, Ryanko Island (Dokdo). This can be the only reasonable interpretation, given the Japanese Foreign Ministry's position on this issue.

To recapitulate, in early 1977, the Japanese Ministry of the Interior and the Dajokan both judged that Ulleungdo and Dokdo were islands in Joseon's possession. This opinion was echoed by the Japanese Foreign Ministry into the 1880s. The opinion was also shared by the Japanese Navy. Hence, all high-level Japanese government agencies with a say on territorial issues, including the Dajokan, the highest government authority of the Meiji administration, indicated that they perceived Dokdo as being a territory outside Japanese control, in other words, as belonging to Joseon.

Several important implications should be highlighted concerning the statement of opinion issued by the Dajokan. First, the 1877 Dajokan directive provides a definitive answer to the question, much debated among both Korean and international scholars, whether Dokdo was included in the scope of the ban on navigation to Ulleungdo imposed by the Tokugawa Bakufu. The Dajokan's statement that "Takeshima and another island lie outside Japan's jurisdiction" clearly indicates the Meiji government's understanding that the seventeenth-century ban by the Tokugawa Bakufu applied to both Takeshima and Matsushima; hence both Takeshima and Matsushima were recognized by Japan as belonging to Joseon. Also, the summary map of Takeshima, Iso-takeshima Ryakuzu, that the Japanese Ministry of the Interior submitted to the Dajokan as a supporting document, depicts Matsushima as being located alongside Takeshima, once again indicating that Joseon's territorial rights, confirmed through this cabinet-level inquiry, applied to both the islands.

Another important point that needs to be underlined is that both the opinion expressed by the Japanese Ministry of Interior concerning the territorial status of Ulleungdo and Dokdo, and the Dajokan's answer to the latter's inquiry that stated that "Takeshima and another island," in other words, Takeshima and Matsushima were "unrelated to our country (Japan)," were based on diplomatic documents that had been exchanged between the two countries. In other words, these documents, which were submitted to the Dajokan by the Interior Ministry as supporting evidence, were so unambiguous concerning the territorial status of the two islands that they permitted no other conclusion than that Takeshima and Matsushima were part of Joseon territory. What this also implies is that the bilateral confirmation procedures that took place between the 10th month, 1696 and the 3rd month, 1699, on the territorial standing of the two islands, were completed in due form. Hence, the Meiji government had no other choice but to uphold the ban on navigation to Takeshima issued by the Tokugawa Bakufu in the late seventeenth century.

The New Meiji Navigation Ban to Ulleungdo and the Repatriation of its Subjects

The Japanese trespassing into Ulleungdo's fishing grounds was an issue that was closely followed by the Joseon government up until the early eighteenth century. After this date, however, the issue ceases to be mentioned in government records. This indicates that Japanese trespassing incidents occurred so rarely after the early eighteenth century that was witnessed, at least by the *suto* officials patrolling the island on a triennial basis. This respite proved only temporary, however, as Japanese intrusion into Ulleungdo's waters appears to have resumed sometime around the mid-nineteenth century, and one such trespassing incident was reported by a *suto* official in 1881 (Gojong 18).

The year 1881 saw the enacting of the early phase of Gojong's modern-ization and reform initiative. Following the decision to establish diplomatic relations with the United State (1880), Gojong set up the Office for Extraor-dinary State Affairs, a new government agency comprehensively responsible for all diplomatic and trade affairs, as well as modernization policies. The government, as advised by the Office for Extraordinary State Affairs, had a let-ter of protest sent to the Japanese Ministry of Foreign Affairs. Meanwhile, the government also sent Yi Gyu-won to Ulleungdo on an inspection mission to assess the local situation (Yi Gyu-won was appointed "Ulleungdo Inspector" on the May 23rd, lunar calendar). Aside from investigating the illegal Japanese presence on the island, he was also charged with assessing how feasible devel-opment and civilian settlement project would be. In sum, the resurgence of Japanese trespassing into Ulleungdo's fishing grounds helped the Joseon gov-ernment move toward a more proactive policy for the territorial management of Ulleungdo. The budding pro-modernization mood in the Joseon govern-ment, disposing it favorably toward opening its ports to foreigners, contrib-uted to this shift in its Ulleungdo policy as well.

The letter of protest, signed by Joseon Minister of Ceremonies and Pro-tocol Shim Sun-taek and addressed to Inoue Kaoru of the Japanese Foreign Ministry, was sent out in the 5th month. The letter stated among other things that (1) 189 years ago, in 1693 (Sukjong 19), there had been a misunder-standing on the Japanese side concerning the name of Ulleungdo, and this confusion had been clarified through a series of letters exchanged between the two countries' government, leading to the Japanese promise to forever ban fishing trips to the island by coastal residents of western Japan, and (2) notwithstanding this promise, Japanese were today sailing to Ulleungdo and logging trees there. The letter urged the Japanese government to strictly en-force the border law on its subjects to put an end to illegal border crossing and logging and withdraw all fishing fleets from this sea area to make sure that no incident of this type ever re-occurred.

This letter did not receive a prompt response. The Japanese Foreign Ministry was apparently confused about the names "Ulleungdo" and "Matsushima" and deemed an investigation necessary before it could issue an official response to the letter from Joseon. This indicates that both Takeshima and Matsushima had become slowly forgotten in Japan following the 1696 navigation ban. Sometime between the late Tokugawa period and the early Meiji period, the two islands were given new names, after the names assigned to them in Map of Japan (1840) by Philipp Franz von Siebold, calling Takeshima (Ulleungdo) "Matsushima" and Matsushima (Dokdo) "Ryanko Island." Meanwhile, since 1876, the Japanese government had been receiving a series of petitions asking for permission to exploit Matsushima, and some others asking for permission to sail to Takeshima. Not knowing which island was which, the Japanese government eventually decided to send the warship Amagi this sea area. The Amagi survey mission in September 1880 found out that Matsushima was, in fact, the Joseon island of Ulleung, and Takeshima, its adjoining island known as "Jukseo." In 1881, when the Japanese Foreign Ministry received the letter of protest about Ulleungdo from Joseon, they were still conducting internal research to ascertain the facts gathered by the Amagi survey team.

Takeshima Kosho I, II, and III by Kitazawa Masanobu for the Japanese Foreign Ministry, and its abridged version Takeshima Hanto Shozokuko, (August, 1881) were the results of an investigation commissioned by the Japanese Foreign Ministry. These reports, citing relevant Korean, Chinese and Japanese documents, and the results of the Amagi survey, conclude with the following remark.

These findings, thus, indicate that the island today known as "Matsushima" is the same island as the one referred to, in Genroku Year 12, as "Takeshima." and further that it lies outside our country's territorial jurisdiction.

Hence, the conclusion drawn by Kitazawa Masanobu from the results of the Amagi survey is that Matsushima was the island known as Takeshima (Ulleungdo), which was the object of the dispute between Joseon and Japan that had ended in 1699 (Genroku 12)-in other words the Ulleungdo Dispute —and that the island, therefore, lay outside Japanese jurisdiction. Without any doubt, the referent of the designation "Takeshima." in this case, includes its dependent island, Dokdo.

The two reports by Kitazawa Masanobu were accepted by the Japanese Foreign Ministry without objection (August), and were soon forwarded to Chancellor of the Realm Sanjo Sanetomi (October). Soon after Kitazawa Masanobu's report, the Japanese Foreign Ministry wrote to Joseon's Ministry of Ceremonies and Protocol, promising to conduct forthwith an inquiry into Japanese trespassing on Ulleungdo and take appropriate actions to ensure that such incidents did not undermine the relationship between the two countries (August). The Japanese Foreign Ministry followed up on this several months later (November) with another letter informing the Joseon authorities that all Japanese logging on Ulleungdo had been halted.

In the 6th month of the following year (1882), however, Yi Hee-jeong, Joseon's new Minister of Ceremonies and Protocol Minister addressed another letter to the Japanese Foreign Ministry, stating that Japanese logging on Ulleungdo was continuing unabated and urging Tokyo to take action to put a stop to these continuing border violations. The letter was written after Ulleungdo Inspector Yi Gyu-won's return form the island and reported that Japanese timber workers were still on the island. Envoy Park Yeong-hyo, in Japan for the ratification of the Treaty of Jemulpo, also strongly protested against the illegal Japanese presence and activities on Ulleungdo (12th month).

Faced with these protests from Joseon, Tokyo took a number of measures, proposed by Foreign Minister Inoue Kaoru. The Japanese government promised in the 1st month, 1883 (Gojong 20), through Takezoe Shinichiro, the Japanese Ministry to Joseon (1883, Gojong 20) that it would take steps to end logging by its nationals on Ulleungdo. Takezoe Shinichiro's letter to the Minister of Ceremonies and Protocol, Yi Byeong-mun stated that since a ban had been already issued, all offenders caught in violation of this ban would be prosecuted and punished in accordance with the relevant provisions of the Joseon-Japan treaty of amity and Japanese law, provided that they were arraigned and transferred to a nearby Japanese consulate by Joseon's local officials. The logging ban that Takezoe Shinichiro said was already in place, however, was not issued until March, two months after this letter was sent.

In February of the same year, the Japanese Advisory Council of State, which deliberated on the Foreign Ministry's proposal for an executive decree banning navigation to Ulleungdo, approved the navigation ban and the proposal to make violations of the ban punishable under the bilateral trade regulations and Japanese criminal law. On March 1 of the same year (1883), therefore, Chancellor of the Realm Sanjo Sanetomi notified Interior Minister Yamada Akiyoshi and Justice Minister Oki Takato of the decision to ban Japanese trips to Matsushima (Ulleungdo) and make the violation of this ban punishable pursuant to Article 9 of the Japan-Joseon trade regulations and Japanese criminal law.

Regardless of this pledge or notification, Japanese navigation to Ulleungdo continued. In the 1st month, 1883 (March), eighty people including Hayase Iwahei from Fukuoka made secretly landed Ulleungdo and logged trees on the island and fished in its surrounding waters. Around this time, other interlopers from Japan's coastal provinces, including Matsuoka from the Yamaguchi Province also clandestinely came to Ulleungdo, raising the total number of intruders to several hundreds.

Under these circumstances, the Japanese government had no choice but to come up with counter-measures. It was concerned about losing the trust of the Joseon government and had no desire to permit this problem to disturb its relations with Joseon. The Foreign Minister Inoue Kaoru ordered Soeda Takashi, the Japanese consul stationed in Wonsan to deliver his message to repatriate eighty people including Hayase Iwahei. He also sent this order to the prefectures of Fukuoka and Yamaguchi where Hayase and Matsuoka were domiciled. As it was difficult to identify the domicile of most of the Japanese illegally staying on Ulleungdo, however, Inoue Kaoru asked the chancellor to send officers to repatriate them.

It was the 8th month (September) when the Japanese Ministry of Interior dispatched an official to Ulleungdo, a total of thirty-one officers including

Higaki Naoe, Secretary of the Ministry and Inspector. They arrived in the 9th month (October 7) on Ulleungdo and left the island on the 14th day, 9th month with the Japanese trespassers onboard after having conducted a survey and inspection. They arrived in Bakan on the 15th day, 9th month. The officials even received a certificate from Jeon Seok-gyu, the head of the island, confirming that there were no Japanese left on the island. Also, Soeda Takshi, the Japanese consul stationed in Wonsan sent an inquiry to Jeong Hyeon-seok, governor of Deokwon, dated the 9th day, 9th month, and informed him that the Japanese government would dispatch officials and arrest and punish any Japanese illegally staying on Ulleungdo. This happened after Echikomaru landed on Ulleungdo.

The number of Japanese repatriated by Japanese officials came to as many as 255. It is not sure whether several tens of people from Yamaguchi Prefecture including Matsuoka were included in this batch or not. However, eighty people from Fukuoka including Hayase were repatriated separately. Even if the several tens of people including Matsuoka were included in the batch of 225, we can find that the number of Japanese who were engaged in illegally logging trees and catching fish reached more than 330. The number is 43 times higher than that of the time when Inspector Yi Gyuwon visited the island.

Among the 255 repatriated Japanese, 243 were transferred to Yamaguchi, another three to Hyogo Prefecture, while nine others were handed over to the Japanese Police. They were tried in the respective courts. The trial continued until 1886 (Meiji 19), as the Joseon government made several official protests, it was inevitable that they be brought to trial. They were all found not guilty, however, and were set free, contrary to the Japanese government's previous pledge.

In the nineteenth century, illegal logging by Japanese emerged as a diplomatic issue between Joseon and the Japanese government form 1881 (Gojong 18). The Joseon government sent official letters to urge the repatriation of Japanese from the island. Every time such a protest was made, the Japanese government procrastinated over the repatriation issue. After two years of delay, all the Japanese interlopers were finally repatriated on the 9th month 1883 (Gojong 20), resulting in the termination of the illegal activities on Ulleungdo, which was a pressing issue between the two government.

Imperial Decree No. 41 of Gwangmu Year 4

In the summer of 1881 (Gojong 18), King Gojong appointed Yi Gyu-won "Ulleungdo Inspector." Yi Gyu-won sailed to Ulleungdo in the following summer, on a mission to assess the local conditions, ahead of a development project. The information brought back by Yi Gyu-won led the government to go ahead with its development plan, and civilian households were shipped out to the island starting from the summer of 1883. The community rapidly grew in size with farmland reclamation quickly gaining momentum. Encouraged by the initial success of the development project, in early 1895 (12th month, Gojong 31) the king ordered the discontinuation of the *suto* program, which by that time had been in place for nearly two centuries, and the appointment of an island chief (*dojang*) go administer the affairs of Ulleungdo (1st month, Gojong 32). The new post of *dojang* was soon renamed *dogam* (island superintendent) (8th month, 1895).

The abolition of the *suto* program and the subsequent creation of the post of island superintendent marked an important turning point in Joseon's territorial management policy on Ulleungdo. The island superintendent, however, was not an official position integrated into Joseon's local administrative system. Ulleungdo's inclusion in the local administrative system took place three years later in May 1898, with the issuance of Imperial Decree No. 12 (Gwangmu 2). The island superintendent was a post filled by a local resident, giving the administration of Ulleungdo the characteristics of self-governed district. The appointment of an official from the mainland to head the administration of Ulleungdo first occurred after Inspection Commissioner U Yong-jeong visited the island in 1900.

The illegal timber logging and smuggling activities by the Japanese, begun in the mid-nineteenth century, were resolved in 1883 (Gojong 20), when the Japanese authorities finally agreed to arrange for the evacuation of Japanese nationals from the island, bowing to pressure from the Joseon side. Although there were several incidents involving timber smuggling, including the Tenju Maru Incident (late 1883) and the Banri Maru Incident (1885, Gojong 22), as well as persistent disruptive behavior by Japanese ships appearing in Ulleungdo's coastal waters (1888, Gojong 25), clandestine incursions and tree logging stopped, at least for the time being. In 1891, however, clandestine incursions on Ulleungdo resumed, and their rapidly increasing occurrence brought the number of Japanese ships routinely berthing along the island's shores to around 200 by 1896 (Geonyang 1). Most of the Japanese illegally present on Ulleungdo were timber workers, drawn there by the abundant zelkova timber available. Needless to say, the felled trees were all smuggled out to Japan.

The rampant tree logging and smuggling on Ulleungdo by Japanese only worsened in the Gwangmu period (1897-1907). Around this time, the Japanese also started to engage in illegal traffic of merchandise. Many engaged in lawless conduct, making their presence on Ulleungdo a constant source of distress for the island community. The government opened an inquiry into these unlawful Japanese activities on Ulleungdo, sending Ernest Laporte, the Acting Commissioner of the Busan Customs, to the island on an investigative mission in 1899. Later in May 1900, in the context of a joint investigation with Japan, U Yong-jeong, an investigator from the Interior Ministry, was dispatched to the island as the Ulleungdo Inspection Commissioner.

Upon his return to Seoul from his trip to Ulleungdo (June), U Yong-jeong drafted a report containing his recommendations to the government and submitted it to Yi Geon-ha, the minister of the interior at that time. He stated in his report that the Japanese presence on Ulleungdo was in violation of the bilateral treaty between the two countries, and that timely action needed to be taken to evacuate all Japanese loggers residing on the island to protect its community and woodlands. He, meanwhile, urged the government to reform the island's administrative system, stating that an island frequently visited by foreigners such as Ulleungdo could not be left to its own devices or remain as a self-governing community.

Heeding U Yong-jeong's recommendations, the government had its Foreign Ministry begin negotiations with its Japanese counterpart to repatriate Japanese loggers from Ulleungdo. On October 22, 1900, the Interior Ministry submitted a petition to the Uijeongbu, asking that Ulleungdo be upgraded to the status of a county. The petition stated that Ulleungdo was less than other inland counties in terms of its mountainous areas, population, farmland and farming production, and that the current post of island superintendent gave the administrator neither authority nor the practical means necessary to properly govern an island that was experiencing a significant influx of foreign goods and people. Soon after receiving this petition, the Uijeongbu adopted the resolution to issue "Imperial Decree No. 41, Gwangmu 4, Relating to the Renaming of Ulleungdo to Uldo and Replacing the Office of Island Superintendent with the Office of County Mayor." The Uijeongbu's decision was approved by the Korean emperor on October 25, and the decree was proclaimed on October 27, through publication in Gwanbo, the government gazette.

The most noteworthy provision in Imperial Decree No. 41 is undoubtedly Article 1. As this article replaced the post of the Ulleungdo island superintendent—a low-ranking clerical position, filled by a local resident—with the office of a county mayor, appointed and sent by the central government, it effectively integrated Ulleungdo into the local administrative system of Korea and also provided its chief with the authority and power he needed to govern properly.

No less remarkable, however, is Article 2 under which it was stipulated that the jurisdiction of the newly-renamed Uldo County should extend not only to the island of Ulleungdo and Jukdo, but also to Seokdo. Jukdo, here, refers to today's Jukdo (Jukseo), and the entire of Ulleung, namely, Ulleungdo and its adjoining islets and rocks. Seokdo, mentioned in Article 2, therefore, designates today's Dokdo. Seokdo would be translated into vernacular Korean as "Dolseom" of "Dokseom," both meaning "rock island." The people of Ulleungdo today still call Dokdo "Dolseom" or "Dokseom." The name "Dokdo" used by Slim Heung-taek, the Mayor of Uldo County in his 1906 (Gwangmu 10) report to the government, for instance, appears to have been a Sino-Korean transcription of the name "Dokseom."

Meanwhile, Seokdo, in other words, Dolseom or Dokseom, was not the standard name for Dokdo, used in Seoul. Although separated from Ulleungdo by a great distance and not familiar with its local reality, people in Seoul had access to geographical literature. Hence, even up until the late nineteenth century to the early twentieth century, when significant progress had already been made in terms of the domestication of Ulleungdo, people in Seoul called Dokdo "Usando," in accordance with the way it was referred to in ancient writings. The name "Seokdo" is likely to have derived from the Jeollanam-do dialect, as was pointed out by the late Professor Bang Jong-hyeon (1947). Jeollanam-do accounted for the vast majority of early settlers on Ulleungdo who came to the island prior to the Gojong-era settlement project, on their private initiatives. Inspector Yi Gyu-won, during his 1882 (Gojong 19) visit to the island, found 140 settlers, residing there on a more or less permanent basis. Of the total 140 settlers, 115 (82%) were from Jeollanam-do, After the start of the government-initiated settlement project, these seamen from the coastal areas of Jeollanam-do visited Ulleungdo yet more frequently. Being simple seamen, most probably illiterate, the chances are that they had never heard of Usando. Hence, when they came upon Dokdo or caught sight of it from a distance, on their way to Ulleungdo, they probably called it "Dokseom." *Dok* is, as is well known, the Jeollanam-do dialect word for *dol* (rock, stone).

In all likelihood, this name "Dokseom," coined by the coastal residents of Jeollanam-do, became the accepted name for the island and remained in use among the new settlers of Ulleungdo. Although no exact statistics are available as to the regional origins of the settlers brought to Ulleungdo in the context of the government-led development project, a great majority of them must have come from Gangwon-do, given this province's proximity to the island, followed by Gyeongsang-do; consistent with the statistical pattern that emerged during the first round of relocation. Dot being the standard word for stone or rock in Gangwon-do and Gyeongsang-do, the name "Dolseom" was likely to have been used at this time together with the name "Dokseom," coined by the Jeollanam-do seamen. Hence, it is likely that Dokdo was known among the early settlers of Ulleungdo as either "Dokseom" or "Dolseom": In other words, "Dolseom," the name used by the new settlers arriving from eastern Korea, eroded the exclusivity of the earlier name "Dokseom," which had originated from the Jeollanam-do seamen frequenting Ulleungdo, and the two names existed side-by-side. As for the name "Seokdo," used in Imperial Decree No. 41, Gwangmu 4, its source must have been U Yong-jeong, who during his visit to Ulleungdo probably heard the above two names and transcribed them into a Sino-Korean name.

"Imperial Decree No. 41, Gwangmu 4 On the Renaming of Ulleungdo to Uldo and Replacing the Office of Island Superintendent with the Office of County Mayor" was published, as has been mentioned earlier, in Gwanbo, on October 27, 1900. The procedural requirement at that for proclaiming a law, ordinance or a decree was that it be published in Gwanbo which makes October 27, the date of publication, also the date of the proclamation of this decree. The date of entry into force of Decree No. 41 is October 27 as well, since it is stated in Article 6 in the Addendum of the decree that it entered into force as of its proclamation. Imperial Decree No. 41, Gwangmu 4, therefore, constitutes a formal reaffirmation by the Korean Empire, issued in due form, of its sovereignty over Seokdo, that is to say, Dokdo.

One month after the granting of county status to Ulleungdo, the Korean government appointed the first mayor of Uldo County (November 1900). This was the first official appointed by the central government to administer Ulleungdo. Bae Gye-ju, the longtime island superintendent of Ulleungdo, was appointed the inaugural mayor of the new county. Three years later, in 1903, the county administration relocated to a new building in Taeha-dong, and its staff now included law enforcement officers, equipping it with the manpower befitting its new status. In April 1903, Shim Heung-taek succeeded Bae Gye-ju to the county mayoral office.

A Study on How the Japanese Government of the Meiji Period Investigated and Disclaimed Jurisdiction over Dokdo

Park Byoung-sup

Representative, 'Dokdo=Takeshima' Issue Research Net

1. Introduction

The newly established Meiji (明治) government, which toppled the Edo (江戸) shogunate (*bakufu* 幕府) in 1868, decided to directly undertake diplomatic negotiations with Korea, affairs previously conducted by the Tsushima (對馬) domain (*han* 藩). To this end, the government's Ministry of Foreign Affairs (*Gaimusho* 外務省) examined the history of the Tsushima domain's diplomatic engagement with Korea. In the course of its investigation, the territorial sovereignty of Takeshima (竹島) and Matsushima (松島), islands located in the East Sea, arose as an issue. The Korean name for the former is Ulleungdo, the latter, Dokdo.

In the 17th century, some Japanese occasionally engaged in fishing activities at the two islands. As Koreans also fished at Ulleungdo, Japanese fishermen ended up abducting Korean fisherman An Yong-bok and his party who were fishing there. In the wake of this incident, the territorial ownership of Takeshima became an issue of contention for Korea and the Tsushima domain. The ensuing diplomatic negotiations are known as the Ulleungdo Dispute in Korea and the Takeshima Incident (*Takeshima Ikken*) in Japan. Based on their detailed study of this history, Moriyama and his colleagues concluded that both Takeshima and Matsushima belonged to Korea. However, most Japanese researchers tend to ignore the details of that study and focus on the conclusion reached by the Meiji government's Ministry of Foreign Affairs. This paper seeks to shed light on how the Ministry of Foreign Affairs conducted its inquiry into the two islands.

Later on, the issue of Takeshima and Matsushima resurfaced when the Japanese government compiled the geographical records (地誌) and land registry of the entire nation. The compilation of Japan's official geographical records and land registry was a project vital to its efforts to transform the former feudal system into one that was suitable for a modern nation state. In order to consolidate centralization, the new government initiated *Haihanchiken* (藩置県), a policy of abolishing feudal domains and establishing prefectures by which the domain system based on autonomous local governing was disbanded and replaced by a system of prefectures that were subject to the control of the central government. Administering all the land through direct state rule required the compilation of a national land registry (地籍) and facilitating local governing required the compilation of geographical records. The geographic compilation on a national scale was the first of its kind in one thousand years. To push ahead with this project, the Meiji government set up the Office of Geography (*Chishika* 地誌課) in 1872 (the 5th year of the Meiji period, or Meiji 5) under the Grand Council of State (*Dajokan* 太政官), which was the highest decision-making body composed of Chancellor (*Daijodaijin* 太政大臣), Minister of the Left (*Sadaijin* 左大臣), Minister of the Right (*Udaijin* 右大臣) and Counselors (*Sangi* 参議), and the equivalent of a present-day cabinet. The Office of Geography was put under the control of the Ministry of the Interior (*Naimusho* 内務省), formed in 1874 as a subsidiary ministry of the Grand Council of State, as was the newly established Office of Land Registry

(*Chisekika* 地籍課).[1]

The territorial sovereignty of Takeshima and Matsushima also became an issue in compiling the entire nation's geographical records. The Ministry of the Interior launched in earnest an inquiry of the history surrounding the two islands and produced the *Isotakeshima Memorandum* (*Isotakeshima Oboegaki* 礒竹島覺書), in which it was articulated that they were not Japanese territory. The same issue loomed large once more when the national land registry of Japan was being put together. In light of the gravity of the territorial issue, the Ministry of the Interior, although construing neither island as Japanese territory, cautiously asked the Grand Council of State to deliberate on the matter. In keeping with the Interior Ministry's assessment, the Grand Council of State asserted in a directive that the two islands had nothing to do with Japan. As this Grand Council of State directive has sparked controversies among researchers of late, this paper intends to throw light on these academic scuffles and examine the way Dokdo was represented on the official Japanese maps that were compiled after the issuing of the directive.

During the Edo period and the early years of the Meiji period, Ulleungdo and Dokdo were designated as Takeshima and Matsushima, respectively, but later on, Ulleungdo also came to be called Matsushima while Takeshima was used to refer to Dokdo from 1905. To avert such confusion in the naming of the islands, in this paper, the current names of the islands are put in round brackets ( ) as the author deems fit, with the exception of quoted passages, in which the author's footnotes are placed in square brackets [ ].

---

1   Sato Sakae (佐藤侊), "Historical Records of the Ministry of the Interior's Geography and Land Registry Offices" (内務省地理局地誌課の事蹟), *Journal of Ancient Maps* (古地図研究) 305 (1999): 4.

2. The Investigation of Takeshima(Ulleungdo) and Matsushima(Dokdo) by the Ministry of Foreign Affairs

At the inception of the Meiji period, the Japanese government had an opportunity to make its judgment on the sovereignty status of Dokdo. The following is an account of how the process of this consideration unfolded. In a bid to directly take up diplomatic exchanges with Korea, which had been carried out solely by the Tsushima domain during the Edo period, the Meiji government sent a diplomatic note informing its Korean counterpart of the restoration of direct imperial rule in Japan (天皇親政). But the Korean government refused to accept it, taking issue with its content. In order to find a way out of the difficult situation while studying the history of exchanges between the two nations and making secret inquiries of Korea's situation, the Japanese government dispatched Foreign Affairs Ministry officials, including Moriyama Shigeru (森山茂), to the Tsushima Itsuhara (嚴原) domain and the Itsuhara House[2] in Busan. In 1869 (Meiji 2) the Ministry of Foreign Affairs secured approval from the Grand Council of State of a proposal titled "Instructions to Be Observed by the Korea Mission"[3] on what the Korea delegation should seek to obtain through investigation and confidential inquiry. However, the survey of Takeshima and Matsushima was not initially included in these instructions. Moriyama and his colleagues departed from Yokohama harbor (横濱港) in December 1869, and reached Tsushima on January 28 of the following year. After the completion of their investigation of the Itsuhara domain, they arrived at the Itsuhara House in Busan on February 22 to secretly study Korea. Their investigation extended the scope of the survey approved in the previous year to include the matter regarding the jurisdiction of Takeshima and Matsushima. The widening of the investigation may have been due to a

---

2   In the Edo period the Tsushima domain was officially called the Itsuhara domain.

3   "朝鮮へ被差遣候もの心得方御達之案," *Japan's Diplomatic Documents* (日本外交文書), vol. 2 (1938): 265.

couple of reasons. In studying the history of relations between the Tsushima domain and Korea, they were bound to read, among other things, historical sources considered fundamental to understanding the history, such as the *Grand Records of Diplomatic Relations with Korea* (*Chosen Tsuko Daiki* 朝鮮通交大紀) and *Good-Neighbor Diplomacy* (*Zenrin Tsuko* 善隣通交), in which the reader would learn about the Genroku Takeshima Incident (Genroku Takeshima Ikken 元禄竹島一件), an affair that caused a seven-year clash between the Tsushima domain and Korea in the 1690s. In addition, toward the end of the Edo period certain Japanese made an attempt to develop Ulleungdo, which was still uninhabited at the time, and in 1860 they went so far as to put forward a development proposal.[4] It is thus likely for the study team, headed by Moriyama, to have investigated the sovereignty status of the two islands in view of these historical developments. It also appears that Japan intended to delimit the boundaries of its territory as a modern nation state through such an investigation.

Moriyama and his associates provided a detailed account of their investigation and confidential inquiry findings in the Takeshima Incident section (Figure 1) of the "Investigation Report of Exchanges between Taishu [Tsushima] and Korea" (對州朝鮮交際取調書 "Taishu Chosen Kosai Dorishirabesho," or "Dorishirabesho" for short). They presented to the Ministry of Foreign Affairs the Investigation Report "Dorishrabesho," attached to their mission report titled *A Confidential Inquiry into the Particulars of Korea's Foreign Relations* (朝鮮国交際始末内探書 *Chosenkoku Kosai Shimatsu Naitansho*, or *Naitansho* for short).[5] Japanese researchers, however, assessed the *Confidential Inquiry* (*Naitansho*) mostly overlooking or disregarding the attached Investigation Re-

---

4   Omino Kiyoharu (小美濃清明), *Sakamoto Ryoma and the Exploration of Takeshima* (坂本龍馬と竹島開拓), Shinjinbutsu Ōraisha (新人物往来社) (2009), 68-69.

5   The following is in Japan's Diplomatic Documents, vol. 3, 138. Here, Taishu (對州) refers to Tsushima. "本文書 (『内探書』, 注) ノ附屬書タル別冊「對州朝鮮交際取調書」ハ省略ス" (The attachment to this document (Naitansho, footnote) "Investigation Report of Exchanges between Taishu and Korea" is omitted).

port. The former document is a summary of the latter prepared for reporting purposes, and as such lacks detailed information. Accordingly, discussing the process by which Takeshima and Matsushima came into Korea's possession necessitates examining the Investigation Report. It seems, however, that hardly any researchers have ever mentioned the report in their studies. The Investigation Report is posted on the National Archives of Japan website[6] and readily available to the public. The account of the Takeshima Incident included in the Investigation Report centers on the six correspondences between Korea in King Sukjong's reign and the Tsushima domain with respect to the dispute over the territorial ownership of Ulleungdo. The following is a summary of each letter. The month and year in round brackets mark the date the summary was put in *Records of Takeshima* (*Takeshima Kiji* 竹島紀事).

1. The letter sent by the Tsushima domain in September 1693 (October 1693) demanding that the Korean fishermen who trespassed onto Takeshima be returned to Korea and fishing activities by Korean nationals be forbidden (the latter part of Figure 1);[7]

---

6   Japan Asian Center for Asian Historical Records, National Archives of Japan (http://www.jacar. go. jp). Search reference code: B03030124800.

7   The translation of the letter is as follows (see Song Byong-gi, *Selected Materials on the Territorial Ownership of Dokdo*, Hallim University [2004], 14-15 for the Korean translation):
　　This year [1692], fishermen from your country have been sailing to Jukdo (竹島) and fishing in secret. However, this is a place where Koreans should never set foot and the land administrator (土官) immediately sent all your fishermen back, explaining in detail our state ban (國禁) on entry to the island and urging them never to come back. Still, this spring, the ban went unheeded yet another time, as about 40 Korean nationals caught fish off the coast of Jukdo, mingling with Japanese.
　　The land administrator detained two of these fishermen in the province office (州司) as hostages to be used as evidence of trespassing committed by Koreans, and the minister (州牧) of Inaba Province (因藩州) received an account of the incident and sent a report (馳啓) to Toto (東都). We have been ordered by Toto to have our village (弊邑) people repatriate the Korean fishermen and to never allow Korean boats to enter the island by enforcing the ban (禁制) more strictly.

148

2. The letter sent by Korea in December 1693 (January 1694) convey-
ing its gratitude for Japan's handling of the Korean fishermen's entry
to Ulleungdo and informing Japan that there was a ban on sailing to
Ulleungdo;[8]

3. The letter sent by the Tsushima domain in February 1694 (March
1694) demanding the deletion of the name "Ulleung" from the Korean correspondence;[9]

4. The letter sent by Korea in September 1694 (September 12, 1694)
protesting the arrest of the Korean fishermen and declaring Takeshima
as Ulleungdo;[10]

---

8   With an extremely strict ban on seafaring in place, our country (弊邦) forbids our fishermen to
    sail out to the ocean. Even voyages to Ulleungdo, which is within our border, are not permitted
    because it is far away from our mainland. How would our people be allowed to go outside of
    our boundaries? We are truly grateful to you for the good neighborliness (隣好) you exhibited in
    taking the trouble to send back (押領) to Korea our fishing boats which had ventured into Jukdo
    in your territory (貴界) and to inform us of your handling of the matter in writing from afar.
        When fishermen have to subsist on fishing, they cannot rule out the possibility of having
    to suffer the hardship of drifting while caught in storms. Even so, they should be rigorously
    prohibited by law (懲治) from engaging in fishing activities while mingling with others by cross-
    ing over the maritime boundary into forbidden territory. We assure you these criminals will be
    punished in accordance to our law (科罪) and that with respect to coastal fishing areas (等處) a
    strict measure (科條) will be established and implemented.

9   Since we never mentioned Ulleungdo in our letter, we find it hard to understand that your last
    reply (回簡) somehow refers to the island as such. We would be grateful if you could only delete
    the designation of Ulleung.

10 The island under the administrative control of Uljin-gun, Gwangwon-do, is called Ulleungdo,
    and the records about the island can clearly be found in the historical chronicles of successive
    generations. Fishermen of our country went to the island and encountered your countrymen
    who had arbitrarily trespassed on our territory. To our surprise, two Koreans were seized and
    taken to Edo. Fortunately, however, thanks to the gracious and lucid consideration of your ruler
    in reviewing the matter, they have been returned home with the gift of a generous amount of
    money for traveling expenses. What words could ever possibly convey our deepest gratitude for
    your lofty act of neighborly goodwill?

5. The letter sent by Korea in March 1698 (April 1698) confirming Ulleungdo as definitively belonging to Korea;[11]

6. The letter sent by the Tsushima domain in January 1699 (January
1699) offering congratulations on the settlement of the Takeshima Incident (Takeshima Ikken).[12]

The letters listed above are all quoted from "Reflections on the Takeshima
Incident (*Koku Takeshima Ikken Jiko* 告竹島一件事考) included in *Good-Neighbor Diplomacy*, vol. 5.[13] The whole collection of *Good-Neighbor Diplomacy* was

---

Nevertheless, it is on the fishing grounds of the island, originally called Ulleungdo, where
our people did fishing. As bamboo is grown there, the island is also called Jukdo (Bamboo
Island). There exist two names, but both refer to the same island. Not only is the fact that the
island is assigned two different names recorded in the historical documents of our nation, but
people of your province (貴州) are also all aware of it. When you have not broached the issue of
your country men's misconduct of trespassing on our boundary and arresting our people while
demanding that we forbid our fishing boats' passage to the island, calling Jukdo your territory in
your letter, how could we not consider the proper way of sincerity and trust as being tarnished?

11   As the interpreter (譯使) who has recently returned from your province relayed to us the personal message from you ruler (左右) in detail, we have come to learn the full account of the
incident.
    That Ulleungdo is our territory is written down in the Map of Korea (*Yeojido* 輿地圖) and
can be found clearly (昭然) in our literature (文跡). Aside from the fact that it is located near us
and far from you, the matter concerning its boundary is self-evident (自別). Previously you have
pledged to ban your fishermen from fishing off the island, for which we are deeply indebted. It
is our sincere hope that this incident (辭意) will help prevent another undesirable incident and
we think it immensely fortunate to see such preventative measures materialize. By conducting
frequent patrolling of the island, we will see to it that people from the two countries will be
forbidden to mingle with each other.

12   Receiving the report (陳達) on the Jukdo issue by the interpreter who came over to our country
last year, Your Lord (左右) sagaciously examined the incident (情由) and expressed his appreciation for the auspicious development in which both the countries vowed to maintain lasting
amicable relations with sincerity and trust. We have already conveyed (啓達) those thoughts to
Tobu (Edo 東武).

13   Preserved in the National Archives of Japan (国立公文書館所蔵).

Figure 1

The Takeshima Incident recorded in the "Investigation Report of Exchanges
between Taishu and Korea," appended to *A Confidential Inquiry into the Particulars
of Korea's Foreign Relations*

edited by Abiru Sobee (阿比留総兵衛) and revised by Matsuura Giemon (松浦
儀右衛門). Abiru, a Tsushima domain high official, was deeply involved in the
Takeshima Incident, and Matsuura wrote the preface to *Records of Takeshima*.
Despite presenting a well-organized description of the Takeshima Incident,
Good-Neighbor Diplomacy omitted some of the correspondence between Korea and the Tsushima domain included in *Grand Records of Diplomatic Relations with Korea* and *Records of Takeshima*. The Moriyama delegation wrote the
following in its *Confidential Inquiry* (*Naitansho*) the findings of its thorough
investigation of the Genroku Takeshima Incident:

The Particulars of How Takeshima and Matsushima Became Korean
Territory.

Matsushima in this case is a neighboring island of Takeshima. No document has so far been filed regarding Matsushima. As for Takeshima,
however, there remain copies of the Genroku (元禄) correspondences

<u>and procedural papers.</u> There was a case in which Koreans were sent to Takeshima for temporary settlement during the Genroku era, but now it is an uninhabited island as before. Bamboo and reeds taller than bamboo grow there, along with wild ginseng. In addition, it is said that the island abounds in marine products.

The copies, underlined above by the author, are what are included in the primary source, that is, *Special Collection of Official Documents* (*Kobun Betsuroku* 公文別録),[14] but missing from the secondary sources, such as *Diplomatic Documents of Japan* (*Nihon Gaiko Bunsho* 日本外交文書), vol. 3 and *Business Documents of Korea* (*Chosen Jimusho* 朝鮮事務書). For this reason, researchers who dealt only with the secondary sources assessed only the *Confidential Inquiry* (*Naitansho*) while overlooking the careful investigation of the Genroku-era materials researched by Moriyama and others. For instance, Tsukamoto Takashi has written, "The report did not include the 'Particulars of How Takeshima and Matsushima Became Korean Territory.'"[15] However, the particulars regarding the former can be found in the "copies of the Genroku-era correspondences and procedural documents," which were underlined for emphasis above. The Takeshima Incident included in the Investigation Report, annexed to the *Confidential Inquiry*, is actually an abridged version of the Genroku Takeshima Incident, the copies of which was used as the template. Hori Kazuo, who also appears to have overlooked these materials, contended regarding the "Particulars of How Takeshima and Matsushima Became Korean Territory" that it "indicates the understanding that, following the Genroku-era incident, Matsushima (Dokdo) was ceded to Korea, but it is only a

---

14   *Public Records: Joseon Incident, Mejii years 1–4* (公文別録 朝鮮事件 明治元年~明治四年), vol. 1, preserved in the National Archives of Japan. The original text for the underlined words is: "元禄 度之往復手続書 写の通ニ有之."

15   Tsukamoto Takashi (塚本孝), "History of the Takeshima Territorial Dispute" (竹島領有権問題 の経緯), *Research and Information* (調査と情報) 244 (1994): 4. The second (1996) and third (2011) editions are the same.

simple report."[16] To the contrary, however, the Takeshima Incident recorded in the Investigation Report was a meticulous survey report, rather than a simple one. In the meantime, Ikeuchi Satoshi (池内敏) remained silent on the matter, perhaps choosing to ignore the "Particulars of How Takeshima and Matsushima Became Korean Territory." The Ministry of Foreign Affairs took the same stance on this. Naito Seichu (内藤正中) wrote regarding the *Confidential Inquiry* that it "reveals the understanding that both Takeshima and Matsushima belong to Korea," adding, "Shimane Prefecture, too, regarded not only Takeshima (present-day Ulleungdo) but also Matsushima (present-day Takeshima) as Korean territory."[17]

While providing a sound description of the circumstances under which Takeshima became Korean territory, however, the Takeshima Incident included in the annex makes no mention of Matsushima. Moriyama's delegation wrote in their *Confidential Inquiry*, "No document has yet been filed regarding Matsushima," but a brief description of the island can be found in literature such as the section dated October Genroku 8 (1695) of *Records of Takeshima* and in *Documents of the Sho Family of Daemado*.[18] The Tsushima domain had viewed Matsushima, Takeshima's neighboring island, also as Korean territory. Moriyama and his associates affirmed Matsushima, too, as part of Korea, lay-

---

16   Hori Kazuo (堀和生), "Japan's 1905 Incorporation of Takeshima Territory" (一九〇五年日本の 竹島領土編入), *Journal of Korean History* (朝鮮史研究会論文集) 24 (1987): 104.

17   *Photo Shimane Feature: Takeshima* (フォトしまね 特集竹島), vol. 161, Shimane-ken (島根縣) (2006): 7.

18   The following is recorded in *Documents of the Sho Family of Daemado* (對馬島宗家文書), National Institute of Korean History, archive catalog #4013.

      There remains a record that during the Genroku (元禄期) era, Abe Bungo no Kami (阿部 豊後守) inquired about Matsushima and received a reply based on the rumor that there was an island called Matsushima near Takeshima and that Japanese fishermen had crossed over to Matsushima to fish. It is believed that crossing and fishing by Japanese are banned for this island, as with Takeshima, but that cannot be confirmed. A look at the map of Korea shows that there exist two islands, Ulleung and Usan. We heard that fishermen from that country have been sailing to Takeshima and building boats using wood abundant on the island, and that it still remains uninhabited.

ing more emphasis on the Tsushima domain's view concerning 'Takeshima's neighboring island' or on the simple description than on the availability of Matsushima-related documents. This all indicates that there was a strong notion that Matsushima was an island ancillary to Takeshima or that the two islands formed a dyad.

Because the report by Moriyama's delegation was naturally submitted to the Grand Council of State,[19] it is highly likely that the Japanese government, too, considered Takeshima and Matsushima (Dokdo) as Korean territory. Eventually, the Meiji government shared with the Edo shogunate the notion of Dokdo being under Korean jurisdiction. The *Confidential Inquiry* (*Naitansho*) and the *Investigation Report* (*Dorishirabesho*) are thus far more than simple reports, but are historical documents that serve to provide understanding in this matter.

3. The Interior Ministry's *Isotakeshima Memorandum*

Any modern nation-state needs a clear demarcation of its territory. Tasked with this endeavor, the Ministry of the Interior embarked on an investigation of the jurisdiction of Takeshima and Matsushima. The *Isotakeshima Memorandum* was published in August 1875[20] by Nakamura Genki (中邨(村) 元起)

19　The Foreign Affairs Ministry's proposal of "Instructions to Be Observed by the Korea Mission" was approved by the Council of State and even the arrival of Moriyama and his associates at the Itsuhara House in Busan was reported to the Council. These facts corroborate the Council of State's great interest in Moriyama's delegation (*Diplomatic Documents of Japan*, vol. 3, 127). Therefore, the study team's report was likely to have been submitted to the Council of State.

20　The National Archives of Japan has (1) *Isotakeshima Memorandum*: Complete (礒竹島覺書 完) and (2) *Isotakeshima Memorandum*: Bureau of Geography (礒竹島覺書 地理局), while the University of Tsukuba (筑波) has (3) a two-volume set of *A Short History of Isotakeshima* (礒竹島事略). The contents of these books are almost identical. At the end of (1) is written "August 8, the 8ᵗʰ year of the Meiji period, proofread by Nakamura Genki" (明治八年八月八日校正 中邨元起), along with the stamped seal of "Genki," showing this text to be the original. Since the Bureau of

on the basis of the Genroku-era Takeshima Incident-related materials from the Tsushima domain, such as *Records of Takeshima*, that were collected by the Office of Geography under the Interior Ministry's Bureau of Geography (*Chiriryo* 地理寮). Isotakeshima refers to Takeshima, that is, Ulleungdo. The *Isotakeshima Memorandum* is a historical material illustrative of Japan's stance regarding the sovereignty of the two islands. The following is the part of the book that describes Matsushima (Dokdo).

In its report dated August 12, 1695, to a Council Elder (*Roju* 老中), one of the highest-ranking government officials in the Edo shogunate, the Tottori domain said the Oya (大谷) and Murakawa (村川) families, who had left Yonago (米子) on March 6 for Takeshima, gave up fishing at the island upon finding many Korean fishermen already there and that "on the return journey they saw an islet called Matsushima and took some abalone from there."[21] Subsequently, the Tsushima domain had its representatives, including Sho Yoshizane (宗義真), sent to Edo for consultation with the Edo shogunate in order to break the negotiation deadlock with Korea. From then on, the Edo shogunate's investigation of Takeshima began in earnest. The Council Elder relayed questions to the Tottori domain pertaining to the jurisdiction of the island. His seventh question was whether there were any other islands under the jurisdiction of the two provinces (Tottori domain) besides Takeshima. To this query, the Tottori domain replied on December 25 that "no islands belong to the two provinces, including Takeshima and Matsushima."[22] Taking interest in Matsushima, mentioned in the Tottori domain's response, the shogunate

---

Geography succeeded the Interior Ministry's Chiriryo (地理寮) in 1877, (2) is a copied manuscript. Since the first head title inside (3) is Isotakeshima Memorandum, it is also judged to be a copied manuscript.

21 "去八月 松平伯耆守方より其節之月番土屋相模守殿江書付差出候寫," *Isotakeshima Memorandum*: Complete. The original text is, "船路に松島と申小島相見 立寄鮑少々取候而歸帆仕候."

22 "同月二十四日 松平伯耆守家来召寄 書付を以尋候事 附右之返答書付來事," *Isotakeshima Memorandum*: Complete. The original text is, "竹嶋之外兩國江付屬之嶋有之候哉," "竹島松島其外兩國江付屬之島無御座候事."

soon asked whether the island called Matsushima did not belong to Inaba (因幡國) or Hoki Province, to which the Tottori domain answered that Matsushima was not and that it was an island lying on the sea route to Takeshima.[23] Having heard the name Matsushima for the first time during the Takeshima Incident, the shogunate confirmed through the Tottori domain's response that Matsushima did not belong to either Inaba or Hoki Province, that is, part of the Tottori domain. In its investigation of the Matsue (松江) domain's possible involvement in the Takeshima voyage project, the Edo shogunate also found out that some Matsue sailors hired by Yonago merchants had sailed to the island and that the domain itself had nothing to do with the voyage project.

Figure 2
The Ministry of the Interior's *Isotakeshima Memorandum*

---

23   "松平伯耆守江重而相尋候書付到來之事," *Isotakeshima Memorandum*: Complete. The original text is, "松島与申島 因幡國伯耆國江付屬之島に候哉," "松島兩國江付屬に而は無御座候 竹島江渡海之筋に在之島に而御座候."

The following year, on January 9, 1696, the Edo shogunate conveyed to the Tsushima domain its intention to ban Japanese nationals from traveling to Takeshima on the basis of its investigation findings. The ban was to be put in place for the reasons (1) that the fishermen of the Tottori domain were granted permission only to undertake fishing activities at Takeshima, a decision that did not appear tantamount to occupying a Korean island; (2) that the island appeared to belong to Korea since it was about 40 *li* from Korea and about 160 *li* from Hoki Province, thereby closer to the former; and (3) that if the island came under Japan's ownership or Japanese lived there, it would be difficult to hand control of the island over to Korea, but there was no evidence that such was the case.[24] Afterwards, the shogunate cautiously asked the Tottori domain again whether provinces, such as Izumo, were engaged in voyages to Takeshima and how the situation was in Matsushima. The Tottori domain replied that both the Oya and Murakawa families had sailed in the same vessel to Takeshima with sailors hired from other provinces, while there was no case of seafaring to the island conducted independently by sailors hailing from other provinces; that they fished and hunted at Matsushima on their return journey as it was located on the sea route to Takeshima; and that they had been told Matsushima did not belong to any province.[25] It is believed that "any province" in the Tottori domain's reply refers to Inaba and Hoki Provinces, that is, the Tottori domain, but it is contextually dubious to regard Inaba as being "any province" because there is no mention of it in the reply.[26] Furthermore, as Tsukamoto contends, the Tottori domain cannot have pro-

---

24　"元禄九年丙午正月九日　宗刑部大輔家老平田直右衛門召寄　書付を以申渡候事," *Isotakeshima Memorandum*: Complete.

25　"同月廿三日松平伯耆守留守居召寄 并相尋候趣伯耆守より書付を以申來事," *Isotakeshima Memorandum*: Complete. The original text is, "松嶋は何連之国江付候嶋に而茂無御座候由承候."

26　Kawakami Kenzo (川上健三), *Historical and Geographical Study of Takeshima* (竹島の歴史地理学的研究): 85; Ikeuchi Satoshi (池内敏), "Concerning the Perception of Takeshima and Matsushima in the Edo Period" (江戸時代における竹島および松島の認識について), *Dokdo Research* (獨島研究) 6, Yeungnam University, Korea (韓国嶺南大学校) (2009): 192.

vided a response as to the ownership of its own territory by using the wording, "had been told," as if relaying a message.[27] Therefore, this "any province" was understood to refer to a province in Japan, and the Tottori domain regarded Matsushima as an island to which Japan had no title. It can be said that the shogunate, too, understood the island ownership issue in the same vein upon the receipt of the Tottori domain's reply.

It is through the investigation of these materials that the *Isotakeshima Memorandum* confirmed Takeshima and Matsushima to be no concern of Japan's. Even with no mention of the name Matsushima in the Edo shogunate's "ban on Takeshima voyages," therefore, sailing to Matsushima, no territory of Japan's, was also forbidden, as was expected.

4. The Government-Compiled *Japanese Geography Summary* (*Nihon Chishi Teiyo* 日本地誌提要)

The Interior Ministry's Office of Geography, having completed the compilation of the *Isotakeshima Memorandum* in August 1875, was placed in the following month under the Division of Geography of the Grand Council of State's Japanese History Compilation Bureau (*Dajokan Shushikoku Chishikakari* 修史局地誌掛). Along with this structural change, Nakamura Genki, the compiler of the *Isotakeshima Memorandum*, too, was transferred to the Division of Geography to participate in the compilation of official Japanese geographical records.[28] He worked for the Grand Council of State and the Of-

---

27   Tsukamoto Takashi, "Old Tottori Domain Documents and Pictures Relating to Takeshima" (竹島関係 旧鳥取藩文書および絵図), *References* (レファレンス) 411, National Diet Library (国会図書館) (1985), 192.

28   Preface to the *Japanese Geography Summary* (Nihon Chishi Teiyo 日本地誌提要) preserved in the National Archives of Japan. Its photoprint is *Japanese Geography Summary*, vol. 1, Rinsen Shoten (臨川書店) (1982).

fice of Geography within the Interior Ministry from 1873 to January 1877.[29] As a matter of course, the latter's notion that Takeshima and Matsushima did not belong to Japan was passed directly on to the Grand Council of State, the transition that is reflected in *Japanese Geography Summary* compiled by the Grand Council of State's Division of Geography. The compilation consists of eight books in all, the first three published in October 1874 by the Interior Ministry's Office of Geography and the remaining five published from 1877 to 1879 by the Office of Geography under the Grand Council of State's Central Chamber (*Seiin* 正院).[30] The following is the record concerning Takeshima and Matsushima that appears in Section 50 titled "Oki" in Book 4 published in April 1877.

- The islands under the jurisdiction of Honshu (本州) number 179 in all, comprising 45 in Chibu District (知夫郡), 16 in Ama District (海士郡), 75 in Suki District (周吉郡) and 43 in Ochi District (穩地郡). They are collectively called the Small Islands of Oki (*Okino Kojima* 隠岐の小島).

- There are also two islands, Matsushima and Takeshima, northwest of Honshu. There are folk tales about them. They are about 69 *li* and 35 *jung* from the Port of Fukuura (福浦港), Ochi District, to Matsushima. The distance from the Port to Takeshima is about 100 *li* and 4 *jung*. It is about 136 *li* and 30 *jung* from the Port to Korea. [1 *li* = 4 km, 1 *jung* = 110m]

In *Japanese Geography Summary*, the total number of islands under the jurisdiction of Inshu (隠州) is recorded to be 179, with Takeshima and Matsushima counted out and separately described. This omission indicates that the

---

29   Sato Sakae (1999): 8.

30   Marked on the cover of *Japanese Geography Summary*, vol. 1.

two islands were under neither Inshu's jurisdiction nor any other province's. In other words, they were not regarded as Japanese territory. Tanaka Akamaro (田中阿歌麻呂), a Meiji-era geographer, held the same view. Despite confusing Takeshima (Ulleungdo) and Matsushima (Dokdo) for some time, he did not alter his assessment that *Japanese Geography Summary* showed the two islands to be outside of Japan's territorial sovereignty.[31] This indicates that the official geographical records compiled by the Grand Council of State judged Dokdo to be outside the nation's jurisdiction.

5. The Grand Council of State Directive on "Takeshima and the Other Island"

As mentioned above, by establishing the Office of the National Land Registry the Ministry of the Interior enlisted local government offices in its national land registry compilation project. As the administrative control of Takeshima and Matsushima emerged as an issue in Shimane Prefecture, the prefecture submitted in October 1876 to the Interior Ministry "An Inquiry on the Compilation of the Land Registry of Takeshima and the Other Island in the Sea of Japan [the East Sea]." It is clearly stated in the document attached to the inquiry that Takeshima was Ulleungdo and "the other island" Matsushima, that is, Dokdo. To this inquiry, the Interior Ministry probably found it easy to make a decision on the issue since it had previously had its Office of Geography compile the *Isotakeshima Memorandum*. It based its judgment of Takeshima and Matsushima being of no concern to Japan on the following four documents.

---

31   Park Byoung-sup, "Analyzing the Commentaries of Shimojo Masao (2)" (Shimojo Masao [下條正男]-ui nonseol-eul bunseokhanda[2]), *Dokdo Research* 7 (2009): 136-139; Park Byoung-sup, "Analyzing the Editorial of Shimojo Masao (2)" (下條正男の論説を分析する[2]), *Dokdo Research* 7 (2009): 105-107.

Document 1: Purpose of District Government Consultation
This is an explanatory record of the ban on travel to Takeshima conveyed to the Tsushima domain by the Council Elder, quoted from the section dated January 28, 1696, of *Records of Takeshima*. The reason for the travel ban was nearly identical to what is described in the *Isotakeshima Memorandum*.

Document 2: Memorandum Sent to the Korean Interpreter
This is a Tsushima domain memo notifying the Korean interpreter of the Edo shogunate's ban on travel to Takeshima, quoted from the section dated October 1696 of *Records of Takeshima*.

Document 3: Letter from Korea
Sent in March 1698 by the Secretary (*Chamui*) of Korea's Ministry of Rites (*Yejo*), this letter confirms the nation's sovereignty over Ulleungdo and expresses satisfaction at the settlement of the Ulleungdo Dispute. It is quoted from the April 1698 section of *Records of Takeshima* or the *Isotakeshima Memorandum*. In addition, it is identical to the fifth letter regarding the Takeshima Incident included in the Foreign Affairs Ministry's *Investigation Report*.

Document 4: Last Letter from the Tsushima Domain
This January 1699 letter was sent to Korea's Ministry of Rites by the Tsushima domain to convey the domain's congratulations on the settlement of the Takeshima Incident, along with a verbal note reflecting the domain's comprehensive assessment of the Incident, both of which are quoted from the section dated January 1699 of *Records of Takeshima*. The copy of the letter corresponds to the sixth letter regarding the Takeshima Incident included in the *Isotakeshima Memorandum* and the Foreign Affairs Ministry's *Investigation Report*.

As shown above, the rigorous investigation of the Genroku Takeshima Incident led the Ministry of the Interior to conclude that Takeshima and Matsushima were not Japanese territory. Considering the acquisition and disposition of national territory as a matter of great importance, the Interior Ministry put much thought into the matter before submitting to the Grand Council of State on March 17, 1877 "An Inquiry on the Compilation of the Land Registry of Takeshima and the Other Island in the Sea of Japan [the East Sea]," an inquiry note with the same title as the one presented by Shimane Prefecture. At the time, under the direction of the Grand Council of State, the national geography compilation project was carried out by the Division of Geography, the successor of the Interior Ministry's Office of Geography, rechristened the Second Office of the Third Bureau under the House of Japanese History Compilation (*Shushikan* (修史館) *Dai 3 Kyoku* (第3局) *Otsuka* 乙科). This made it easy for the Grand Council of State to review the Ministry's inquiry note. In reality, despite the gravity of the matter, it was only three days before the Grand Council of State drafted a directive proclaiming, "Our country (本邦) has nothing to do with Takeshima and the other island." Within ten days, it was approved and ratified by high government officials. Iwakura Tomomi (岩倉具視), the Minister of the Right, instructed the Interior Ministry on March 29 to issue the directive in its original form. The prompt handling of the matter can be attributed to the fact that Interior Ministry research reports such as the *Isotakeshima Memorandum*, in which Japan was indicated to have nothing to do with Takeshima and Matsushima, were in the possession of the Grand Council of State's House of Japanese History Compilation.

6. Controversies over the Grand Council of State Directive

Hori Kazuo, who discovered the Grand Council of State Directive on "Takeshima and the Other Island," wrote drawing on the Directive that "the other island" was specified in the document as Matsushima, with its location and form correctly described.[32, 33] Following the publication of Hori's paper in 1987, the view that the island referred to as "the other island" was Matsushima, that is, Dokdo, remained unchallenged for a long time, with the support of such academics as Tsukamoto Takashi[34] and Naito Seichu.[35]

It was Shimojo Masao (下條正男), however, who took issue with this line of interpretation. In 2004, he wrote that it was not clear whether "the other island" referred to present-day Takeshima [Dokdo],[36] but he put forth an entirely different view in 2006, contending that "the other island" was regarded as the then Matsushima and present-day Takeshima [Dokdo].[37] Altering his stance anew in March 2007, he maintained that while Shimane Prefecture identified "the other island" as Dokdo, Takeshima and the other island, which the Grand Council of State Directive indicated to have nothing to do with Japan, were actually two Ulleungdos.[38] Hardly had six months passed before he changed his position yet again, this time asserting that Shimane Prefec-

---

32   Hori Kazuo (1987): 103.

33   For photoprints of relevant material, see Park Byoung-sup and Naito Seichu, *The Dokdo/Takeshima Controversy* (trans. Yuji Hosaka), Bogosa (2008), 322-323; Naito Seichu and Park Byoung-sup (内藤正中・朴炳渉), *The Dokdo/Takeshima Controversy* (竹島＝独島論争), Shinkansha (新幹社) (2007), 324-325.

34   Tsukamoto Takashi (1985), 5.

35   Naito Seichu, *Japan-Joseon Relations Concerning Takeshima (Ulleungdo)* (竹島(鬱陵島)をめぐる日朝関係史), Taga Shoten (多賀書店) (2000), 131.

36   Shimojo Masao, *Japan or Korea, Where Does Takeshima Belong?* (竹島は日韓どちらのものか), Bunshunshinsho (文春新書) (2004), 123.

37   Shimojo Masao, *Message from Takeshima, Toward a Sincere Japan-Korea Friendship: the Embers Remaining from the Meiji Period (2), the Second "Edict vs. Council's Decision"* (発信竹島-真の日韓親善に向けて-: 第2部 "勅令vs閣議決定"－明治時代－(2)残った火種), San-in Shimbun (山陰新聞), August 24, 2005.

38   Shimojo Masao, "Regarding the Final Report Two Years after the Ordinance of 'Takeshima Day'" (最終報告にあたって'竹島の日'条例から二年), *Final Report on the "Study of the Takeshima Dispute"* ("竹島問題に関する調査研究" 最終報告書), Takeshima Research Center (竹島問題研究会) (2007), 2.

ture viewed both Takeshima and Matsushima as Ulleungdo.[39] Then, in 2011, with another change of heart, he stated that "Takeshima and the other island" referred to Argonaut (竹島) Island and Ulleungdo (松島), respectively.[40] Although he recognized "the other island" as Dokdo, it is extremely unusual for a scholar to change his view no fewer than four times without offering any explanation.[41]

Apart from Shimojo, controversy has recently been caused by some Japanese researchers who regard "the other island" as Ulleungdo. Citing "An Inquiry on the Development of Matsushima in the Sea of Japan," submitted to the Ministry of the Interior by Shimane Prefecture in 1881 (Meiji 14), four years after the issuing of the Grand Council of State Directive, Sugihara Takashi (杉原隆) stated that the Meiji government had recognized Matsushima as Ulleungdo since the phrase "Takeshima and the other island" came into use in Meiji 10, adding that both Takeshima and Matsushima referred to the same island, that is, Ulleungdo.[42] To this argument, Takeuchi Takeshi (竹内猛) took Sugihara to task, pointing out that when one said in Japanese the phrase "Takeshima and the other island," it clearly meant two islands, that the problem with Sugihara's contention had to do with not so much his interpretation of relevant historical materials as his Japanese proficiency (comprehension), and that he failed to present his own interpretation of the written report of

---

39 Shimojo Masao, "To Those Manipulating the History of Japanese Territory 'Takeshima'" (日本 の領土「竹島」の歴史を改竄せし者たちよ'), *Shokun* (諸君) (2007), 103.

40 Shimojo Masao, "Regarding the Territorial Criticism by the Foreign Affairs Division of the Silsagusi 32nd Hangyere Newspaper Electronic Edition" (実事求是 第32回 ハンギョレ新聞電子 版の外務省の固有の領土論批判について), *Report on the 'Study of the Takeshima Dispute'* (竹島問 題に関する調査研究報告書), Shimane-ken (島根県) (2013), 29.

41 Park Byoung-sup, "Analyzing the Commentaries of Shimojo Masao" (下條正男の論説を分析す る), *Dokdo Research* 4 (2008): 89-90.

42 Sugihara Takashi (杉原隆), "Regarding the 'Application to Pioneer Matsushima' by Shizoku Oya Kensuke and One Other of Asaimura" (浅井村士族大屋兼助他一名の '松島開拓願'について), *Kyodo Iwami* (郷土石見) 83 (2010): 23.

Meiji 9 [the Inquiry Note of Shimane Prefecture].[43] In Shimane Prefecture's inquiry note, attached to the Interior Ministry's "An Inquiry on the Compilation of the Land Registry of Takeshima and the Other Island in the Sea of Japan," the part titled "A Summary of Reasons" (原由の大略) stated, "Then there is an island called Matsushima. It is located on the same sea route as Takeshima and its circumference is 30 *jung* [3.3 km]. It is 80 *li* [320 km] from Oki." Takeuchi concluded that along with the map titled Simplified Map of Isotakeshima (Isotakeshima Rakyuzu 磯竹島略圖) (Figure 3), which was enclosed in the inquiry note, the quoted passage clearly indicated "the other island" to be Matsushima and that there was no room for that kind of interpretation, such as Sugihara's one-island theory, to establish a foothold.

As briefly mentioned before, Tsukamoto Takashi, concurring with Hori Kazuo, maintained in 1994 that Matsushima (Dokdo) became of no concern to Japan.[44] In his recent paper, however, he set forth an idea that in Shimane Prefecture's inquiry note Matsushima referred to the island called by this name of Matsushima in the Edo period, (present-day Takeshima). He went on to contend that it was likely for the central government to judge the island under consideration to be outside Japanese territory on the basis of thinking that it was "an island (Ulleungdo) designated as either Takeshima or Matsushima" rather than Takeshima (Ulleungdo) and Matsushima (Takeshima today).[45] Tsukamoto's argument, which unfolds in a manner similar to Sugihara's, is grounded on literature of the later period, such as the 1833 Grand Council of State Decree (諭達) and the aforementioned "Inquiry on the Development of Matsushima in the Sea of Japan," and does not offer an analysis of the Interior

43   Takeuchi Takeshi (竹内猛), "Regarding the Debate Surrounding the Interpretation of 'Takeshima and the Other Island'" ("竹島外一島"の解釈をめぐる問題について), *Kyodo Iwami* (郷土石見) 87 (2011): 43.

44   Tsukamoto Takashi (2011): 5.

45   Tsukamoto Takashi, "Protection and Amalgamation in Korea, and the Territorial Views of Japan and Korea" (韓国の保護・併合と日韓の領土認識), *Modern East Asian History* (東アジア近代史) 14 (2011): 58.

Ministry's notion at the time of the issuing of the Grand Council of State Directive. In connection with Tsukamoto's paper, Naito Seichu stated, "By 1877, both Shimane Prefecture, which made a clear distinction between Takeshima and Matsushima in its inquiry note, and the Ministry of the Interior, which, in receiving the inquiry note, recognized Takeshima by the name used in the past, considered Matsushima as "the other island." He suggested the previously mentioned Summary of Reasons and Simplified Map of Isotakeshima for the grounds of the inference that "the other island" was Dokdo.[46] Naito's view is valid. Furthermore, as shown below, Ikeuchi Satoshi, too, has mounted a searing criticism of late on what Sugihara and Tsukamoto sought to do.

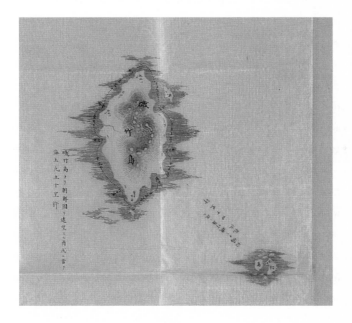

Figure 3

Part of the Simplified Map of Isotakeshima

46   Naito Seichu, "Takeshima Controversy in 1905" (一九〇五年の竹島問題), *Studies of the Cultures in Northeast Asia* (北東アジア文化研究) 34 (2011): 11.

The views espoused by Sugihara and Tsukamoto are intended to stir up confusion in the interpretation of "An Inquiry on the Compilation of the Land Registry of Takeshima and the Other Island in the Sea of Japan." Subjecting this historical material to strict textual interpretation leads to only one conclusion that in Meiji 10 the Japanese central government indicated in its official documents that Takeshima (Ulleungdo) and Takeshima [Dokdo] were outside of Japanese territorial sovereignty. This is a historical fact that those intent on asserting Japan's ownership of Takeshima [Dokdo] in view of history find hard to accept. Unable to confront head-on a historical fact that they are reluctant to accept, they ended up persisting with arguments fraught with contradictions by resorting to an element extraneous to the discussion, that is, the impact of confusing the name of an island that did not exist there in the first place.

Despite such criticism, Tsukamoto still has not renounced his position that "the other island" could well be Ulleungdo.[47] To fundamentally debunk this kind of controversy, Park (2013) demonstrated by examining official documents that for Shimane Prefecture, the Ministry of the Interior and the Grand Council of State, Matsushima invariably meant the same island. That is to say, he stated that regarding the location of Takeshima and Matsushima, Shimane Prefecture's, the Ministry of Home Affairs, and the Grand Council of State's notions were represented in the Simplified Map of Isotakeshima, the *Isotakeshima Memorandum* and *Japanese Geography Summary* respectively, and that the location of the two islands shown in these materials nearly corresponded to each other as listed in Table 1 below.[48] From this it can be con-

---

47 Tsukamoto Takashi, "Council of State Directive in Meiji 10 Surrounding the Genroku Takeshima Incident" (元禄竹島一件をめぐって 一付、明治十年太政官指令), *The Journal of Islands Studies* (島嶼研究ジャーナル) 2-2 (2013): 48-54.

48 Park Byoung-sup, "The Problem of Dokdo's Territoriality in the Modern Era" (Geundaegi Dokdo-ui yeongyugwon munje), *On Establishing the Territoriality of Dokdo* (Dokdo yeongyugwon hwangnip-eul wihan yeongu), Seonin Publishing (Doseochulpan Seonin) (2013), 168.

cluded that Matsushima mentioned in these documents refers to the same island, and therefore, the views advocated by Tsukamoto Takashi and others like him hardly cohere with the facts.

Table 1

Japanese Government Office Notions of the Location of Takeshima and Matsushima

(1 *li* = 4 km, 1 *jung* = 110 m)

	Shimane Prefecture	Ministry of the Interior	Grand Council of State
Oki – Matsushima	80 *li*	80 *li*	69 *li* and 35 *jung*
Matsushima – Takeshima	40 *li*	40 *li*	30 *li* and 5 *jung*
Takeshima – Korea	50 *li*	40-50 *li*	36 *li* and 26 *jung*
Data Source	Simplified Map of Isotakeshima	*Isotakeshima Memorandum*	*Japanese Geography Summary*
Publication Date	October 1876	August 1875	January 1877 (Vol. 50)

7. Government-Compiled Maps of the Meiji Era

There exist numerous maps created by such countries as Korea and Japan that show Dokdo, but delving into any discussions on territorial sovereignty requires one to consult maps compiled by the authorities in charge of territorial jurisdiction. In Japan, the Ministry of the Interior takes charge of such matters. In the Meiji period, it defined the administrative control of each area in Japan and decided on the acquisition and disposition of territory. Therefore, maps compiled by the Ministry reflect the official position of the Japanese government on territory. It can be said that the absence of Dokdo on such maps indicates an understanding that the island was situated outside Japanese territory.

With this in mind, maps compiled by the Ministry of the Interior will be examined. Based on the "*Maps of Greater Japan's Coastal Areas*" (*Dai Nihon Enkai Yochi Zenzu* 大日本沿海輿地全圖) by Ino Tadataka (伊能忠敬), the compilation of which was sponsored by the Edo shogunate, the Ministry's Bureau of Geography created the *"Map of Greater Japan's Prefectural Jurisdictions"* (*Dai Nihon Fuken Gankatsuzu* 大日本府県管轄圖) in 1879, the *"Complete Map of Greater Japan"* (*Dai Nihonkoku Zenzu* 大日本國全圖) in 1880 and the *Map of Greater Japan's Prefectural Divisions* (*Dai Nihon Fuken Bunkatsuzu* 大日本府県分轄圖) in 1881. These official maps, including Ino Tadataka's, neither marked Takeshima/Matsushima nor treated them as Japanese territory even when they were marked.[49] Furthermore, Dokdo was missing from all of the twelve maps in the Ministry's collection of maps published around 1883 that indicated the changes in each area's jurisdiction. It was based on the *"Complete Map of Greater Japan"* and also titled the *Complete Map of Greater Japan*. This collection shows the yearly changes that took place in each area's jurisdiction from 1871 to 1882 with the implementation of the policy of abolishing domains and establishing prefectures. For instance, the north of the Kuril Islands, that is, the Chishima Islands (千島), was not regarded as Japanese territory on the map compiled prior to May 1875 (Figure 4), the time when it became part of Japan, but was marked as belonging to Japan in the later map (Figure 5). The fact that the 1883 *Complete Map of Greater Japan* did not include Dokdo leads one to believe that the Ministry of the Interior did not consider the island as Japanese territory at least from 1871 and 1882.[50]

This notion of Dokdo continued into later decades. In particular, when a fisherman named Nakai Yozaburo (中井養三郎) submitted a petition in 1904 to the Interior, Foreign Affairs, and Agriculture & Commerce Ministries (農商務省), seeking the incorporation of Liancourt [Dokdo] into Japan's territory and requesting to lease it, the Ministry of the Interior raised vehement objections to the petition on the grounds that the idea of including the mere

49   Park Byoung-sup, "The Meiji Government's Takeshima=Dokdo Perception" (明治政府の竹島＝独島認識), *Studies of the Cultures in Northeast Asia* (北東アジア文化研究) 28 (2008): 41-42.

50   Park (2013), 169.

Figure 4

1871 map from the Interior Ministry's *Complete Map of Greater Japan*: on this map the
north Kurile Islands are not shown as Japanese territory and Dokdo is not marked at all

Figure 5

1882 map from the Interior Ministry's *Complete Map of Greater Japan*: on this map, the
north Kurile Islands are marked as Japan's territory, whereas Dokdo is absent

rocks, no better than a piece of barren terrain, which might belong to Korea, at this time [in the midst of the Russo-Japanese War] would lead many nations watching Japan to suspect that it was nurturing the ambition to annex its neighbor and that provoking such suspicion would not yield many benefits while dealing with the petition would be no easy feat. Given the instructions of the Grand Council of State Directive, objecting to the petition was a natural course of action for the Interior Ministry.

To sum up, there are historical precedents whereby Japan viewed Dokdo as the territory of Joseon or Korea, whereas prior to 1905 the island was never judged to belong to Japan. Therefore, the argument advanced by the Ministry of Foreign Affairs that Dokdo is part of Japan does not stand to reason.

8. Conclusion

The 17th century Ulleungdo Dispute (the Genroku Takeshima Incident) had a great influence on the issue of Dokdo that would arise later. While investigating Takeshima (Ulleungdo), the Edo shogunate came to learn Matsushima (Dokdo) was located near Takeshima, regarding both islands as part of Korea. This idea of the two islands' jurisdiction continued into the Meiji period.

At the inception of the Meiji period, the Japanese government dispatched a delegation headed by Moriyama Shigeru in 1870 to the Tsushima domain and the Japan House in Busan. Based on its careful examination of the Genroku Takeshima Incident, the delegation produced a piece of writing titled the "Particulars of How Takeshima and Matsushima Became Korean Possession" in its report, *A Confidential Inquiry into the Particulars of Korea's Foreign Relations*. The process in which Takeshima (Ulleungdo) became Korean territory was well explained in the section titled the "Takeshima Incident" that was included in the "Investigation Report of Exchanges between Taishu and Korea," the annex to the aforementioned *Confidential Inquiry*, while an account of Matsushima (Dokdo) was not provided. However, the delegation judged that Matsushima became Korean territory, too, by placing more importance on the Tsushima domain's notion of "Matsushima lying close to Takeshima" than on the availability of records on the former. This indicates that the idea of Matsushima being an island ancillary to Takeshima was deeply rooted.

It is likely that the Grand Council of State had the same understanding, since the Ministry of Foreign Affairs reports were submitted to it. In the meantime, the Ministry of the Interior, overseeing Japan's territorial jurisdictions, embarked on the compilation of the national land registry and maps in order to lay the foundation for a modern nation state. In the midst of creating official Japanese geographical records, the Interior Ministry's Office of Geography probed into the sovereignty status of Takeshima and Matsushima and compiled in 1875 the *Isotakeshima Memorandum*, the document indicating in the wake of the Genroku Takeshima Incident that the two islands were outside Japan's jurisdiction.

Subsequently, placed under the control of the Division of Geography, which was supervised by the Grand Council of State's Japanese History Compilation Bureau, the Office of Geography compiled *Japanese Geography Summary*. At the time, Nakamura Genki, who undertook the compilation of the *Isotakeshima Memorandum*, also joined the project. Needless to say, the Interior Ministry's understanding concerning Takeshima and Matsushima was reflected in the making of official Japanese geographical records. The two islands, albeit recorded in Oki, vol. 50 of *Japanese Topography Summary*, were described separately from Oki and not regarded as part of the province. To be sure, they did not belong to any other part of Japan, either. Taken together, this indicates that they were viewed as being outside Japanese jurisdiction. In addition, Tanaka Akama, a Meiji-period geographer, shared the same understanding. This line of thinking was continued into the Grand Council of State's 1877 Directive, which declared that "Takeshima and the other island," that is, Ulleungdo and Dokdo, had nothing to do with Japan.

In the meantime, the Interior Ministry's Bureau of Geography made the "Complete Map of Greater Japan" in 1880, with Dokdo not marked. In 1883, the Geography Bureau expanded the 1880 map into a collection of maps also called the *Complete Map of Greater Japan*. It is made up of twelve maps illustrating the changes in each area's jurisdiction from 1871 to 1882. In none of these maps may Dokdo be found. Therefore, it can be said that the maps compiled by the Japanese government treated Dokdo as territory outside of Japan's administrative control at least during this period. Even at a later time, the Interior Ministry never considered Dokdo as Japanese territory, either. Not unexpectedly, it mounted a strong objection on the grounds that "Liancourt is suspected of being part of Korea," when the "Petition for Incorporation of Liancourt into Japanese Territory and Its Leasing" was submitted by the fisherman, Nakai Yozaburo, to the Interior, Foreign Affairs, and Agriculture & Commerce Ministries in 1904.

As indicated above, there were many occasions where the Edo shogunate and the Meiji government regarded Dokdo as Korean territory. Prior to 1905, it was never viewed as part of Japan. Therefore, the argument advanced by the Foreign Affairs Ministry that Dokdo belongs to Japan does not stand to reason.

References

Documents of the Sho Family (宗家文書). Preserved in the National Institute of Korean History. No date.

Hori, Kazuo (堀和生). "Japan's 1905 Incorporation of Takeshima Territory" (一九〇五年日本の竹島領土編入). *Journal of Korean History* (朝鮮史研究会論文集) 24 (1987).

Ikeuchi, Satoshi (池内敏). *What is the Takeshima Controversy?* (竹島問題とは何か). Nagoya: Nagoya University Press (名古屋大学出版会), 2012.

Inabashi (因幡志). [Historical record of Inaba Province]. No date.

Isotakeshima Memorandum: Complete (礒竹島覚書完). No date.

Japanese Geography Summary (*Nihon Chishi Teiyo* 日本地誌提要), vol. 50. Preserved in the National Archives of Japan. No date.

Japanese Geography Summary, vol. 1 (photoprint). Rinsen Shoten (臨川書店), 1982.

Kawakami, Kenzo (川上健三). *Historical and Geographical Study of Takeshima* (竹島の歴史地理学的研究). Tokyo: Kokonshoin (古今書院), 1966.

Ministry of Foreign Affairs of Japan. *Diplomatic Documents of Japan,* vol. 3 (日本外交文書, 第3巻). No date.

Ministry of Foreign Affairs of Japan. *10 Issues of Takeshima* (竹島問題を理解するための十のポイント). Northeast Asia Division, Asian and Oceanian Affairs Bureau, MOFA, February 2008.

Naito, Seichu and Park Byoung-sup (内藤正中・朴炳渉). *The Dokdo/Takeshima Controversy* (竹島＝独島論争). Shinkansha (新幹社), 2007.

Naito, Seichu (内藤正中). "Takeshima Controversy in 1905" (一九〇五年の竹島問題). *Studies of the Cultures in Northeast Asia* (北東アジア文化研究) 34 (2011).

Omino, Kiyoharu (小美濃清明). *Sakamoto Ryoma and the Exploration of Takeshima* (坂本龍馬と竹島開拓). Shinjinbutsu Ōraisha (新人物往来社), 2009.

Park, Byoung-sup. "The Meiji Government's Takeshima=Dokdo Perception" (明治政府の竹島＝独島認識). *Studies of the Cultures in Northeast Asia* (北東アジア文化研究) 28 (2008).

Park, Byoung-sup. "Analyzing the Commentaries of Shimojo Masao (2)" (Shimojo Masao [下條正男]-ui nonseol-eul bunseokhanda[2]). *Dokdo Research* 7 (2009).

Park, Byoung-sup. "Analyzing the Editorial of Shimojo Masao (2)" (下條正男の論説を分析する[2]). *Dokdo Research* 7 (2009).

Park, Byoung-sup. "The Problem of Dokdo's Territoriality in the Modern Era" (Geundaegi Dokdo-ui yeongyugwon munje). In *On Establishing the Territoriality of Dokdo* (Dokdo yeongyugwon hwangnip-eul wihan yeongu). Seoul: Seonin Publishing (Doseochulpan Seonin), 2013.

Park, Byoung-sup and Naito Seichu. *The Dokdo/Takeshima Controversy* (trans. Yuji Hosaka). Seoul: Bogosa, 2008.

Public Records: Joseon Incident, Meji years 1-4 (公文別録 朝鮮事件 明治元年~明治四年), vol. 1. No date.

Sato, Sakae (佐藤侊). "Historical Records of the Ministry of the Interior's Geography and Land Registry Offices" (内務省地理局地誌課の事蹟). *Journal of Ancient Maps* (古地図研究) 305 (1999).

Shimane-ken. *Photo Shimane Feature: Takeshima* (フォトしまね 特集竹島), vol. 161. Shimane-ken (島根縣), 2006.

Shimojo, Masao (下條正男). *"Takeshima": History and Territorial Issues* ("竹島"その歴史と領土問題). Shimane Prefectural Conference for Reclaiming Takeshima and the Northern Territories (竹島・北方領土返還要求運動島根県民会議), 2005.

Shimojo, Masao. "Regarding the Final Report Two Years after the Ordinance of 'Takeshima Day'" (最終報告にあたって '竹島の日'条例から二年). In *Final Report on the "Study of the Takeshima Dispute"* ("竹島問題に関する調査研究" 最終報告書). Takeshima Research Center (竹島問題研究会), 2007.

Shimojo, Masao. "To Those Manipulating the History of Japanese Territory 'Takeshima'" (日本の領土 「竹島」の歴史を改竄せし者たちよ). *Shokun* (諸君), 2007.

Shimojo, Masao. "Regarding the Territorial Criticism by the Foreign Affairs Division of the Silsagusi 32nd Hangyere Newspaper Electronic Edition" (実事求是 第32回 ハンギョレ新聞電子版の外務省の固有の領土論批判について). *Report on the 'Study of the Takeshima Dispute'* (竹島問題に関する調査研究報告書). Shimane-ken (島根県), 2013.

Sugihara, Takashi (杉原隆). "Regarding the 'Application to Pioneer Matsushima' by Shizoku Oya Kensuke and One Other of Asaimura" (浅井村士族大屋兼助他一名の '松島開拓願'について). *Kyodo Iwami* (郷土石見) 83 (2010).

Takeshima Official Documents (*Takeshima No Kakitsuke* 竹島之書付). No date.

Takeshima Records (*Takeshima Kiji* 竹島紀事). No date.

Takeuchi, Takeshi (竹内猛). "Regarding the Debate Surrounding the Interpretation of 'Takeshima and the Other Island'" (「竹島外一島」の解釈をめぐる問題について). *Kyodo Iwami* (郷土石見) 87 (2011).

Tsukamoto, Takashi (塚本孝). "Old Tottori Domain Documents and Pictures on Relating to

Takeshima" (竹島関係 旧鳥取藩文書及び絵図). *References* (レファレンス) 411. National Diet Library (国会図書館), 1985.

Tsukamoto, Takashi. "Protection and Amalgamation in Korea, and the Territorial Views of Japan and Korea" (韓国の保護・併合と日韓の領土認識). *Modern East Asian History* (東アジア近代史) 14 (2011).

Tsukamoto, Takashi. "History of the Takeshima Territorial Dispute, 3rd Edition" (竹島領有権問題の経緯[第3版]). In *Research and Information* (調査と情報) 701 (2011).

The World Knows the Truth

A Draft of the Peace Treaty with Japan by the British Ministry of Foreign Affairs, the Formation of the Attached Map (March 1951) and a Reconfirmation of Korea's Possession of Dokdo

Jung Byung-joon

Professor, Ewha Womans University

In September 1951, the Allied Forces led by the United States and Great Britain concluded the San Francisco Peace Treaty with Japan to end their hostile post-World War II relations. As a result, Japan regained its sovereignty and, at the same time, became separated from its previous colonies and occupied areas, and obtained its current territory. The peace treaty's territorial definitions, however, were very ambiguously worded. Afterwards, Japan came to have territorial disputes with Russia regarding the four northern islands, with China regarding the Diaoyu (Senkaku) islands, and with Korea regarding Dokdo.

The Dokdo dispute arose from the preparations preceding the San Francisco Peace Conference. Japan's claim is that the decision for Dokdo to become Japanese territory was made at that conference and, as a result, Dokdo was not included as Korean territory in the provisions of the peace treaty. The counterargument, of course, is that there was no provision declaring Dokdo as Japanese territory in the treaty either.

There has never been any indication that a map was used to deal with territorial matters during the San Francisco conference. The US government

Jung Byung-joon   A Draft of the Peace Treaty with Japan by the British Ministry of   **179**
Foreign Affairs, the Formation of the Attached Map (March 1951)
and a Reconfirmation of Korea's Possession of Dokdo

never published an official map leading up to the conference and no such map was included in the San Francisco Peace Treaty. If there had been a map included in the treaty, the many territorial disputes surrounding Japan would not have arisen.

There are already several well-known maps that verify Dokdo is Korean territory. For example, the map attached to SCAPIN (Supreme Command for the Allied Powers) Document No. 677 in 1946 and the map the United States used in 1950 while preparing for the San Francisco conference have been used to indirectly prove that Dokdo belongs to Korea. The US government prepared many drafts for the conference beginning in 1949 but an official map dealing with territorial matters was never drawn up. It is well known that in the lobby documents of William J. Sebald, who was MacArthur's political advisor in Japan, Dokdo is variously marked as belonging to both Korea and Japan, or is left unmarked.[1]

In February 2005, the author of this paper publicized a map relating to Dokdo which was produced by the British Ministry of Foreign Affairs in 1951. This map created quite a stir[2] because it clearly excluded Dokdo from Japan and marked it as Korean territory. This map was attached to the only official draft (April 7, 1951) prepared by the British Ministry of Foreign Affairs for the peace treaty with Japan.[3] The official British Draft was already

---

1   Byung-Joon Jung, "William J. Sebald-wa 'Dokdobunjaeng'-ui Sibal" (William Sebald and His Role in the Beginning of So-called Dokto [sic] Dispute), *Yeoksabipyeong* (Historical Criticism) 71, yeoreum-ho (Summer Edition) (2005): 140-170.

2   Reported by Yonhap News on February 27, 2005 and the next day by major news channels, including KBS, MBC, SBS, YTN and MBN, with headlines, "Discovery of British Ministry of Foreign Affairs Map Ruling Dokdo is Korean Territory," "Discovery by Prof. Jung Byung-Joon of British Ministry of Foreign Affairs Map Showing Dokdo as Korean Territory," "Japanese Government Lobbied to Make Ulleungdo Japanese Territory in 1947," and "US State Department Official in Charge of Geography Declared Dokdo Korean Territory in 1951."

3   For convenience, the draft of the peace treaty with Japan prepared by the British Ministry of Foreign Affairs will henceforth be abbreviated as the British Draft, and the map attached to that British Draft abbreviated as the British Map.

well known among Korean scholars, but the existence of the British Map was largely unknown and being publicized for the first time.

The purpose of this paper is to introduce and analyze the British Draft and its accompanying map as discovered by this author. Specifically, the paper will focus on explaining why the British Ministry of Foreign Affairs produced this map and what its significance is with regard to Dokdo's dominium. At the same time, the British Ministry's position concerning Korea's interests in the peace treaty with Japan will also be explained.

1. Details of the Discovery of the British Map

The British Map was first discovered while archival work was being carried out at the National Archives and Records Administration (NARA) in the United States in January 2005. It had been made at the Research Department of the British Ministry's Foreign Office, and it was first found in John Moore Allison's files, stored at the State Department.[4] Allison had been an assistant to John Foster Dulles, the State Department official heading the US delegation in the peace treaty negotiations with Japan. He had accompanied Dulles on visits to Japan, the Philippines and Australia, and he also represented the US while visiting England, with responsibility for working with British representatives in writing the joint US-UK draft. Allison's files show details of the various drafts and revisions of the peace treaty with Japan, and also how the changes were made. The British Map found in Allison's files is a scaled-down copy, source of origin not determined. The map's legend is smudged as well and could not be deciphered.[5] The title is "The Territory under Japanese Sov-

---

4   The Allison files are officially identified as RG 59, Records Relating to the Treaty of Peace with Japan 1947-1951 (John Moore Allison file), Lot File 56D527, 7 boxes.

5   "The Territory under Japanese Sovereignty as Defined in Art.1 of Peace Treaty," Research Dept. F. O., March, 1951, RG 59, Records Relating to the Treaty of Peace with Japan 1947-1951, Lot File 56D527, box 4, folder "Peace Treaty (Press-Speeches)."

Jung Byung-joon   A Draft of the Peace Treaty with Japan by the British Ministry of   **181**
Foreign Affairs, the Formation of the Attached Map (March 1951)
and a Reconfirmation of Korea's Possession of Dokdo

ereignty as Defined in Art. 1 of the Peace Treaty," the producer identified as "Research Dept. F. O.," and the date marked as "March 1951." It was conjectured that F. O. might stand for the British Foreign Office but the evidence was not conclusive.

Another map was then discovered, one in perfect condition, during an examination of Dulles's Japanese peace treaty files.[6] Because many people access these files, NARA officially allows the viewing only of microfilm copies and not the original documents, but the map was not included in the microfilm. The author was able to access the original map with the assistance of the archivist in charge of documents at the State Department. The condition of the map was satisfactory but, again, determining its origin was problematic. Other than the map, no documents to which it may have been originally attached were found. However, the result of careful examination of the box containing the relevant files and folders led the author to conclude that the map was attached to British documents classified on April 4, 1988. One reason for this conclusion was that, in the folder that contained the map, a withdrawal notice for Document FJ 1022/222 sent by the British Ministry of Foreign Affairs dated April 7, 1951, classified and kept separately, was also discovered. Another reason was that the notation "Research Dept. F. O." indicating the producer of the map was ascertained to refer not to a US government department but to the Research Department of the British Foreign Office. These findings thus indirectly confirmed that the map had been attached to British Ministry of Foreign Affairs Document FJ 1022/222, dated April 7, 1951.

The next step was to determine the contents of FJ 1022/222 and whether the map had actually been attached to the document. Fortunately, with the help of Jin-Hui Park, who had been dispatched to England in 2004 from the National Institute of Korean History, the author managed to obtain the col-

---

6   RG 59, General Records of the Department of State, Entry Japanese Peace Treaty1947-1952, Japanese Peace Treaty Files of John Foster Dulles, 1947-1952, Lot file 54D423, box 12, folder "Treaty Drafts, May 3, 1951."

lection of British government documents relating to the Japanese Peace Treaty. An examination of these documents showed that FJ 1022/222 was an official draft prepared by the British Ministry of Foreign Affairs in preparation for the Japanese Peace Treaty.[7] The title of the document is "Provisional Draft of Japanese Peace Treaty (United Kingdom)" and it is dated April 7, 1951. The document is kept at the National Archives in Britain and registered as FO 371/92538, FJ 1022/222. The map was attached to the document as Appendix I. In the original draft kept at the National Archives it is stated that a map representing Japanese territory is included as an appendix, but the appendix itself states that the map is not printed. The National Archives also did not have the actual map in its possession.

This rather complicated situation can be summarized as follows. Currently, the United Kingdom's Provisional Draft of the Japanese Peace Treaty dated April 7, 1951 is kept as a classified document at NARA, with only the map attached to the document accessible to the public. In contrast, the provisional draft may be freely accessed at the National Archives in Britain, but it does not include the map. In the end, the map in the United States had to be compared with the document in Britain before the two could be identified as belonging together.

The UK provisional draft was already well known in Korea. What was not known, due to the complicated situation outlined above, was the fact that the British government had officially produced a map and attached it to the document. The existence of this map was also not known in Korea. It was confirmed, however, that Tsukamoto Takashi (塚本孝) of Japan's National Diet Library, well known as an expert on the Dokdo issue, had seen this map. In "The Peace Treaty and Takeshima," he mentions in small print in the latter part of the paper that he referenced the map of the British provisional draft

---

7   "Provisional Draft of Japanese Peace Treaty (United Kingdom)," April 7, 1951, 15-50, National Archives, FO 371/92538, FJ 1022/222.

Jung Byung-joon   A Draft of the Peace Treaty with Japan by the British Ministry of   **183**
Foreign Affairs, the Formation of the Attached Map (March 1951)
and a Reconfirmation of Korea's Possession of Dokdo

from Dulles' files.[8] However, he did not publicize this map, which is disadvantageous to Japan's interests. His paper was already known in Korea, but the relationship between the provisional draft and the map and the details of its contents remained completely unknown.

2. Preparation of the British Provisional Draft

Working in conjunction with the United States, Britain wanted to quickly conclude the Japanese Peace Treaty. The United States began to formulate the Japanese Peace Treaty in early 1947 and completed its first provisional draft in March.[9] Britain also began to work on the Peace Treaty starting in 1947.

The Commonwealth nations of Britain, Australia and New Zealand discussed the Peace Treaty through three rounds of conferences: the Canberra Prime Ministers' Conference in August 1947; the Colombia Foreign Ministers' Conference in January 1950; and the London Prime Ministers' Conference in January 1951. Also, in May 1950, a "Commonwealth Working Party of Officials on the Japanese Peace Treaty" was held in London, where all issues concerning the treaty were studied.[10]

Once Dulles became the President's special envoy in charge of the peace treaty with Japan in May 1950, movement to conclude the peace treaty accelerated. The Commonwealth nations continued to advance the dialogue at the working level after September 1950. Dulles visited Tokyo three times

---

8   Tsukamoto Takashi (塚本孝), 1994 「The Peace Treaty and Takeshima (Review)」 National Assembly Library, Research and Legislative Reference Bureau (The Reference, March 1994, no. 518), 55, footnote 38.

9   See William Sebald's memoir, "Chapter 11: The Peace Treaty," in *With MacArthur in Japan: A Personal History of the Occupation* (New York: W. W. Norton, 1965), 242-268; Ronald L. McGlothlen, *Controlling the Waves: Dean Acheson and U.S. Foreign Policy in Asia* (New York, London: W. W. Norton, 1993), 40-47.

10   "Parliamentary Question," February 19, 1951, National Archives, FO 371/92532, FJ 1022/91.

within a year, in June 1950 and in February and April 1951, with his February visit proving especially influential in putting the peace treaty on a specific schedule. On February 9, 1951, based on the understanding reached between Dulles and Japanese Prime Minister Yoshida Shigeru (吉田茂), John Allison and Iguchi Sadao (井口貞夫), Vice-Minister of Foreign Affairs, signed a joint statement on the five annexed drafts dealing with the peace settlement.[11] At this stage, it was confirmed regarding territorial matters that Japan would renounce all right, title and claim to Korea, Taiwan and the Pescadores, and that it would accept the trusteeship of the United Nations, with the United States acting as the administering authority, concerning the Ryukyu Islands south of 29 degrees north latitude, Rosario Island, the Volcano Islands (硫黄島), Parece Vela (沖ノ鳥島), Marcus Island (南鳥島) and the Bonin Islands (小笠原諸島).[12] They also agreed that Japan was to have a general waiver of war claims, with certain exceptions.[13]

Dulles left Tokyo for Australia on February 15 for a three-party meeting with the representatives of Australia and New Zealand. Afterwards, the British government began to compose its own draft of the peace treaty with Japan. The British Ministry of Foreign Affairs notified Washington (telegram No. 753) on February 24 that, if possible, it would present a first draft to the United States by mid-March. Later, Director C. H. Johnston of the Japan & Pacific Department began to compose a draft together with the Ministry's legal advisors.[14] As is well known, a total of three drafts were composed.

---

11   "John Foster Dulles to Dean Acheson (Tokyo),"February 10, 1951, NARA, RG 59, State Department Decimal File, 694.001/2-1051.

12   Provisional Memorandum, February 8, 1951, 694.001/2-1051.

13   Annex I: Elaboration of Exception to General Waiver of War Claims, 694.001/2-1051.

14   "Letter from C. H. Johnston to A. E. Percival," March 1, 1951, National Archives, FO 371/92532, FJ 1022/97.

Jung Byung-joon   A Draft of the Peace Treaty with Japan by the British Ministry of   **185**
Foreign Affairs, the Formation of the Attached Map (March 1951)
and a Reconfirmation of Korea's Possession of Dokdo

Table 1. A Comparison of the Three British Drafts[15]

	Official Name	Date	Contents	Characteristics	Notes
First Draft	Japanese Peace Treaty	Feb. 28, 1951	89 articles, 22 pages	Internal draft of the Japan & Pacific Department	A very rough preliminary draft
Second Draft	2nd Draft of Japanese Peace Treaty	March 1951	48 pages	Reflecting the opinions of relevant Ministry of Foreign Affairs departments	Examined by 18 people from 7 government departments
Third Draft	Provisional Draft of Japanese Peace Treaty (United Kingdom)	April 7, 1951	9 Parts, 40 clauses, 20 pages	Official draft by the British government given to the United States	Examined by 18 Foreign Affairs Office departments and 13 government ministries

The first draft had been composed by February 28, 1951. Johnston, who was in charge of the drafting, stated that it was "a very rough preliminary draft" in his letter to A. E. Percival at the Board of Trade on March 1, 1951.[16] The draft was submitted exactly as typed. The official title was "Japanese Peace Treaty" and it was made up of 89 articles over 22 pages.[17] The most important motivation for preparing the draft was that one had been promised to the United States, but it was also intended to clarify the stance of the British government. The primary focus was on commerce and economics, with the draft being mainly distributed to departments dealing with economic matters. This draft from the Japan & Pacific Department was to be reviewed and its

15   First draft: "Japanese Peace Treaty," February 28, 1951,102-123, FO 371/92532, FJ 1022/97; second draft: "Japanese Peace Treaty: Second revised draft of the Japanese Peace Treaty," March 1951, 70-117, FO 371/92535, FJ 1022/171; third draft: "Provisional Draft of Japanese Peace Treaty (United Kingdom)," April 7, 1951, 15-50, FO 371/92538, FJ 1022/222.

16   "Japanese Peace Treaty," March 1, 1951, FO 371/92532, FJ 1022/97, C. H. Johnston to A. E. Percival, Esq., Board of Trade.

17   "Japanese Peace Treaty,"102-123, FO 371/92532, FJ 1022/97.

economic contents were to be agreed upon by March 7 or 8.[18] Other contents of the draft were to be reviewed by two separate groups within the Ministry of Foreign Affairs, likely on March 9. Thus this draft was indeed a very preliminary document the Japan & Pacific Department composed with legal advisors for the purpose of internal review by Foreign Affairs and other related government ministries.

On March 16, with G. G. Fitzmaurice acting as chairman, 18 people gathered from seven ministries—four from Foreign Affairs, two from Treasury, one from Commonwealth Relations, three from the Colonial Office, six from Commerce, one from Communications and one from Miscellaneous—to discuss the Japanese peace treaty. At this meeting it was decided that Foreign Affairs would set the exact stipulations to be applied in the Japanese peace treaty for the Allied Powers and prepare the necessary details using the peace treaty with Italy as a model.[19] The second draft was composed as a result. It was 48 pages, including an 8-page appendix, and was titled "2nd Draft of Japanese Peace Treaty."[20] While it was still being prepared, a conference between US representative Allison and Britain's Robert H. Scott, Assistant Under-Secretary of Foreign Affairs, took place on March 21. The main topic was China's involvement, with Korea being discussed as well.[21]

The British government's final official draft was completed on April 7, 1951. It was 20 pages, composed of 9 parts, 40 articles, 5 appendices, and

---

18 The first draft was distributed to the Colonial Office, the Department of Defense, the Chief of Staff, the Ministry of Civil Aviation, the Army and the Navy, the Ministry of War, the Ministry of Transport, and the Ministry of Home Affairs.

19 "Japanese Peace Treaty: Record of Meeting held at the Foreign Office on the 16th March 1951," 53-60, FO 371/92535, FJ 1022/167.

20 "Japanese Peace Treaty: Second revised draft of the Japanese Peace Treaty," March 1951, 70-117, FO 371/92535, FJ 1022/171.

21 Won-deok Yi, *Hanil Gwageosa Cheori-ui Wonjeom* (A Starting Point for Dealing with Korea and Japan's Past Affairs) (Seoul: Seowuldaehakgyo Chulpanbu, 1996), 30-31.

Jung Byung-joon   A Draft of the Peace Treaty with Japan by the British Ministry of   **187**
Foreign Affairs, the Formation of the Attached Map (March 1951)
and a Reconfirmation of Korea's Possession of Dokdo

titled "Provisional Draft of Japanese Peace Treaty (United Kingdom)."[22] According to the report Johnston sent to Sir R. Makins, Permanent Under-Secretary, on April 5, this draft had been presented to legal counsel and had gone through all related departments at the working level within Foreign Affairs, and also 13 other government ministries. Johnston stated that, once Foreign Affairs approved the draft, he would send it to the US government on April 7.[23] Assistant Under-Secretary R. H. Scott, who had worked on the draft with Johnston, also expressed his satisfaction with the draft and stated that it was based on decisions made by the cabinet and had the approval of 18 departments within the Ministry of Foreign Affairs, and that it was the product of difficult negotiations and adjustments.[24]

The British government's drafting process for the peace treaty thus began with the Japan & Pacific Department of Foreign Affairs (first draft on February 28, 1951) and the final draft, after having been approved by 18 Foreign Affairs departments and 13 other government ministries, was sent to the US State Department on April 7, 1951. According to British Foreign Minister Morrison, this was a provisional draft prepared at the working levels and subject to change. Nevertheless, it was officially sent to the Commonwealth nations of Canada, Australia, New Zealand, South Africa, India, Pakistan, and Ceylon.[25] The British government judged its draft to be longer than the

---

22   "Provisional Draft of Japanese Peace Treaty (United Kingdom)," April 7, 1951, 15-50, FO 371/92538, FJ 1022/222. The third British draft was edited in a way that it could be compared to the American draft page by page. As a result, the 14 pages of the American draft (March 17, 1951) were included in the British draft. Including the 14 pages of the American draft and the 2 pages of explanatory memorandum at the beginning, 1 page for a table of contents, and 2 pages of distribution lines at the end, this draft totals 39 pages.

23   "C. H. Johnston to Sir R. Makins (Permanent Under Secretary)," April 5, 1951, 4-5, FO 371/92538, FJ 1022/222.

24   "Memorandum by R. H. Scott," April 5, 1951, FO 371/92538, FJ 1022/222.

25   Although Morrison stated that the draft was a provisional, working-level document and not the agreed, expressed opinion of the Commonwealth of Nations, it was, practically, the product of the continually coordinated opinions of member nations. "Mr. Morrison to Sir O. Franks

American draft for the reason that the British version was based on the Italian Peace Treaty.

Around the same period, on March 17, 1951, the United States also completed its provisional draft of the Japanese treaty. This first official draft, which was "suggestive only" for the purpose of consulting with other nations, was sent to the British government through the British Embassy on March 23. However, the British Ministry of Foreign Affairs did not take this American draft into consideration in composing its final draft.[26]

3. Contents in the British Draft Relating to Korea

3.1. First Draft (February 28, 1951) (Appendix 1)

According to the files at the British Ministry of Foreign Affairs, there was a preliminary document which was used to draft the first version of the peace treaty. Johnston revised this preliminary document to produce his first draft. The preliminary draft and the first draft of the peace treaty did not greatly differ. The draft he made was, as Johnston himself said, a very rough preliminary draft. One common characteristic of the British drafts was that they clearly stipulated Japan's war responsibilities.

In the preamble of the first draft, the parties to the contract are introduced as the Allied and Associated Powers of the one part and Japan of the other. According to the proceedings of the joint meeting between the United States and the United Kingdom in May 1951, the Allied Powers referred to the major powers that could participate in the drafting of the Japanese Peace

---

(Washington)," no. 401, April 7, 1951, FO371/92538, FJ 1022/222.

26   "Memorandum by the United States Government (Communicated by the State Department to His Majesty's Embassy in Washington on 23rd March, 1951," FO 371/92538, FJ 1022/222; "Mr. Morrison to Sir O. Franks (Washington)," (no. 401, Secret), Foreign Office, April 7, 1951, FJ 1022/222.

Jung Byung-joon   A Draft of the Peace Treaty with Japan by the British Ministry of   **189**
Foreign Affairs, the Formation of the Attached Map (March 1951)
and a Reconfirmation of Korea's Possession of Dokdo

Treaty, namely the United States and Britain, and the Associated Powers referred to other countries that fought against Japan.[27] The draft begins as follows:

1. The United Kingdom of Great Britain and Northern Ireland, the United States of America, Australia, Canada, the Netherlands, New Zealand, and …, hereinafter referred to as "the Allied and Associated Powers," of the one part, and Japan, of the other;

2. Whereas Japan under the militarist regime became a party to the Tripartite Pact with Germany and Italy, undertook a war of aggression and thereby provoked a state of war with all the Allied and Associated Powers and with other United Nations, and bears her share of responsibility for the war.

Because the first draft was "very rough," it contained many errors and loopholes. It stated the following concerning Japanese territories:

Territories

6. Japanese sovereignty shall continue over all the islands and adjacent islets and rocks lying within an area bounded by a line …. the line should include Hokkaido, Honshu, Shikoku, Kyushu, the Suisho, Yuri, Akijiri, Shibotsu, Oki and Taraku islands, the Habomai islands, Kuchinoshima, Utsuryo (Ulling) island, Miancourt rocks (Take island) Quelpart (Shichi or Chejudo) island and Shikotan. The line

---

27 Britain distinguished between "main parties" who could participate in the drafting of the peace treaty and "lesser belligerents" who could only make comments, which seems to be the distinction between the Allied Powers and the Associated Powers. The reference to Associated Powers was eliminated in the seventh joint US-UK meeting on May 1, 1951. See "Anglo-American meetings on Japanese Peace Treaty, Summary Record of Seventh meeting," May 3, 1951, British Embassy, Washington to C. P. Scott, O. B. E., Japan and Pacific Department, Foreign Office no. 1076/357/5IG, FO 371/92547, FJ 1022/376.

above described is plotted on the map attached to the present Treaty (Annex 1). In the case of a discrepancy between the map and the textual description of the line, the latter shall prevail.

Regarding its stipulations of Japanese territory, the first draft had the following characteristics. First, it identified the northern boundary beyond the four main islands of Honshu, Hokkaido, Shikoku, and Kyushu as Habomai (齒舞) and Shikotan (色丹) islands north of Hokkaido; the southern boundary as Kuchinoshima (口之島) adjacent to the Ryukyu Islands; the western boundary toward Korea as Oki (殷岐), Dokdo, Ulleungdo, and Jejudo.

Second, by naming the islands to be included in stipulating Japanese territory, it chose a method of naturally excluding areas not mentioned. This was in character with the way the treaty aimed to restore the territories taken through acts of aggression as stated in the Potsdam Declaration, as well as to punish Japan by clearly stating its war crimes and requiring accountability for those acts. If the Allied nations forced these provisions on Japan, it had no choice but to accept them. In other words, the articles concerning territories were one-sided and disadvantageous to Japan.

Third, the first draft was a rough and error-ridden document containing a serious error concerning Japan's western boundary. It stated that Dokdo was Japanese territory, and further included Ulleungdo and Jejudo as part of Japan. This was a clear mistake. Not only are Dokdo, Ulleungdo and Jejudo all historically Korean territory, but SCAPIN 677 (January 29, 1946) had also confirmed these areas as belonging to Korea. From these errors, it can be seen that the draft was poorly informed. It also misspelled many place names. For example, it misspelled Dokdo, which was internationally identified as Liancourt, as Miancourt, and Akiyuri (秋勇留) as Akijiri.

Lastly, the first draft was composed without a clear idea of island affiliation. Suisho (小晶), Yuri (勇留), Akijiri [sic] (秋勇留), Shibotsu (志癸), and Taraku (多樂島) islands are all part of the Habomai (齒舞) islands, but they were listed serially, thus misrepresenting their locations and relation-

Jung Byung-joon   A Draft of the Peace Treaty with Japan by the British Ministry of   **191**
Foreign Affairs, the Formation of the Attached Map (March 1951)
and a Reconfirmation of Korea's Possession of Dokdo

ships. Also, Kuchinoshima (口之島) is an island above the Ryukyu Islands and located south of 30° North Latitude, and Oki (殷岐) is the westernmost island from Shimane, both listed as Japanese territory in SCAPIN 677, while the same memorandum excluded Dokdo, Ulleungdo and Jejudo. In the first draft, however, all these islands were mixed together and listed as Japanese territory, and the order of their listing and their affiliations are also problematic. A map was referenced as well "(Annex 1)" but no map had been produced. An actual map had been made only by the time of the second draft.

Meanwhile, the first draft states the following regarding Korea's independence:

> 7. Japan hereby renounces any claim to sovereignty over, and all right, title and interest in, Korea, and undertakes to recognise and respect all such arrangements as may be made by or under the auspices of the United Nations regarding the sovereignty and independence of Korea.

What is notable here is the emphasis placed on the role of the United Nations. This was likely because the Korean War was still raging at the time, with the status and fate of Korea unknown, and the drafter was mindful of the possibility that the Korean Peninsula might be unified by the UN.

3.2. Second Draft (March 1951) (Appendix 2)

As discussed above, the British Ministry of Foreign Affairs composed its second draft of the peace treaty through consultations among its internal departments and other relevant government ministries. The preamble of the second draft remained unchanged, as did the article concerning Korea's independence and its relationship with Japan. The most significant changes occurred in the section dealing with territorial matters.

(6) Japanese sovereignty shall continue over all the islands and adjacent islets and rocks lying within an area bounded by a line from Latitude 30° N in a North-Easterly direction to approximately Latitude 33° N 128° E, then northward between the islands of Quelpart, Fukue-Shima bearing North-Easterly between Korea and the island of Tsushima, continuing in this direction with the islands of Oki-Retto to the South-East and Take Shima to the North-West curving with the coast of Honshu, then Northerly skirting Rebun-Shima passing Easterly through Soya Kaikyo approximately 145°40' N, ... The line above described is plotted on the map attached to the present Treaty (Annex I). In the case of a discrepancy between the map and the textual description of the line, the latter shall prevail. (p. 72)

Unlike in the first draft, the description in the second draft regarding Japanese territory was more clearly stated. In contrast to the ambiguities present in the former, the latter more concretely stipulated Japanese territory and areas that were to be excluded.

The characteristics of the second draft are as follows. First, the boundary line surrounding Japanese territory was clearly drawn using longitudes and latitudes and specific geographical names. Second, the errors of the first draft were corrected and Jejudo, Ulleungdo and Dokdo were clearly marked as excluded from Japanese territory. Third, Japanese territory as defined in the second draft remained unchanged in the third and final draft. Fourth, territory was marked using a boundary line. Such a method had already been used in SCAPIN 1033 (June 22, 1946), titled "Area Authorized for Japanese Fishing and Whaling," in which a so-called "MacArthur Line" was drawn. In this regard, it is highly possible that in terms of representing the overall contours and contents of the boundary line, the second draft actually utilized the MacArthur Line. Lastly, an accompanying map clearly showing the territorial stipulations was officially produced. Although some misrepresented geographical information in the text of the second draft was corrected in the

Jung Byung-joon   A Draft of the Peace Treaty with Japan by the British Ministry of   **193**
Foreign Affairs, the Formation of the Attached Map (March 1951)
and a Reconfirmation of Korea's Possession of Dokdo

third draft, the same map was used without alteration.

3.3. Third Draft (April 7, 1951) (Appendix 3)

When the British government's third and final official draft was compared with the second draft, some differences were observed. First of all, the preamble was significantly revised. In the second draft, only seven nations were mentioned as members of the Allied and Associated Powers, with other nations left undetermined, but this was changed to 16 specific nations. Because Britain had already recognized Communist China, it included China as a member of the Allied Powers, in contrast to the United States, whereas it excluded Korea.[28] The section on Korea and its relationship to Japan was left unchanged.

The territorial clauses were not significantly altered from those of the second draft. Other than a few minor revisions, the content of the second draft remained unchanged. The parts regarding Korea are as follows:

Article 1
Japanese sovereignty shall continue over all the islands and adjacent islets and rocks lying within an area bounded by a line from latitude 30° N. in a *north-westerly direction* to approximately latitude 33° N. 128° E. then northward between the islands of Quelpart, Fukue-Shima bearing north-easterly between Korea and the island of Tsushima, continuing in this direction with the islands of Oki-Retto to the south-east and Take-Shima to the north-west curving with the coast of Honshu, then northerly skirting Rebun-Shima passing easterly through Soya Kaikyo approximately *142° E.* ... The line above described is plotted on the map attached to

---

28   The names of the Allied and Associated Powers were as follows: the Union of Soviet Socialist Republic, the United Kingdom of Great Britain, Northern Ireland, the United States of America, China, France, Australia, Burma, Canada, Ceylon, India, Indonesia, the Netherlands, New Zealand, Pakistan, and the Republic of the Philippines.

the present Treaty (Annex I). In the case of a discrepancy between the map and the textual description of the line, the latter shall prevail. [italics added]

Here, the changes from the second draft include "North-Easterly direction" being revised to "north-westerly direction" and "145°40' N" being revised to "142° E." As can be seen by examining the map, these were corrections of mistakes made in the second draft.

In the third draft it was stated that a map was included as "Annex I." Currently at Britain's National Archives, the third draft exists in two forms: a typewritten manuscript and a print copy of its published form. In the print copy there is an explanation stating that the Annex I map was not published with the printed document. In the typewritten manuscript it is stated that there is an accompanying map, but no such map is kept at the National Archives. Currently, the only existing map that has been confirmed to be the Annex I map of the third draft is the one discovered at NARA in the United States.[29]

4. UK Map and Confirmation of Korea's Possession of Dokdo

The map attached to the third draft is 72 cm in width, 68.5 cm in length, and titled "The Territory under Japanese Sovereignty as Defined in Art. 1 of the Peace Treaty." The producer is the "Research Department" of the British Ministry of Foreign Affairs, and the date of production is "March, 1951" (Appendix 4). The date of production shows that the map was prepared at the time of the second draft in March. Furthermore, when we consider which parts of the

---

29   The printed copy is "Provisional Draft of Japanese Peace Treaty (United Kingdom)," April 7, 1951, 15-50, FO 371/92538, FJ1022/222; the typewritten manuscript is "Provisional Draft of the Japanese Peace Treaty and list of contents" (undated), 90-140, FO 371/92538, FJ 1022/224.

Jung Byung-joon   A Draft of the Peace Treaty with Japan by the British Ministry of   **195**
Foreign Affairs, the Formation of the Attached Map (March 1951)
and a Reconfirmation of Korea's Possession of Dokdo

second draft were revised in the third draft, it is likely that the map was used first to determine the boundaries of Japanese territory and then, based on the map, the documentation work proceeded.

The overall characteristics of the map and its contents regarding Dokdo can be summarized as follows. First, it defines Japanese territory as centering round its four main islands. This is common to all versions of the British drafts and can be viewed as adhering to the way Japanese territory was defined in the Potsdam Declaration.

Second, Japanese territory is stipulated precisely so as to prevent any controversy, with boundaries clearly represented by a solid line surrounding Japan. While in the first draft a strict method of naming islands belonging to Japan was used in order to naturally exclude islands that were not named, the second and third drafts used the more flexible method of drawing a boundary line. However, this method was still more disadvantageous to Japan than the method ultimately used in the San Francisco Peace Treaty, which entailed specifically naming the islands that were to be excluded from Japan.

Third, Britain likely chose to define Japanese territory using a boundary line for three reasons. The main reason had to be the stipulations in the Potsdam Declaration, Article 8 of which defined Japanese territory as follows: "The terms of the Cairo Declaration shall be carried out and Japanese sovereignty shall be limited to the islands of Honshu, Hokkaido, Kyushu, Shikoku and such minor islands as we determine." Based on this, Britain likely identified the "minor islands" as those around the four main islands. The second reason is that, by drawing a boundary line, Britain likely aimed to forestall any territorial disputes that might arise. In other words, this method had the advantage of overcoming any textual ambiguities and inaccuracies and removing any grounds for conflict with neighboring countries by showing a clear boundary. In fact, if a map such as the one attached to the British draft clearly showing the Japanese territorial boundary had been included in the San Francisco Peace Treaty, the so-called "territorial disputes" that Japan is currently engaged in with its neighbors could have been avoided. The final reason for the use of a boundary line was to indict Japan and call it to account for its war crimes and aggression. In other words, Britain can be seen as putting forth as a precondition for the "peace" treaty being led by the United States the identification and restoration of what Japan had taken through its territorial aggression.

Fourth, and most important for Korea, Dokdo is excluded from Japan and clearly shown as Korean territory. The boundary line also shows that, among the four northern islands Japan is currently disputing with Russia, Shikotan and Habomai are stipulated as Japanese territory while Ryukyu, which was under a trusteeship administered by the United States, is excluded from Japanese territory.

In interpreting the Potsdam Declaration, Britain and Japan had directly opposite positions. Britain wanted the contents of the Declaration to be strictly applied, while Japan focused on trying to stop the Declaration from being interpreted too broadly against its territorial interests. As Yoshida Shigeru recorded in his memoir, the Japanese government had gathered an enormous amount of material, seven volumes of documents altogether,[30] in preparation for the territorial discussions at the peace treaty. The core areas that Japan insisted it possessed were Okinawa (沖縄), Hokkaido (北海島), Kuril (千島), Habomai (歯舞) and Ogasawara (小笠原諸島). Of these, Okinawa, Kuril and Ogasawara were excluded in the British draft.

The map attached to the British draft is significant with respect to the Dokdo issue for several reasons, which can be summarized as follows. First, it was the only official map produced by the British government during prepara-

---

30 Dr. Seon-Ju Bang, who recently visited the National Archives in Britain to conduct a detailed examination of this matter, stated that he combed several times through all the files related to the San Francisco conference but did not find the map. As Dr. Bang is one of the top experts in this area, the results of his research indicate that, at this point, the National Archives does not have this map in its possession. Meanwhile, it has been confirmed that Japan collected microfilm copies of all records related to the San Francisco conference. Dr. Bang has sent relevant records to the National Institute of Korean History.

Jung Byung-joon   A Draft of the Peace Treaty with Japan by the British Ministry of   **197**
Foreign Affairs, the Formation of the Attached Map (March 1951)
and a Reconfirmation of Korea's Possession of Dokdo

tions for the San Francisco conference. It was also the only map produced by the Allied Powers that deals with Japanese territorial matters. The US State Department, which played the most central role, did use a map during the process of preparing for the conference but never produced an official map, and there was no map attached to the San Francisco Peace Treaty itself. Accordingly, the British map uniquely reflects the opinion of the Allied Powers.

Second, because the map reflects Britain's opinion regarding territorial matters rather than that of the United States, which Japan had been lobbying, it more objectively reflects the third-party perspective of the Allied Powers. During this period, while Japan meticulously prepared and methodically lobbied the United States in order to acquire territorial rights to Dokdo, the Korean government was embroiled in a war and its national priorities lay in the nation's survival. Its lack of diplomatic capacity, structure and experience also contributed to its diplomatic incompetence and ignorance. The Korean government had no cognizance of Japan's lobbying over Dokdo, while Japan was using all its strategic resources to persuade the United States. As a result, the United States came to hold an inaccurate view shaped by Japanese bias.[31] However, because the British government was relatively free of the influence of Japan's lobbying and doctored documents produced at the state level, the map that Britain produced shows the more rational and impartial perspective of the Allied Powers at the time.

Third, the map unambiguously marks Dokdo as excluded from Japanese territory and belonging, together with Ulleungdo, to Korea. This representation is especially significant due to the fact that this is not an antique map from the pre-modern West, or a military or administrative map produced by SCAP during the 1945 to 1950 period, or a map drawn up by the US State

---

31   Yoshida Shigeru (吉田茂), Ten Years in Retrospect Volumes 1-4 Tokyo: Shinchosha, 1959. See *Dokdo Museum Report* (December 20, 2001) by Jong-Hak Yi (former Director of the Dokdo Museum), accessed April 16, 2005, http://www.tokdo.co.kr. By examining and analyzing the *Japanese National Assembly Stenographic Records*, Yi made it possible for others to investigate Japan's lobbying activities in the United States.

Department or military authorities or some other governmental department, but rather reflects the officially confirmed opinion of the British government during the period between March and April 1951, just before the San Francisco Peace Treaty was signed. In other words, in terms of who produced it, it is the only map attached to an officially confirmed draft of the peace treaty presented by the British government, and in terms of when it was produced it has close proximity to the San Francisco conference. The map thus serves as the clearest piece of evidence reconfirming Korea's possession of Dokdo since SCAPIN 677.

Fourth, an even more important fact to take note of is that Britain mistakenly identified Dokdo, Ulleungdo, and even Jejudo as Japanese territory in the first draft, then corrected these mistakes and excluded these islands from the second draft onwards. This indicates that the British government did not identify Dokdo as Korean territory accidentally or out of carelessness, but made a deliberate decision to change a previous representation that it knew to be wrong. Accordingly, the argument does not hold water that because the map was following SCAPIN 677, its exclusion of Dokdo was a simple oversight.[32] The final draft by the British government was composed with the assistance of legal and economic advisors, and was then approved by the 18 internal departments of the Ministry of Foreign Affairs and 13 other government ministries. Because of this, the draft can be said to be based on all the information and data at the British government's disposal. It can be concluded from this that the reconfirmation of Dokdo as part of Korea was based on the British government's independent preparatory work and information analysis.

Fifth, although the British map was not included in the final Peace Treaty's official territorial presentation, it clearly has the significance of reconfirming Korea's ownership of Dokdo. Because the Dokdo issue was not mentioned in the Treaty of San Francisco, Japan has argued that such an absence of any statement excluding Dokdo from Japanese territory is proof that it is Japa-

---

32   Jung, "William J. Sebald-wa 'Dokdobunjaeng'-ui Sibal," 153-164.

Jung Byung-joon   A Draft of the Peace Treaty with Japan by the British Ministry of   **199**
Foreign Affairs, the Formation of the Attached Map (March 1951)
and a Reconfirmation of Korea's Possession of Dokdo

nese. The British draft, however, demonstrates through its production and the changes made to the earlier drafts that Japan's argument lacks merit. Britain's first draft followed the method of actually stating the territories to be included within Japanese territory centering on its four main islands, its second and third drafts drew a boundary line around the four main islands to mark Japanese territory, while the final peace treaty listed the areas to be excluded from Japan. From this it can be seen that the modifications were generally favorable to Japan. Since the territorial stipulations being proposed in the official peace treaty were the most advantageous yet to Japan, it strongly opposed the territorial boundary method proposed by Britain. Before Japan could engage in any lobbying, however, the British government corrected its initial mistake of identifying Dokdo as Japanese, thus making it clear that Dokdo was Korean and to be excluded from Japan. Therefore, while Japan did succeed in negotiating with the United States to adopt in the peace treaty the method of explicitly stating the territories to be excluded from Japan, thus giving itself the pretext for disputing the territorial ownership of Dokdo, it failed to reverse the British government's stance of affirming Dokdo as part of Korea.[33]

5. US-UK Meetings and Discussions Relating to Korea

The issues that most concerned Britain between March and April of 1951 were: 1) Russia and China's nonparticipation in the conference; 2) Japan's participation; and 3) Japan's renunciation of its claim on Taiwan.[34] During this

---

33   Tsukamoto Takashi (塚本孝), 1994. "The Peace Treaty and Takeshima (Review)" National Assembly Library, Research and Legislative Reference Bureau The Reference, March 1994, no. 518, 46.

34   Further research is needed to fully examine the reasons for why Dokdo was not listed in the territories to be excluded from Japan in the Treaty of San Francisco. To summarize the discussions that have taken place so far, firstly, because Dokdo is an uninhabited, rocky island, it was viewed differently from inhabited islands such as Jejudo, Geomundo and Ulleungdo that were being

period, Britain and the United States had different positions regarding Korea. Their two main discussion points were: 1) Korea's status as a signatory of the peace treaty with Japan and participant in the negotiations; and 2) territorial rights to Dokdo. Regarding Korea's participation, the United States agreed with the idea, while Britain opposed it. Regarding Dokdo's territorial rights, while they did not have a detailed discussion on the matter, Britain recognized Korea's ownership of the island, while the United States declined to commit itself to any position.

The United States' provisional draft of the Japanese treaty produced on March 17, 1951 was the US government's first official draft, "suggestive only" for the purpose of negotiating with the other participating nations. This initial draft reflected a fair number of the opinions of many governments, including those of Korea.[35] At a meeting of 14 major Allied Powers and Korean representatives in Washington, Dulles presented copies of this draft and requested quick responses from the participating governments.[36] This was the first official document that was conveyed to the Korean government regarding the Japanese peace treaty. Korea received this draft because it was recognized as a participating signatory nation of the treaty.

---

discussed in the treaty. In other words, there were numerous rock masses like Dokdo but were generally not mentioned for the sake of simplifying the peace treaty and making it more succinct. Secondly, for the same reason of brevity, Dokdo was treated not as an independent island but as a satellite island of Ulleungdo. In the same manner, when Jejudo was being discussed, Marado, located at the southern end of Jejudo, was not mentioned, just as all the numerous islands around Ulleungdo were also not mentioned. The many islands near Taiwan could be seen as not being mentioned in the peace treaty for the same reason.

35 "Comments on the Japanese angle of the problem of Chinese & Russian non participation & the question of Japanese participation of Japanese Peace Treaty," March 22, 1951, FO 371/92535, FJ 1022/174.

36 "Memorandum"; "Provisional Draft of a Japanese Peace Treaty (Suggestive Only); Revised on March 17, 1951," NARA, RG 59, Decimal File FW694.001/3-1751.

Jung Byung-joon   A Draft of the Peace Treaty with Japan by the British Ministry of   **201**
Foreign Affairs, the Formation of the Attached Map (March 1951)
and a Reconfirmation of Korea's Possession of Dokdo

When the official British draft (April 7, 1951) was conveyed to the US government, Dulles was visiting Tokyo again (April 7-23, 1951). It was his third visit. According to Sebald, "Dulles' last day in Japan, April 23, 1951, was devoted to an intensive review of a British draft treaty" that they had just received.[37] Dulles and his team conferred for several hours with Prime Minister Yoshida, Vice Foreign Minister Iguchi Sadao (井口貞夫), and Nishimura Kumao (西村熊雄), the head of the Japanese Treaty Bureau of the Foreign Ministry. When they were shown the British draft, the Japanese expressed a preference for the American draft, even though the British version was more technically accurate and comprehensive.[38] It can be guessed that the Japanese strenuously opposed having their territory clearly marked with a boundary line on the map produced by the British Ministry of Foreign Affairs, with Dokdo excluded, and that they succeeded in persuading the US representatives to agree.

One of the most significant characteristics of the preparations for and the signing process of the Japanese peace treaty was that Japan, although considered a war criminal nation before its defeat, was recognized as a signatory partner at the conference. After World War I, Germany only had the right to sign the treaty presented by the Allied Powers and could not take part in negotiations or revise any part of the treaty. It had to either accept the "dictated peace" or face another war. In leading up to the Japanese peace treaty, however, the United States presented multiple drafts of the treaty to Japan and listened respectfully to the opinions of the Japanese government and leading politicians and political parties. It also tried to reflect Japan's opinions through the active mediation of William J. Sebald, who served as a political advisor to the State Department on US-Japan relations. The American government even went so far as to examine the British draft of the peace treaty together with

---

37   William Sebald's memoir, 263.

38   William Sebald's memoir, 266.

Japanese representatives. The British government insisted until the end that the phrase "war responsibilities" should be included in the final treaty, and people such as Sebald who were pro-Japanese argued vehemently against it because such language would destroy the whole concept of the treaty as being a non-punitive document, and that such a phrase would cause great difficulty with the Japanese people in accepting the treaty.[39] As a result, the San Francisco Treaty declared the restoration of peace with Japan, but made no mention of criminal acts committed by Imperialist Japan and subsequent responsibilities, let alone of any commonly employed statements concerning "militaristic mistakes." Since Korea's participation in the conference was uncertain, it was inevitable that issues pertaining to Korea's interests should be marginalized by Japan's lobbying and interventions.

Korea's participation in the Japanese peace treaty as a signatory and the territorial issue of Dokdo were all discussed in a joint US-UK working group session held in Washington from the end of April to the beginning of May, 1951. The working group was chaired by John M. Allison from Dulles' delegation and the head of the British delegation was Johnston, Director of the Japan Bureau of the Ministry of Foreign Affairs. The working group examined the existing British and American drafts and, regarding territorial matters, the delegates agreed at their seventh meeting on May 1, 1951 to explicitly state only those territories of which Japan was to renounce possession.[40] In other words, by specifically selecting the areas to be excluded from Japan, the treaty put Japan in an advantageous position regarding territorial claims. Based on the American draft, the treaty included three Korean islands that were to be excluded from Japan: Jejudo, Geomundo, and Ulleungdo. The United States was extremely conciliatory toward Japan and took the position that although Okinawa was to be under American trusteeship, it should still be removed

---

39   William Sebald's memoir, 266.

40   William Sebald's memoir, 265.

Jung Byung-joon   A Draft of the Peace Treaty with Japan by the British Ministry of   **203**
Foreign Affairs, the Formation of the Attached Map (March 1951)
and a Reconfirmation of Korea's Possession of Dokdo

from the list of territories to be excluded from Japan because it was expected to be returned to Japan someday. It is not clear what exactly was decided on the issue of Dokdo during the meetings. What is clear is that, instead of the explicit stipulations of the British draft, the ambiguous and noncommittal method favored by Japan was adopted of stating the areas to be excluded, thus providing fodder for future international territorial disputes.

The joint US-UK working group session in Washington was also significant with respect to Korea's participation as a signatory nation at the conference. As is well known, the United States' position on the matter from the end of 1949 was favorable to Korea. This opinion only strengthened after the start of the Korean War. Then, in July 1951, the United States' position turned against allowing Korean participation. In this, Britain and Japan's opposition was certainly influential.[41] The United States had argued for Korea's signatory status even until May, during the joint US-UK working group meetings, but at a certain point afterwards, it came to have a negative view of Korea's participation. Its resolve was ultimately shaken by Britain and Japan's persistent arguments of the following: 1) Korea was not a part of the Allied Powers; 2) if Korea were to be given the status of an Allied Power, Communist-leaning Japanese-Koreans would be empowered and the Japanese government would face difficulties;[42] and 3) if Korea were allowed to participate while China was

---

41 "Anglo-American meetings on Japanese Peace Treaty, Summary Record of Seventh meeting,"
May 3, 1951, British Embassy, Washington, to C. P. Scott, O. B. E., Japan and Pacific Department, Foreign Office, no. 1076/357/5IG,FO 371/92547, FJ 1022/376.

42 Tae-Gi Kim, "1950nyeondaecho Miguk-ui Daehan Oegyojeongchaek: Daeilganghwa Joyake-seo-ui Hankuk-ui Baeje Mit Je-1cha Hanil Hoedam-e Daehan Miguk-ui Jeongchijeok Ipjang-eul Jungsimeuro" (The U.S. Foreign Policy toward Korea at the Beginning of 1950s: The U.S. Political Position on the Exclusion of Korea from Japanese Peace Treaty and First Korea-Japan Negotiations), *Hankguk Jeongchihakhoebo* (Korean Political Science Review) 33, no. 1 (1999): 362-363; Won-deok Yi, *Hanil Gwageosa Cheori-ui Wonjeom*, 27-28.

excluded, other Asian nations such as Burma and Indonesia might protest.[43] Finally, on July 9, 1951, Dulles notified Korean Ambassador Yang Yu-chan of the United States' position that Korea could not be a signatory because it was not part of the Allied Forces that had fought against Japan. With that, Korea was excluded from the peace conference.[44]

Through the joint US-UK meetings, Britain's opinions were integrated into the two countries' unified document on May 3, 1951. In this way the first joint US-UK draft was prepared, but differing views on such matters as what to do with Taiwan and choosing between Communist China and the Chinese National Party as a signatory still needed to be arbitrated.[45] The joint draft was circulated among the 13 other nations for their opinions and Korea, as just noted, was excluded at the end.

Most governments that received temporary drafts from the United States during April and May sent back to Washington their opinions and positions. The United States and Britain resolved all their differences and completed their final joint draft by July 3, 1951, which was sent to the 13 other nations that had fought against Japan, excluding the two Chinese governments, on July 9.[46] With further minor modifications, the final draft was readied and distributed on August 13 and signed at the San Francisco Conference on Sep-

---

43   "Korea and Peace Treaty" by Yoshida Shigeru, Japan Prime Minister, April 23, 1951, NARA, RG 59, Japanese Peace Treaty Files of John Foster Dulles, 1947–1952, Lot File, 54D423, Box 7.

44   "Japanese Peace Treaty: Records of meeting between our representative and Mr. Dulles," no. 393(s), May 3, 1951, Sir O. Franks, Washington, to Foreign Office, FO 371/92547, FJ 1022/370; "Anglo-American meetings on Japanese Peace Treaty, Summary Record of ninth and final meeting held on 4th May," May 4, 1951, British Embassy, Washington, to Foreign Office, no. 1076/366/5IG, FO 371/92547, FJ 1022/378.

45   Memorandum of conversation, Subject: Japanese Peace Treaty, July 9, 1951, NARA, RG 59, Decimal File, 694.001/7-951.

46   William Sebald's memoir, 267.

Jung Byung-joon   A Draft of the Peace Treaty with Japan by the British Ministry of   **205**
Foreign Affairs, the Formation of the Attached Map (March 1951)
and a Reconfirmation of Korea's Possession of Dokdo

tember 8. Article 2a of the treaty states: "Japan, recognizing the independence of Korea, renounces all right, title and claim to Korea, including the islands of Quelpart (Jejudo), Port Hamilton (Geomundo) and Dagelet (Ulleungdo)."

Received: July 1, 2005
Accepted: August 10, 2005

Key Words

San Francisco Peace Treaty, British draft of Japanese peace treaty, Dokdo, Liancourt Rocks dispute, British map on the territory of Japanese Sovereignty

Appendix 1
First British Draft of the Japanese Peace Treaty (February 28, 1951)

102

Secret.

JAPANESE PEACE TREATY

Preamble

1. The United Kingdom of Great Britain and NorthernIreland, the United States of America, Australia, Canada, the Netherlands, New Zealand, and ...., hereinafter referred to as "the Allied and Associated Powers", of the one part, and Japan, of the other;

2. Whereas Japan under the militarist régime became a party to the Tripartite Pact with Germany and Italy, undertook a war of aggression and thereby provoked a state of war with all the Allied and Associated Powers and with other United Nations, and bears her share of responsibility for the war; and

3. Whereas in consequence of the victories of the Allied Forces, the militarist régime in Japan was overthrown and Japan, having surrendered unconditionally, in accordance with the Potsdam Proclamation, signed an Instrument of Surrender on the 2nd September, 1945; and

4. Whereas the Allied and Associated Powers and Japan are desirous of concluding a Treaty of Peace which, in conformity with the principles of justice, will settle questions still outstanding as a result of the events hereinbefore recited, will enable Japan freely to accept and apply the principles of the Universal Declaration of Human Rights and will form the basis of friendly relations between them /thereby enabling the Allies and Associated Powers, when they shall deem the time appropriate, to support Japan's application to become a member of the United Nations and other International Organisations;7

5. Have therefore agreed to declare the cessation of the state of war and for this purpose to conclude the present Treaty of Peace, and have accordingly appointed the undersigned Plenipotentiaries, who, after presentation of their full powers, found in good and due form, have agreed on the following provisions:

/Territories

Jung Byung-joon   A Draft of the Peace Treaty with Japan by the British Ministry of
Foreign Affairs, the Formation of the Attached Map (March 1951)
and a Reconfirmation of Korea's Possession of Dokdo   **207**

-2-   103

Territories

6.   Japanese sovereignty shall continue over all the islands and
adjacent islets and rocks lying within an area bounded by a
line ....

/The line should include Hokkaido, Honshu, Shikoku, Kyushu,
the Suisho, Yuri, Akijiri, Shibotsu, Oki and Taraku islands,
the Habomai islands, Kuchinoshima, Utsuryo (Ulling island),
Liancourt rocks (Take island) Quelpart (Shichi or Chejudo)
island and Shikotan_7.

The line above described is plotted on the map attached to the
present Treaty (Annex 1). In the case of a discrepancy between
the map and the textual description of the line, the latter shall
prevail.

7.   Japan hereby renounces any claim to sovereignty over, and all
right, title and interest in, Korea, and undertakes to recognise
and respect all such arrangements as may be made by or under the
auspices of the United Nations regarding the sovereignty and
independence of Korea.

8.   Japan hereby cedes to the Union of Soviet Socialist Republics
in full sovereignty the Kurile islands, that portion of South
Sakhalin over which Japan formerly exercised sovereignty and the
Habomai group of islands, and agrees to the arrangements respecting
these territories set out in /Annex 7.

9.   Japan hereby cedes to China, in full sovereignty, the island of
Formosa and the Pescadores islands, and agrees to the arrangements
respecting property in these territories set out in /Annex 7.

10.   Japan renounces sovereignty over, and all right, title to and
interest in the Ryukyu-Bonin and Volcano islands, and Marcus island.

11.   Japan takes note of the intentions of the United States Government
to negotiate a United Nations trusteeship agreement in respect of the
Ryukyu and Bonin islands, once this present Treaty has come into force.

Appendix 2

Second British Draft of the Japanese Peace Treaty (March 1951)

70

ecret.

2nd DRAFT OF JAPANESE PEACE TREATY

Preamble

1.   The United Kingdom of Great Britain and Northern Ireland, the United States of America, Australia, Canada, the Netherlands, New Zealand, and ...., hereinafter referred to as "the Allied and Associated Powers", of the one part, and Japan, of the other;

2.   Whereas Japan under the militarist régime became a party to the Tripartite Pact with Germany and Italy, undertook a war of aggression and thereby provoked a state of war with all the Allied and Associated Powers and with other United Nations, and bears her share of responsibility for the war; and

3.   Whereas in consequence of the victories of the Allied Forces, the militarist régime in Japan was overthrown and Japan, having surrendered unconditionally, in accordance with the Potsdam Proclamation, signed an Instrument of Surrender on the 2nd September, 1945; and

4.   Whereas the Allied and Associated Powers and Japan are desirous of concluding a Treaty of Peace which, in conformity with the principles of justice, will settle questions still outstanding as a result of the events hereinbefore recited, will enable Japan freely to accept and apply the principles of the Universal Declaration of Human Rights and will form the basis of friendly relations between them;

5.   Have therefore agreed to declare the cessation of the state of war and for this purpose to conclude the present Treaty of Peace, and have accordingly appointed the undersigned Plenipotentiaries, who, after presentation of their full powers, found in good and due form, have agreed on the following provisions:

/Preliminary

Jung Byung-joon   A Draft of the Peace Treaty with Japan by the British Ministry of
Foreign Affairs, the Formation of the Attached Map (March 1951)
and a Reconfirmation of Korea's Possession of Dokdo   **209**

72

PART I - TERRITORIAL CLAUSES
Section I. Japan.
Article I.

(6) Japanese sovereignty shall continue over all the islands and
adjacent islets and rocks lying within an area bounded by a line
from Latitude 30° N in a North-Easterly direction to approximately
Latitude 33° N 128° E, then northward between the islands of
Quelpart, Fukue-Shima bearing North-Easterly between Korea and the
island of Tsushima, continuing in this direction with the islands
of Oki-Retto to the South-East and Take Shima to the North-West
curving with the coast of Honshu, then Northerly skirting Rebun
Shima passing Easterly through Soya Kaikyo approximately 145°40'N,
then in a South-Easterly direction parallel to the coast of
Hokkaido to 145°30' E. entering Nemero Kaikyo to the South-West
passing the Western end of Kunashiri bearing South-Easterly and
passing through the Goyomai Channel between Suisho Shima and
Hokkaido at 43°25' N, then in a South-Westerly direction with the
coastline towards the Nanpo Group of Islands curving South to
include Sofu-Gan (Lot's Wife) at 29°50' N., veering to the North-
West towards the coast of Honshu, then at approximately 33° N.
turning South-Westerly past Shikoku to 30° N. to include Yaku Shima
and excluding Kuchina Shima and the Ryukyu Islands South of
latitude 30° North.   The line above described is plotted on the
map attached to the present Treaty (Annex I).   In the case of a
discrepancy between the map and the textual description of the
line, the latter shall prevail.

/Section II

Appendix 3

Third British Draft of the Japanese Peace Treaty (April 7, 1951)

- 15

PROVISIONAL DRAFT OF JAPANESE PEACE TREATY
(UNITED KINGDOM)

PREAMBLE

1. The Union of Soviet Socialist Republics, the United Kingdom of Great Britain and Northern Ireland, the United States of America, China, France, Australia, Burma, Canada, Ceylon, India, Indonesia, the Netherlands, New Zealand, Pakistan, the Republic of the Philippines; hereinafter referred to as " the Allied and Associated Powers," of the one part, and Japan, of the other;

2. Whereas Japan under the militarist régime became a party to the Tripartite Pact with Germany and Italy, undertook a war of aggression and thereby provoked a state of war with all the Allied and Associated Powers and with other United Nations, and bears her share of responsibility for the war; and

3. Whereas in consequence of the victories of the Allied Forces, the militarist régime in Japan was overthrown and Japan, having surrendered unconditionally, in accordance with the Potsdam Proclamation signed an Instrument of Surrender on 2nd September, 1945; and

4. Whereas the Allied and Associated Powers and Japan are desirous of concluding a treaty of peace which, in conformity with the principles of justice, will settle questions still outstanding as a result of the events hereinbefore recited, will enable Japan freely to accept and apply the principles of the Universal Declaration of Human Rights and will form the basis of friendly relations between them;

5. Have therefore agreed to declare the cessation of the state of war and for this purpose to conclude the present treaty of peace, and have accordingly appointed the undersigned plenipotentiaries, who, after presentation of their full powers, found in good and due form, have agreed on the following provisions:—

PRELIMINARY ARTICLE

As from the date of the coming into force of the present treaty, the state of war between Japan and each of the Allied and Associated Powers which ratify or accede to the Treaty is hereby terminated.

Part I.—Territorial Clauses

ARTICLE 1

Japanese sovereignty shall continue over all the islands and adjacent islets and rocks lying within an area bounded by a line from latitude 30° N. in a north-westerly direction to approximately latitude 33° N. 128° E. then northward between the islands of Quelpart, Fukue-Shima bearing north-easterly between Korea and the island of Tsushima, continuing in this direction with the islands of Oki-Retto to the south-east and Take Shima to the north-west curving with the coast of Honshu, then northerly skirting Rebun Shima passing easterly through Soya Kaikyo approximately 142° E., then in a south-easterly direction parallel to the coast of Hokkaido to 145° 30′ E. entering Numero Kaikyo at approximately 44° 30′ N. in a south-westerly direction to approximately 43° 45′ N. and 145° 15′ E., then in a south-easterly direction to approximately 43° 35′ N. 145° 35′ E., then bearing north-easterly to approximately 44° N., so excluding Kunashiri, and curving to the east and then bearing south-westerly to include Shikotan at 147° 5′ E., being the most easterly point, then in a south-westerly direction with the coastline towards the Nanpo Group of Islands curving south to include Sofu-Gan (Lot's Wife) at 29° 50′ N., veering to the north-west towards the coast of Honshu, then at approximately 33° N. turning south-westerly past Shikoku to 30° N. to include Yaku Shima and excluding Kuchino Shima and the Ryukyu Islands south of latitude 30° North. The line above described is plotted on the map attached to the present treaty (Annex I).(¹) In the case of a discrepancy between the map and the textual description of the line, the latter shall prevail.

(¹) Not printed.

Jung Byung-joon   A Draft of the Peace Treaty with Japan by the British Ministry of   **211**
Foreign Affairs, the Formation of the Attached Map (March 1951)
and a Reconfirmation of Korea's Possession of Dokdo

17

BRITISH DRAFT

ARTICLE 2

Japan hereby renounces any claim to sovereignty over, and all right, title and interest in Korea, and undertakes to recognise and respect all such arrangements as may be made by or under the auspices of the United Nations regarding the sovereignty and independence of Korea.

ARTICLE 3

Japan hereby cedes to the Union of Soviet Socialist Republics in full sovereignty the Kurile Islands, and that portion of South Sakhalin over which Japan formerly exercised sovereignty.

ARTICLE 4

Japan hereby cedes to China, in full sovereignty, the Island of Formosa and the Pescadores Islands.

ARTICLE 5

1. Japan renounces sovereignty over, and all right, title and interest in the Ryukyu Bonin and Volcano Islands, and Marcus Island.
2. Japan takes note of the intention of the United States Government to negotiate a United Nations trusteeship agreement in respect of the Ryukyu and Bonin Islands when this present treaty has come into force.

ARTICLE 6

Japan renounces all rights, titles, interests and claims to territories or islands formerly administered by her under League of Nations mandate, and all other rights, titles, interests and claims deriving from the League of Nations mandate system or from any undertakings given in connexion therewith, together with all special rights of the Japanese State in respect of any territory now or formerly under mandate.

ARTICLE 7

Japan renounces all political and territorial claims in or relative to the Antarctic Continent and the islands adjacent thereto, and undertakes to forego and not to assert any such claims in the future.

ARTICLE 8

Japan renounces on behalf of the Japanese Government and Japanese nationals all rights, titles and interests in and all claims in respect of any property which is or was situated in any of the territories mentioned in Articles 2, 3, 4, 5, 6 and 7.

Part II.—Political Clauses

Section I.—Undesirable Political Societies

ARTICLE 9

Japan which, in accordance with the directives issued by the Supreme Commander for the Allied Powers (Memorandum No. A.G. 091 (4th January, 1946) G.S., &c.) has taken measures to dissolve all ultra-Nationalist and terrorist societies and organisations in Japan, shall not permit the resurgence on Japanese territory of such societies and organisations, whether political, military or para-military, or of any other society or organisation whose purpose it is —

(a) To deprive the people of their democratic rights.
(b) To perpetuate militarism or ultra-nationalism in Japan.
(c) To alter the policy of the Japanese Government by assassination or terrorism or the encouragement or justification of a resort to such methods.
(d) To oppose the free exchange of intellectual or cultural ideas between Japan and foreign countries.

Appendix 4

Map Attached to the British Draft of the Peace Treaty with Japan (March 1951)

Jung Byung-joon   A Draft of the Peace Treaty with Japan by the British Ministry of   **213**
Foreign Affairs, the Formation of the Attached Map (March 1951)
and a Reconfirmation of Korea's Possession of Dokdo

Abstract

The British Government drew up an official draft in the process of preparing a peace treaty with Japan in 1951. The draft indicated that Dokdo (Dok Island) was excluded from Japanese territory, being a part of Korea. The characteristics of the map are as follows:

First, it identified Japanese territory as being centered round its four main islands. Second, not only was Japanese territory narrowly and strictly prescribed, it was clearly delineated with a boundary line. Third, England chose this method of delineating Japanese territory with a boundary line because it wanted to prevent future territorial disputes, to punish Japan and, in line with the Potsdam Declaration, to call Japan to account for the war by confining its boundaries to territory centered on its four main islands. Fourth, and most important for Korea, the map excluded Dokdo from this delineation of Japanese territory, affirming that it was part of Korea.

The meaning of the map in relation to Korea's possession of Dokdo is as follows:

First, it was the only official map made by the British government in preparation for talks in San Francisco. It was also the only map made by an allied nation regarding the delineation of the territory of Japan. Second, it did not reflect the American opinion, which had been shaped by intense Japanese lobbying, but rather the British, which was the more objective, third-person viewpoint of the allied nations. Third, as part of an official draft prepared by Britain, a member of the allied nations, it indisputably indicated and confirmed that Dokdo was not part of Japanese territory but rather belonged to Korea. Its date is also significant, it having been produced immediately before the conclusion of the San Francisco Peace Treaty in 1951, making it the most current and most pertinent map with regard to the Dokdo dispute. Fourth, and even more importantly, Britain initially erred in its first draft in identifying Dokdo, Ulleungdo and even Jejudo as part of Japan, and then officially affirmed that they were excluded from Japan and part of Korea in the map appended to the corrected second draft. Fifth, even though the map was not adopted as the official territorial provision in the final peace treaty, it explicitly reconfirmed Korea's possession of Dokdo.

Japan's Incorporation of Takeshima into Its Territory in 1905[1]

Kazuo Hori[2]

Professor, Kyoto University

I. Introduction

Territorial issues have been the cause of many international disputes not only in ancient times but also today. Moreover, as shown in the dispute over the Falklands some years ago, a territorial dispute intrinsically tends to numb rational reasoning and leads to an outburst of anti-foreign nationalism.

At present, Japan continues to be involved in territorial disputes over the three islands of the Kuriles (Chishima retto), Senkaku shoto, and Takeshima; none of which is likely to be settled any time in the near future. One practical way to resolve a territorial dispute is to resort to international law. However, if the international law is to be applied in a manner acceptable by the countries concerned, there must first be a common basis on which to perceive the facts

---

1   This article was originally published in Japanese in 1987 under the title "1905年日本の竹島領 土編入,"『朝鮮史研究会論文集』, vol. 24, 1987, pp. 97-125. An earlier English version of this article appeared in the Korea Observer (Vol. 38, No.3, Autumn 1997, pp. 477-525).

2   Professor of Kyoto University, Faculty of Economics, Japan.

per se concerning the dispute.

Therefore, I think it is important to provide some forward-looking suggestions by inquiring in a concrete and objective manner into the history of a disputed area in order to aid in the settlement of Japan's territorial question that has come to a deadlock due to the conflicting national interests of the two sides and their national sentiments.

The ownership of Takeshima (Koreans call it Tokdo)[3] has been a bone of contention between Japan and the Republic of Korea and between Japan and North Korea. This postwar dispute at the international level surfaced immediately after the establishment of the so-called Syngman Rhee Line in 1952, around the conclusion of the Republic of Korea-Japan Basic Agreement in 1965 again and also in 1977 when the establishment of 200-nautical- mile territorial waters became an issue. Not a small number of documents regarding Takeshima were made public at these times.[4]

As methodology in writing this article, a critical examination is made of *Takeshima no rekishi chirigakuteki kenkyu* (Historical and Geographical Study of Takeshima) (Tokyo: Kinkoshoten, 1966) by Kawakami Kenzo. This article develops an argument as opposed to Kawakami's claims. Kawakami's study is chosen because:

(1) It is the most extensive study made in Japan on the history of Takeshima; (2) its author was a researcher at the Japanese Foreign Ministry at the time of its writing and the study was made at the request of the government; and (3) it is used by Japan today as the most cogent basis in claiming its sovereign

---

3   Takeshima and Ullŭngdo have been called by many different names in Korea and Japan. In order to avoid confusion, the names used today are given in addition to the old ones. The island consists of tiny, rocky uninhabitable islets of about 56 acres with no trees and potable water.

4   See Yang T'ae-jin, *Tokdo kwangye munhŏn mongnok* (A List of Documents concerning Tokdo), (1978); Oguchi Satoko, *Takeshima (Tokdo) kankei shiryo mokuroku* (A List of Data on Tokdo), vol. 17, no. 11: "Azia afrika shiryo tsuho (Materials on Asia and Africa)," (Tokyo: the National Diet Library), 1980.

right to Takeshima.[5]

This study is intended to shed light on Japan's relations with Takeshima since the Meiji Restoration in 1867 and on what grounds Japan managed to place Takeshima into its territory in 1905. To help understand the situation more clearly, a brief overview is also made of the events before that period. No discussion will be made on international law. Kawakami repeatedly asserts that in his study he attempted to inquire into the history of Takeshima from a purely academic perspective without being affected by the actual territorial dispute on the islets. Is his assertion true?

II. Knowledge and Consciousness of Takeshima as a Territory

A. The Government of the Chosŏn Dynasty, Korea from 1392 to 1910 and the Edo Government of Japan from 1615 to 1867

The reference to Takeshima/Tokdo was first made in Korean documents approximately 200 years before it was first made in Japanese documents. *Sejong sillok chiriji*, or the gazetteer in the *Annals of King Sejong* (actually compiled in 1432 and formally published in 1454), refers to Takeshima/Tokdo in the entry on Uljinhyŏn, Kangwŏndo as follows: "There exist two islands, Usan and Mŭllung, in the sea off the east coast of this county. The islands are not far away from each other, so one can be seen from the other on a clear day."

In other words, separate from Ullŭngdo that was known to Koreans as early as the Silla Dynasty, there exists another island, and Ullŭngdo and this island are visible from each other on a clear day. In Korea, Usando has been known as Takeshima/Tokdo.

---

5   In his paper entitled "Takeshima/Tokdo mondaito nihon kokka "The Issue of Takeshima/Tokdo and Japan" *Chosen Kenkyu* (Study on Korea), no. 182, 1978, Professor Kajimura Hideki criticizes Kawakami's study mainly from a logical point of view.

However, Kawakami maintains that Usando does not exist and that it does not make sense to say that Usando is Takeshima/Tokdo today.[6] He cites the following two historical records:

First, the section on Uljinhyŏn in the *chiriji* (Gazetteer) in *Koryŏsa* (History of Korea, 1451) which reads "Ullŭngdo is situated in the midst of the East Sea and was called Usan'guk during the Silla Dynasty. It is also known as Mullŭng or Ullŭng... According to one theory, Usan and Mullŭng were originally two separate islands; they were not far apart, and were visible from each other on a clear day."

Second, in the entry on Uljinhyŏn, *Tongguk yŏji sŭngnam* (Augmented Survey of the Geography of Korea, 1531), notes as follows: "There are two islands, Usando and Ullŭngdo which is also called Mullŭng or Ullŭng, are in the midst of the East Sea... One theory has it that Usando and Ullŭng, are one and the same island."

As noted above, *Koryŏsa* describes Usan and Mullŭng as two different names of the same island, whereas *Sinjung tongguk yŏji sŭngnam* (Revised and Augmented Survey of the Geography of Korea) treats Usan and Mullŭng as two different islands. Kawakami believes the one-and-same—island theory for Usan and Mullŭng is more convincing. He holds that the treatment of Usan and Mullŭng as two different islands as seen in other historical records was the result of overstretching the meaning of an erroneous note given in *Koryŏsa*.

The primary basis on which Kawakami places his assertion is the point of time in which the two historical records, *Sejong sillok* (Annals of King Sejong) and *Koryŏsa* were compiled. Kawakami admits that as a whole *Sejong sillok* is the older data than *Koryŏsa*. However, when it comes to the description of Ullŭngdo, *Sejong sillok* notes an incident concerning the island that took place during the reign of King Sejong, an incident that is not mentioned in *Koryŏsa*. For that reason, Kawakami says that as far as the issue of Takeshima/Tokdo is concerned, *Koryŏsa* represents an older basic record than *Sejong sil-*

---

6   Kawakami *op. cit.*, pp. 94-120.

lok... The fact, however, is that it is only natural that *Koryŏsa* should not treat the Chosŏn period that follows the Koryŏ period it covers.

As the second basis for his assertion, Kawakami states that since Takeshima/Tokdo cannot be seen from Ullŭngdo what is described as Usando in *Sejong sillok* cannot be Takeshima/Tokdo. He also argues that the part of *Koryŏsa* which says that "on a clear day they can be seen from each other" does not involve two separate islands, but rather it refers to Ullŭngdo and the mainland of the Korean Peninsula. In making this assertion, however, Kawakami apparently disregards the context and misreads the subject in the above-cited portion of *Koryŏsa*. Furthermore, that Takeshima/Tokdo can be seen from Ullŭngdo has been already proved.[7] Even Japanese documents state that "on a clear day one can see Takeshima/Tokdo from a high spot on the mountain of Ullŭngdo"[8] and that "Takeshima/Tokdo, 50 *ri* (one *ri* is about 2.44 miles, 3,937 meters) away from Ullŭngdo can be seen from Ullŭngdo on a day when the sea is calm."[9] These remarks concur not only with what is said in *Sejong sillok*, but even with the configuration sketched by a Japanese warship in Chart 3 (See page 512).

Although the description in the text of *Koryŏsa* is somewhat confusing, it is clear that in the early 15th century, Koreans already knew that apart from Ullŭngdo there existed in its vicinity a separate island. And the fact that these islands are recorded in the official gazetteer is considered to indicate Korea's consciousness of them as its possessions.

The more serious defect in Kawakami's book is that because of his as-

---

7   Physically, at an altitude of 120 meters or more on Ullŭngdo, one can see Takeshima/Tokdo. Lee Han-ki, *Han'guk ŭi yŏngt'o* (Korea's Territories) (Seoul: Seoul National University (SNU) Press, 1969) pp. 232-234. The altitude of the highest peak of the mountain on Ullŭngdo is 985 meters. Kawakami, however, says (p. 281) that it is very difficult to climb to this height at Ullŭngdo because the island is thickly covered by shrubs and trees.

8   See Katsuo Shukichi, *Kankai tsugyo shishin* (Guidelines for Fishing in the Korean Seas) (Tokyo: Kokuryukai Shuppanbu, 1903), p. 123.

9   See *Chigaku zasshi* (Journal of Earth Science), no. 210, 1906, p. 415.

sumption that this Usando does not exist, he has to deny the existence of every Usando that appears in many documents and maps of the 16th century and thereafter.[10] Vol. 30 of *Sukchong sillok* (Annals of King Sukchong, 1728), for example, reads in part that An Yong-bok, who visited Japan a couple of times for talks with Japanese authorities over disputes involving Ullŭngdo toward the end of the 17th century, is quoted as stating "Songdo, also called Chasando, is our territory," and "By the islands of Ullŭngdo and Chasando, the boundary of Chŏson is set."

Kawakami, although he admits that An Yong-bok knew of the existence of Takeshima/Tokdo, refuses to accept An's testimony as anything of historical value, saying that the testimony is fictitious in many parts. However, even putting aside the authenticity of An's testimony, the simple fact that he called Takeshima/Tokdo Usando and stated that the island and Ullŭngdo were Choson's territory is enough to confute Kawakami's assertion that Usando does not exist.

The *Yŏjigo* (Gazetteer) in *Chungbo munhŏn pigo* (Augmented Reference Compilation of Documents on Korea), published in 1908, points out that "what is cited in the *yojiji* as Ullŭng and Usan belong to Usan'guk, and Usan is what Japanese call "Matsushima," thus accurately stating that Usando is Takeshima/Tokdo today. In view of the fact that *Chungbo munhŏn pigo* is the result of the 200-year long Korean government project to compile its annals continuously, it is obvious that the Chŏson government had long been conscious of Usando as part of its territory.

---

10   Originally, Usan and Ullŭng were the different transcriptions of the same word in Chinese characters, but they had come to be established as the names of two different islands. For Usan (于山) different or erroneous characters are used: 于山, 牛山, 子山, 芋山, 亏山 etc. Some Japanese scholars say that Usando is Takesho. (Boussole Rock), an island one nautical mile east of Ullŭngdo. However, their view cannot substantiate the description that "on a clear day, it can be seen." Their assertion also does not agree with a report made by E. Laporte, a Frenchman working for the Pusan Customs Office after surveying Ullŭngdo in June 1899, It cited Usando and Takeshima as being two big islands appendant to Ullŭngdo. See the *Hwangsŏng sinmun*, Sept, 23, 1899.

There are many other Korean and Japanese references that show Takeshima/Tokdo as Usando. For instance, *Taehan sinjiji* (A New Treatise on Korean Geography, 1907), by Chang Chi-yŏn states that there is Usando southeast of Ullŭngdo. Also in *Chosenkoku chirishitekiyo* (A Summary of Korean Geography, 1876), by Kondo Horoku, and *Shinsen chosenchirishi* (A New Geography of Korea, 1894) by Ota Saijiro it is noted that Usando exists separate from Ullŭgdo in the East Sea.

Chart 1

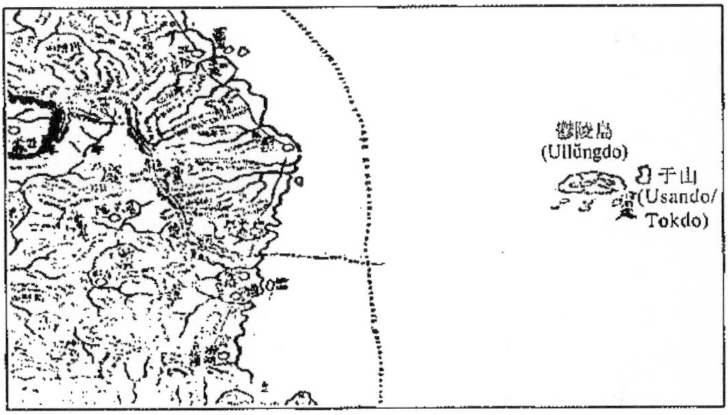

Ministry of Education, the Empire of Korea, ed., *Taehan yŏchido* (Korean Gazetteer, 1899), Seoul: The Kyujang-gak library, Seoul National Univ.

The Korean map that first showed Usando separate from Ullŭngdo is a map included in *Tongguk Yŏji sŭngnam*, 1499.[11] Since then, it is said, Usando has appeared in several hundred other Korean maps that have been made thus far. These old maps may not be accurate about the location and size of Ullŭngdo and Usando. Nonetheless, the single fact that so many old maps show Ullŭngdo and Usando suggests that the existence of Usando had been widely known among Koreans.

---

11   Ch'oe Suh Myun, "Kochizu kara mita dokdo (Tokdo Seen from Old Maps), *Toitsu nippo* (Unification Daily), May 27-29, 1981, pp, 28-29.

Especially by the end of the 19th century, Korea had come to have more accurate knowledge about Usando as the Korean government began to develop Ullǔngdo, Korea's knowledge of Takeshima/Tokdo of this time is well illustrated by *Taehan yǒjido* (Korean Gazetteer) edited by the Ministry of Education, the Empire of Korea, in 1899 and is kept in the Kyujang-gak Library, Seoul National University (See Chart 1). For an old map, Ullǔngdo and Takeshima/Tokdo are shown in almost accurate positions on the map. Given all these facts, it is clear that Kawakami's assertion that no Usando exists cannot be upheld. In other words, as early as the 15th century, the Korean government regarded Takeshima/Tokdo, then called Usando, as its territory, and in the late 19th century its consciousness of ownership again became pronounced although there had been some period of confusion.

The Japanese document that mentions Takeshima/Tokdo for the first time ever is a book *Onshu shicho goki* (Records on Observations in Oki Province) by Saito Hosen, a retainer of Izumo in 1667. By the name of Matsushima, it is shown along with Takeshima/Ullǔngdo. Since then the configurations of these islands have become known in detail among Japanese as they found their way to Ullǔngdo.

Beginning in the mid-15th century, the Korean government evacuated people from Ullǔngdo as it enforced a vacant island policy.[12] In 1617, the merchant ship of Otani Jinkichi of Yonago, was wrecked and drifted to Ullǔngdo... Drawn to the rich products of island, he, together with Murakawa Ichibei, applied to the Japanese government for a license to navigate to the island. Receiving permits from the Japanese authorities in the following year, 1618, the families of Otani and Murakawa alternately dispatched ships to Ullǔngdo for lumbering and gathering products.

The two Japanese families falsely claimed the "enfeoffment of Takeshima," but what the Shogunate gave them were "permits for passage" to the

---

12 One reason was that the island was often ransacked by Japanese pirates and another was that people sought to live in the island to evade taxation.

island. It appears that the Japanese families engaged in fishing for some time off Matsushima/Tokdo on their way to Takeshima/Ullŭngdo. In 1661, they received from the Japanese government a new permit for passage to Matsushima/Tokdo. However, the Japanese families' main destination, or main area of activity, was Takeshima/Ullŭngdo, and Matsushima/Tokdo was only incidental to this operation.

Apparently because of the different sizes of Takeshima/Ullŭngdo and Matsushima/Tokdo, historical records written at that time variously describe Matsushima/Tokdo as "being situated within Takeshima,"[13] or "being located near Takeshima"[14] or "being an islet close to Takeshima.[15] Thus they treat Matsushima as an adjunct to Takeshima. During the period when Japanese were repeatedly navigating to Ullŭngdo, Japan apparently was unaware of the fact that the island was Korea's territory.

In 1693, there occurred at Ullŭngdo a major clash between a group of Japanese from the Otani-family and An Yong-bok and other Korean fishermen who were on a fishing venture from Kyŏngsangdo. As the Otanis and Murakawas brought the matter before the Shogunate, this developed into the so-called "Takeshima Incident" pitting Japan against Korea through diplomatic channel over the fishing rights and ownership of the island. In the process of diplomatic negotiation, the lord of Tsushima, Japan, plotted a scheme to take Ullŭngdo away from Korea, plunging the Korean authorities into confusion for a time as they sought to counter the Japanese scheme.

However, after An Yong-bok went to Japan again to assert that Ullŭngdo and Usando were Korean territory, the hard-liners against Japan became dominant within the Korean government. Because it was historically evident that Ullŭngdo belonged to Korea since the Silla period, the Japanese government eventually restrained Tsushima's lord from making any reckless attempt against

13   Kawakami, *op. cit.*, p. 74.

14   *Ibid.*, p. 80.

15   *Ibid.*, p. 78

Korea and adopted a cooperative policy toward Korea. More specifically, in January 1696, the Japanese authorities prohibited the Otani and Murakami families from going to Takeshima/Ullŭngdo anymore. In January 1699, "the Takeshima Incident" was settled as the Japanese authorities formally recognized in an official document[16] that Ullŭngdo belonged to Korea.

The Japanese document does not specifically mention the name of Matsushima/Tokdo, but regards the island as an appendant of Takeshima/ Ullŭngdo, and thus its ownership is considered to have been treated likewise. Japanese fishing activity at Matshushima/Tokdo in the 17th century was only incidental to their advance to Takeshima/Ullŭngdo. Therefore, with the Japanese government decision to prohibit Japanese fishermen from going over to Takeshima/Ullŭngdo, their passage to Matsushima/Tokdo had to come to an end, too. As a matter of fact, none from the Otanis and Murakawas sailed to Matsushima/Tokdo as their sole destination thereafter.

Still, it appears that some other Japanese fishermen from the San'in area secretly crossed to Ullŭngdo.[17] Some private Japanese books[18] describe Matsushima/Tokdo as belonging to Okinokuni, Japan. There is also another Japanese book[19] that does not seem to know even that Takeshima/Ullŭngdo is Korea's island. However, these irresponsible civilians' knowledge and information have no bearing at all on the question of territorial sovereignty.

Among Japanese data that indicate Japan's consciousness of its sovereign territory are maps made by the Japanese government. Of these maps, the one which shows Matsushima/Tokdo for the first time is *Nihon yochirotei jenzu*,

---

16   Kitazawa Shosei, *Takeshima kosho* (A Study of Takeshima), 1881, vol. 2 (out of three vols,) kept in the National Archives, Japan. Kitazawa also understands Ullŭngdo and Usan as Takeshima and Matsushima, See vol. I.

17   Toda Keigi, "Takeshima no zu (The Map of Takeshima)" attached to "Takeshima tokai negai (Application for Voyage to Takeshima)" in *Takeshima kosho, op, cit.*

18   Hokugen Tsuan, ed., *Takeshima zusetsu* (Illustrated Record of Takeshima), published during the Horei nenkan (1751-1764).

19   Matsuura Takeshiro, *Takeshima zasshi* (An Encyclopedia of Takeshima), 1854.

a map drawn by Nagakubo Sekisui in 1773. It is the first Japanese map that used latitude and longitude. Nagakubo also published *Nippon rotei yochizu*, another map printed in color from wood blocks in 1778. What makes this map particularly notable is that while the Japanese mainland and its attached islands are shown in color, Takeshima/Ullŭngdo and Matsushima/Usando, along with the Korean Peninsula, are not colored.[20] Thus, after the Takeshima incident, the official maps do not treat Takeshima Ullŭngdo and Matsushima/ Tokdo as Japan's possessions.

A more recent official Japanese map, *Tainippon enkai yochi zenzu*, a map of Japan's coastal waters by Ino Tadataka in 1821, considered to mark a complete break from the older maps, also shows Takeshima/Ullŭngdo and Matsushima/Tokdo as not being Japan's territory. Japan's attitude toward Matushima/Tokdo, was somewhat ambiguous around the mid-17th century, but it became fairly clear after the governmental negotiations between Korea and Japan. In the Genroku era, in other words, in the late 17th century and there-after, Japan did not treat Matsushima/Tokdo as part of its territory, though it became aware of the existence of the island.

As we have seen so far, it was by advancing to Korea's island, Ullŭngdo, that Japanese came to know much about Matsushima/Tokdo. When the governments of Korea and Japan settled the Korea's ownership of Ullŭngdo, Matsushima/Tokdo, as its appendant island, quite naturally was excluded from the domain of Japan.

B. Cognizance of Takeshima/Tokdo by the Meiji Government (1868-1912)

Japan, as it came into contact with European countries and the United States from the early Meiji era, found its cognizance of Ullŭngdo and Takeshima/ Tokdo, thrown into great confusion. To begin with, French and British vessels

---

20   Ch'oe Suh Myun, *op.cit.*

that came into the Sea of Japan (East Sea) toward the end of the 18th century discovered Ullŭngdo one after another. However, due to their inaccurate measurement of the geographical location of Ullŭngdo, they, introduced Ullŭngdo as two separate islands of Dagelet and Argonaut. Later in 1849 Takeshima/Tokdo was found by a French vessel that named it Liancourt Rocks. Hence the maps in Europe in the mid-19th century showed Ullŭngdo as two separate islands in the Sea of Japan (East Sea) or showed Ullŭngdo as consisting of two such islands plus another island of Takeshima/Tokdo. This European information and Japan's knowledge of Takeshima and Matsushima from times past combined to cause confusion as to the way Japan viewed these two island. These developments have already been clearly known by a number of studies.

On *Chosen jenzu*, a map of Korea made by the Army Staff Bureau in 1875 and *Nihon jenzu*, a map of Japan by Japan's Ministry of Education in 1877, Ullŭngdo is shown as two separate islands, Takeshima and Matsushima and the present Takeshima/Tokdo is omitted. Soon the existence of Argonaut was negated and turning away from the Edo period representation, Ullŭngdo was now called Matsushima, and there appeared only one island in the Sea of Japan (East Sea) on maps.

Another civilian map showed three islands. Thus, from the '70s to the early '80s. Japan's knowledge of the two islands became considerably confused. With a three-island view, a two-island view, or one-island view, few accurately grasping the locations of the two islands. This is counter evidence refuting a view that Takeshima/Tokdo was an inherent part of Japanese territory in ancient times.

In the process of overcoming such confusion and putting things in order, the Japanese government began to settle the question of title to these islands. As no unified action was taken among the agencies, let us examine the separate actions one by one. The Japanese Ministry of Home Affairs was the first to take action on the ownership of these two islands. In October 1876, the Office of Geography, the Japanese Ministry of Home Affairs, sent an inquiry to Shimane prefecture for information about Takeshima/Tokdo in the course of the compilation of a cadastre.[21]

Shimane prefecture examined the particulars of the development of Takeshima/Ullŭngdo by the Otani and Murakawa families, and sent a reply entitled *Nihonkainai takeshima hoka itto chiseki hensan kata ukagai* (An Inquiry about the Compilation of the Land Register on Takeshima and Another Island in the Sea of Japan) to the Japanese Ministry of Home Affairs, together with a rough sketch of Takeshima/Ullŭngdo and Matsushima/Tokdo. In the reply, Shimane prefecture treated the two islands together as it understood Matsushima/Tokdo was attached to Takeshima/Ullŭngdo.

The Japanese Ministry of Home Affairs examined on its own the record on the Takeshima/Ullŭngdo incident of the late 17th century as well as the reply from Shimane prefecture and concluded that the two islands were Korea's, not Japan's. However, "the acquisition or abandonment of a territory being a matter of great importance," the Ministry, on March 17, 1877, referred the matter to the Dajokan for judgment. In the documents attached to the inquiry, "another island" was clearly stated as referring to Matsushima/Tokdo, and its shape and location were described correctly.

The Research Bureau of the Dajokan drafted the following: (See the photostatic copy of the script of this decision)

Re. the compilation of the cadastre for Takeshima and another island in the Sea of Japan as per Home Office inquiry.

Knowing that our country has nothing to do [with the islands] as the result of the communication between our old government and that country involved after the entry into the island by the Korean in the fifth year of the Genroku, and having examined the view stated in the inquiry, the following

---

21　*Nihonkainai takeshimahoka itto chiseki hensan kata ukagai* (An Inquiry about the Compilation of the Land Register on Takeshima and Another Island in the Sea of Japan) in *Kohunroku* (Official Documents), Dajokan, ed. Section on the Home Ministry, 1877 (Tokyo: National Archives).

draft instruction has been made for deliberation and sanction.

Draft Instruction

Re. Takeshima and another island, it is to be understood that our country has nothing to do with them.

This draft was signed and approved by Minister of the Right Iwakura Tonomi, Vice Minister Okuma Shigenobu, Terajima Munenori, and Oki Takato. In other words, the Dajokan (the Council of State), the highest government organ in Japan at that time, formally declared, on the basis, of the report of both Shimane prefecture and the Ministry of Home Affairs and treating Takeshima/Ullŭngdo and Matsushima/Tokdo as an integral whole, that these two islands were not Japan's territory. This instruction was sent from the Ministry of Home Affairs to Shimane prefecture on April 9 of the same year, and the question was settled at the prefecture, too.

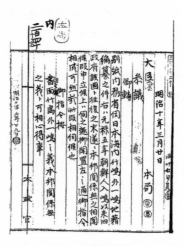

Dajokan decision: The script of the decision by the Japanese Dajokan (Council of State) dated March 20, 1877 states: "Takeshima/Ullŭngdo and Matsushima/Tokdo have nothing to do with our country." The Japanese side has far withheld this document from the public.

It is presumed that the Foreign Ministry came to know about the islands through the report by Sada Hakubo *et al.* temporarily in the service of the Ministry who inspected the islands in 1870. In his report *Chosenkoku kosai shimatsu naitansho* (Report on the Confidential Inquiry into the Particulars of the Relations with Korea), Sada writes:

1. Circumstances under which Takeshima and Matsushima have become Korea's possessions.

Regarding this case, Matsushima is an island adjacent to Takeshima and there has been no document on them to date; concerning Takeshima, Korea sent people to settle there for a while after the Genroku era...[22]

This, too, views that Matsushima/Tokdo was given to Korea in the settlement of the "Takeshima Incident" in the Genroku period, but this is simply a report.[23]

The Japanese Foreign Ministry was prompted for its independent judgment on these two islands in connection with the development of the Matsushima question from 1876. In June of that year, Muto Heigaku proposed to the Ministry the development of Matsushima. In the two following years, some civilians such as Kodama Sadayasu, Saito Sichirohei and Shimomura Rinsaburo, and Commercial Attache Wakise Hisato in Vladivostok submitted one after another similar proposals or applications.[24]

They pointed out the rich resources on the island and requested that they be permitted to develop Matsushima in the Sea of Japan (East Sea) which was

---

22   Japan Foreign Ministry Research Div. (Chosabu), ed., *Nihon gaiko bunsho* (Japanese Diplomatic Documents), vol. III, p. 137.

23   See vol. II of the two-volume book *Takeshima, kosho op. cit.*

24   In a separate development, Toda Keiji submitted to the Governor of Tokyo in January 1877 "an application for voyage to Takeshima." It was turned down in June of the same year. The action must have been taken swiftly because the matter came under the jurisdiction of the Ministry of Home Affairs. Here again Takeshima is Ullŭngdo.

either Japanese territory or whose ownership was unknown. They stirred up a sense of crisis, stating in common that Great Powers were trying to take over the island. Here Matsushima is Ullŭngdo.

On these applications the officials of the Japanese Foreign Ministry had several different opinions among themselves. While admitting Takeshima/ Ullŭngdo to be Korea's, Director Watanabe Kouki, Records Department of the Ministry, asserted that if there should exist another Matsushima separate from Takeshima/Ullŭngdo it might be considered Japan's territory. This view draws special attention in that it separated the ownership of Takeshima from that of Matsushima and is the precursor of the theoretical basis for the later incorporation of Takeshima/Tokdo into Japan's territory. However, he knew about Usando as an ancillary to Ullŭngdo and was at a loss as to how to handle Usando.[25] He was not sure either whether there were two or three separate islands in the Sea of Japan (East Sea). More than anything else he did not know that Matsushima was in fact Ullŭngdo in the applications for development.

Official "A" opposed development on the grounds that Matsushima belonged to Korea's Ullŭngdo and its development would amount to an act of aggression. Official "B" proposed to inspect Matsushima and Takeshima before they decided whether they were Ullŭngdo, Usando or ownerless. Official "C," without mentioning the ownership, but citing information on world powers' movement, proposed to survey Matsushima, disregarding the Koreans living there.

Director Tanabe Taiichi of the Communication Department, the Foreign Ministry, knew from the very beginning that Matsushima, the target island for development in the applications, was Ullŭngdo. Amidst pros and cons, Tanabe stated that if Matsushima was Usando its development would not be granted and that if the island were ownerless they had better negotiate with Korea.

In short, although there was Watanabe's opinion to take in an island

---

25   He believed Usando was Takeshima.

called Matsushima, it was the minority view. The majority view recognized Korea's rights to Matsushima or conceded at least Korea's involvement in the island, although they differed among themselves as to whether "Matsushima" should be regarded as Ullŭngdo or Usando. As no decision was made, the Japanese Foreign Ministry proceeded to conduct an on-site survey of Matsushima, the target area for development in the applications.

The survey was made by the Japanese warship *Amagi* in July 1880, and it was confirmed that Matsushima was Ullŭngdo.[26] As it became unquestionably clear that Matsushima, whose rich natural resources had long attracted Japanese attention, was Korea's territory, all the applications were turned down and the issue was put to an end. Takeshima/Tokdo was a completely barren island and could not be an object of any interest and concern. On November 29, 1881, the Japanese Ministry of Home Affairs made an inquiry to the Japanese Ministry of Foreign Affairs about the situation in Ullŭngdo, attaching thereto the afore-mentioned instruction of the Dajokan which excluded Takeshima and Matsushima from the Japanese territory.[27] The Foreign Ministry raised no objection whatsoever to this. From then to 1905, the Japanese Foreign Ministry never treated the ownership of Takeshima/Ullŭngdo and Mat- sushima/Tokdo.

As for the Navy, no original documents have survived, and we will have to rely on its publications to infer its knowledge of the land. Already in the 1860s, a British marine chart on which the Japanese Navy's Hydrographic Department depended heavily, showed the two islands at their accurate locations. By the end of the 1870s the Japanese Navy seemed to have become fully convinced of that fact and marine charts made in Japan in the 1880s likewise showed the accurate locations of the two islands. However, marine charts usu-

26   *Suiro zasshi* (Journal of Sea Routes), no. 41, pp. 34-37.

27   See *Naimu shokikan nishiyama sutezo no gaimushokikan ate shokai* (Inquiry of Secretary Nishiyama Sutezo of Home Ministry to the Foreign Ministry Secretary) *Gaimusho kiroku* (Foreign Ministry Documents), 3824, *Gaimushogaiko shiryokan* (Foreign Ministry Archives of Historical Materials on Diplomacy).

232

ally show geographical features and do not specify sovereign rights to islands in them. As for sovereign rights to islands, therefore, one has to consult a guide to sea routes, an expounder of a chart.

In March 1880, the Japanese Navy began to compile periodically and publish *Kan'ei suiroshi* (Sealanes of the World)[28] covering the world. Of these publications, Volume 2, Edition 2 (Korea and Russia) was published in 1886, showing Ullŭngdo and Liancourt Rocks. The publication, being a guide to world sealanes, is not decisive in determining the territorial ownership.

In March 1889, Japan ceased publication of the *Kan'ei suiroshi* and switched its emphasis to the Japan-centered northeast Asian seas. First, Japanese territorial waters were separated from others and *Nihon suiroshi* (Japanese Sealanes) was made independent and was published successively from 1892.[29] This publication shows not only Taiwan and Hoko shoto (Pescadores) which Japan gained as its new territory under the Shimonoseki Peace Treaty in 1895, but also the northernmost island of Senshuto in the Chishima retto (Kuriles). But it does not include the other side of the Taiwan Strait and the Kamchatka Peninsula. In other words, the geographical coverage in the publication is limited to Japan's territory and territorial waters.

What is important is the fact that Liancourt Rocks/Tokdo does not appear in the Sea of Japan (East Sea) in this publication. Given the fact that the Japanese sea maps at that time accurately show the position of the island, it is unthinkable that the Navy did not know its location. As shown in Chart 2, if we compare the map attached to the 1897 edition of the *suiroshi* (Sealanes) with that after the incorporation of Liancourt/Tokdo into Japanese possession, the picture becomes clear.

In other words, as of 1900 the Japanese Navy clearly excluded the island from Japan's territory. Moreover, the 1894 and 1897 editions of the *Chosen suiroshi* (Korea's Sealanes) by the Japanese Navy show Liancourt Rocks/

---

28   Japan Maritime Safety Agency, ed., *Nihon suiroshi* (Japan's Sealanes), 1971, pp. 69-70, 122-123.

29   *Ibid.*

Chart2

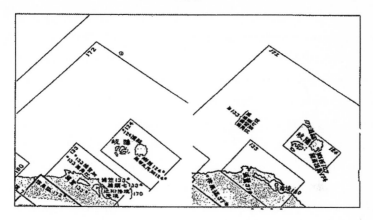

Sakamoto Kazu (Japan, Ministry of Navy, Hydrographic Dep't), ed., *Japanese Sealanes* (Tokyo: 1907), Vol. 4, from the indexes of the relevant maps.

Kimotsuki Kenko (Japan, Ministry of the Navy, Hydrographic Dep't), ed., *Japanese Sealanes* (Tokyo: 1897), Vol. 4, from the indexes of relevant maps.

Tokdo,[30] along with Ullŭngdo. There is no doubt the Japanese naval hydrographic authorities were aware Takeshima/Tokdo belonged to Korea around the end of the 19th century. In brief, after the Meiji Restoration the Japanese government had not expressed any particular interest in Takeshima/Tokdo. It is clear that all the Japanese government organs involved regarded the island as Korea's, along with Ullŭngdo though the degree of their cognizance of the island differed.

---

30   The Japanese Navy conducted on-site surveys of Ullŭngdo on several occasions, but all its information about Liancourt Rocks was acquired from the British Navy's publications on sea routes.

III. Japan's Invasion of Korea's Outlying Islands

A. Korea-Japan dispute over Ullŭngdo

Riding on the tide of external expansion following the Meiji Restoration, the Japanese started crossing the sea to Ullŭngdo on their own initiative. In 1881, a Korean inspector discovered that many Japanese trespassed on this island for logging and fishing. The Korean government promptly countered this by sending an official note to the Japanese government, demanding prohibition of such voyages. The Japanese Foreign Ministry apologized to the Korean side by acknowledging the wrongdoing, as it had confirmed Ullŭngdo to be Korean territory in the question of the development of Matsushima mentioned above.

However, the Japanese government did not take any concrete measures while the Japanese trespassing on Ullŭngdo continued ceaselessly. The Korean government repeatedly protested. As the Japanese government feared that this might develop into a diplomatic dispute, Japanese Ministries of Home Affairs and Justice each issued an unofficial notification banning voyages to Ullŭngdo.

In September 1883, the Japanese government directly sent a secretary of the Home Ministry and a ship to pull out the Japanese on Ullŭngdo. and forcibly brought back all of the 254 Japanese engaged in logging. This was the first diplomatic negotiation the Japanese government conducted on Ullŭngdo.[31] Those Japanese withdrawn from the island were all criminals of illegal departure from Japan and illegal trading, but they were all released after being judged not guilty. It is noteworthy that the Japanese Foreign Ministry at that time raised an objection to the acquittal of all of them out of consideration for the Korean government on the matter.[32]

---

31   *Chosenkoku utsuryoto e hojin toko kinshino ken* (On the Prohibition of Japanese Voyages to Ullŭngdo of Korea) *Nihon gaiko bunsho* (Japanese Diplomatic Documents), Vols. 14, 15, 16.

32   *Chosenkoku utsuryoto e hankin toko no nihonjin hikimotoshi shobun* (On the Disposition of Re-

This incident of numerous Japanese clandestinely intruding into the Korean territory made the Korea government change its policy on Ullŭngdo: the vacant island policy enforced for several hundred years was abolished, and instead, an active development policy was implemented. Thus, in May 1882, Inspector Yi Kyu- wŏn was dispatched to Ullŭngdo and on the basis of his report an ordinance was enacted for the development of Ullŭngdo in December of the same year.[33] This was followed by the appointment of the chief of island of Ullŭngdo in the same year and the policy of settling the island started. Now Ullŭngdo became a real Korean territory, not just a Korea territory on maps.

In 1883, Kim Ok-kyŭn was appointed Commissioner for the Development of Southeast Islands and Whaling to push for an ambitious development of Ullŭngdo, but this did not come to fruition because of his fall from power.

After that the administrative structure of Ullŭngdo was reorganized several times, and in 1895, the island chief was upgraded to island supervisor; the Korean population increased gradually as the government offered tax exemption and encouraged migration to the island.[34] In October 1900, Ullŭngdo was elevated to the status of kun (county) whose magistrate was appointed from the central government. Ullŭngdo was transformed into a stabilized Korean society from a completely undeveloped state.

However, as the administrative structure was less well maintained than on the mainland, Ullŭngdo was subject to Japanese aggression ahead of other regions. Even after the Japanese withdrawal in 1883, the people from various parts of Japan continued sailing to Ullŭngdo without permission. Their purpose was originally to take out timber, but when worthy trees were exhausted

---

patriation of the Illegal Japanses Voyagers to Ullŭngdo of Korea) *Gaimusho Kiroku* (Foreign Ministry Records 3824), vol. 4.

33   According to his report, *Ullŭngdo kamch'al ilgi* (Diary of Inspection Trip to Ullŭngdo), the Japanese there thought the island was a Japanese possession, and they even built a pole stating "Matsushima of Great Japan." Yi Kyu-wŏn is furious and cites the incident of An Yong-bok. Taehan Kongnonsa (Korean Public Information Service), ed., *Tokdo* (Seoul: 1965), pp. 126-148.

34   There were about 2,500 people at the end of the 19th century.

by their logging, an increasingly greater number of Japanese fishermen came to the fishing grounds around Ullŭngdo.

The Korean government requested repeatedly in 1888, 1895, 1898, and 1899 that the Japanese government evacuate the Japanese from Ullŭngdo. This shows how persistent the Japanese trespassing was. According to an early investigation by the Japanese government, some 200 Japanese were staying at Ullŭngdo about the year 1900, and the number rose to over 1,000 depending on the season.[35]

These Japanese settled down gradually on Ullŭngdo. The Japanese government's policy towards the Japanese settlers also changed. As stated above, in the early 1880s the Japanese government formally apologized to the Korean government and took measures to ban such voyages in one way or other. However, after the Sino-Japanese War, the government ignored the Korean demand for withdrawal and gradually came to confront the Korean demand.[36]

This corresponds with Japan's overall intensification of aggression in Korea in the late 19th century. During the period, Japanese acquisition of railway and mining concessions and encroachment on monetary rights in Korea became more undisguised. The fishing situation under review in this article was no exception either.

The Japanese government in 1889 forced the Japan-Korea Fishing Regulations stipulating extraterritoriality and various unequal treatment. The Japanese fishing vessels invaded Korean coastal waters on a large scale and engaged in overfishing in a robber baron-like manner. A number of studies have shed light on frequent clashes that occurred between Korean fishermen with their livelihood threatened and the trespassing Japanese fishermen.[37]

---

35 *Utsuryoto ni okeru batsuboku kankei zikken* (Miscellaneou Cases Involving Felling on Ullŭngdo). *Gaimusho kiroku* (Foreign Ministry Records) 3532. Reference is made to the various records of the Foreign Ministry.

36 In September 1899, the Japanese government ordered the withdrawal of the Japanese on Ullŭngdo as part of its policy on Russia.

37 Pak Ku-byŏng, *Hanil Kŭndae ŏŏp kwan'gye yon'gu* (Study on Korea-Japan Fishery Relations

Towards the end of the 19th century, the Japanese government did not only left this advance of Japanese fishermen to their own initiative, but pushed its fishery policy harder and further.[38] A deep-sea fishing promotion law was implemented in 1898, and subsidized the development of pelagic fishing. At the same time, the highest official in the fishery administration, Director Maki Bokushin of the Agriculture-Commerce Ministry Fishery Department, inspected Korean coastal areas for one month beginning in June 1899. Then a Chosen Sea Fishing Cooperative was organized in every prefecture and a Federation of Chosen Sea Fishing Cooperatives in the capital city.

Further, in 1902, a Fishery Cooperative Law for Foreign Territorial Waters was enacted to develop the simple deep-sea fishing of the past into the settlement of the fishermen who had migrated. Under this government policy, each prefecture also carried out a policy of protecting fishing operations in the Korean coastal waters. In other words, the government and the people were united as one body to swarm into Korean fishing grounds from the end of the 19th century. There was no consideration at all that Korea was a foreign country and there were Korean fishermen.

Ullŭngdo was a case in point. What would happen when as many as 1,000 Japanese surged there during seasons as mentioned earlier? Kawakami says Japanese fishing at Ullŭngdo was legitimate under the "Korea-Japan Fishing Regulations."[39] But, in reality, even this unequal agreement cannot justify Japanese activities at Ullŭngdo because they did not pay the fishing tax stipulated in the regulations and were poachers. According to the regulations, if Japanese fishermen wanted to go to Ullŭngdo for fishing, they had to pay the

---

in Modern Times) *Pusan suscm dae yon'gu pogo* (Research Reports of Pusan Fishery College), (Pusan: 1967), vol. 7, no. 1. K Han U-gŭn, *Kaehanghu ilbon. ŏminŭi ch'imt'u* (Japanese Fishermen's Infiltration after the Opening of Ports), Tan'gukdae tongyanghak (Tan'guk University Oriental Study), no. 1, 1971.

38   Yoshida Keishi, Chosen *suisan kaihatsushi* (History of Korean Fishery Development), 1954, pp. 165-174.

39   Kawakami. *op. cit.*, pp. 198-199.

fishing tax first to the Korean government through the Japanese consulate in Pusan every year and receive licenses at the same time.

Also, according to the "trade regulations," they were supposed to pay export duties for their catch. The Japanese fishermen at Ullŭngdo did not follow this procedure and this clearly means that the Japanese consul in Pusan did not control them at all. As many Japanese data show, the Japanese fishermen came directly from their ports to the island and went back directly with their catch. Their fishing off Ullŭngdo was unjust, even in view of this unequal agreement. This is true of their logging and "export" of the timber too. It is clear that all Japanese logging on Ullŭngdo at the beginning was illegal. It seems that later some prices were to have been paid to local Koreans. Even so, since Ullŭngdo was not an open port, export could not have been carried out there. Therefore, Japanese taking out lumber involved tax evasion and smuggling. The Japanese who lived on this island which was not a Japanese concession were, therefore, all illegal residents.

In short, the Japanese activities on Ullŭngdo, whether fishing or lumbering, were all wrongful acts of aggression. It was not only a legal issue, but frequent clashes between the Japanese trespassers and the local Koreans occurred.[40]

This became widely known as Ullŭngdo Chief Pae Kye-ju brought charges. According to his report, "the Japanese come to the island every year, strut around with swords and guns; threaten people; chase after women; rob their goods; and indulge in unlawful acts, causing much harassment to islanders."[41]

Island Chief Pae went to Japan in July 1898, and demanded the police authorities of Shimane and Tottori prefecture control Japanese acts of

---

40 A report by Japanese government officials said relations between the peoples of the two countries were peaceful on Ullŭngdo, but it could not be trusted since they were instructed to return home with such a report. Hayashi Gonsuke, "Nikkun kanri utsuryoto shutcho ni kansuru ken (On an Official Trip to Ullŭngdo by Japanese and Korean Officials)," *Foreign Ministry Records*, 3532.

41 *Japanese Diplomatic Documents*, vol. 32, pp. 287-288.

violence, and he also brought charges of illegal tree felling and theft against several Japanese to the Matsue District Court. The Japanese prosecutor who investigated the case states: "at times there are said to be those who overpower them [Koreans] and if this trend continues, we cannot predict what would happen there."[42]

Chief Pae also made a detailed report on the situation to the Korean government, and this became a diplomatic issue between the two governments.[43] This was also frequently reported in the Korean newspaper of that time, *Hwangsŏng sinbum* (Capital Gazette). The Korean government demanded the Japanese withdrawal from Ullŭngdo anew, but the Japanese government took a position that no such dispute existed.

Then a joint on-the-spot investigation was conducted by inspector U Yong-jŏng of the Ministry of Home Affairs and Japanese Pusan Vice Consul Akazuka Masasuke; this did not settle the matter. So, the Korean government again requested the Japanese pullout from Ullŭngdo in accordance with the treaty between the two countries, whether or not a dispute existed.

The Japanese government acknowledged that the Japanese residents on Ullŭngdo were in violation of the treaty provisions but claimed that it did not have any obligation to evacuate them directly. Furthermore, the Japanese government argued that the Korean government should be held responsible for acquiescing in the Japanese residence in Ullŭngdo for more than 10 years and demanded that they accept this *fait accompli* and formally allow the Japanese to live there.

The two governments' charges and counter-charges were repeated thereafter. In December 1901, Japanese Minister Hayashi proposed to station Japanese police under the pretext of a need to control the Japanese as trouble

---

42 "*Honponin no toko narabi zairyu torishimarino ken* (On the Control of Japanese Voyage and Sojourn)," *Foreign Ministry Records*, 3532.

43 "Utsuryoto batsuboku ni kansuru ken (Re. Logging on Ullŭngdo)," *Japanese Diplomatic Documents*, vol. 32.

between the two peoples occurred frequently.[44] Under the treaty, Japan had no right to station its police on Ullŭngdo, but he proposed to solve the local issue by posting the Japanese police there since the Korean government was not powerful enough to make the Japanese leave Ullŭngdo.

It was a thief's logic, but as the Korean government was at a loss to cope with the frequent troubles and did not positively oppose it, Japan implemented it forcibly. In March 1902, a police inspector and three policemen from the Pusan Japanese consulate were dispatched to the island and stationed there permanently. They professed to protect and control the Japanese nationals in conformity with the Japanese laws, but it is clear what role these Japanese police played at the scene of aggression.

From a fragmentary report by the Japanese police inspector one can infer that the Japanese police confronted County Chief Sim Hŭng-t'aek who tried to block the Japanese smuggling of lumber and pushed their way to protect them.[45] In 1904, Japan set up a post-office on Ullŭngdo and opened a ferry service between the island and Hamada on the western coast of Japan.[46]

Thus, immediately before the Russo-Japanese War, the Japanese had built a firm position on Ullŭngdo, with the support of the Japanese government. Under the protection of the Japanese police, many Japanese openly lived on Ullŭngdo illegally, smuggled out lumber, and engaged in illegal fishing. In short, Ullŭngdo's sovereignty was infringed by Japanese imperialists earlier than the mainland as it was Korea's frontier and was placed under Japanese domination.

---

44 "*Utsuryoto keisatsukan chuzaisho setchino ken* (On the Establishment of a Police Station on Ullŭngdo)," *Foreign Ministry Records*, 3532.

45 Police Inspector Arima Takanori, "Report Dated April 28, 1903," *Foreign Ministry Records*, 3532.

46 Many of the Japanese on Ullŭngdo were from Shimane prefecture, mostly from Oki Island. Also, the ratio between the Japanese residents and the Koreans was overwhelmingly in favor of the Japanese, the best in Korea, providing an excellent place for Japanese emigrants. Yoshida Keishi, *op. cit.*, pp, 469-470.

B. Japanese Fishing off Takeshima/Tokdo

As in the 17th century, the Japanese passage to Ullŭngdo was followed by their use of Takeshima/Tokdo, and that eventually became the basis for Japan's claim to territorial incorporation. Let us now look into Japan's "effective management" of the island.

From the end of the 19th century, Japanese fishermen from the San'in region sailed to Ullŭngdo for fishing and made a brief stopover at Takeshima/Tokdo for some fishing.[47] This fact can be confirmed by a recollection of the Japanese fisherman of the time.[48]

Nakai Yozaburo of Saigocho of Okinoshima was one of those fishermen. He took note of sea lions inhabiting Takeshima/Tokdo, when the prices of leather and oil rose immediately before the Russo-Japanese War. Not as part of catching fish and gathering shells, he started to hunt sea lions in earnest on Takeshima/Tokdo, beginning in 1903.[49] Concerning Takeshima/Tokdo fishing at the beginning of the 20th century, the *Chosen suiroshi* (Korean Sealanes) published by the Japanese Navy's Hydrographic Department states as follows:

> Takeshima [the Liancourt Rocks]: Koreans call this island Tokdo and Japanese fishermen, Liancoto. When the warship *Tsushima* surveyed this island, November in the 37th year of Meiji (1904), there were small thatched huts for fishermen on the East Islet, but they were said to have been destroyed by wind and waves. Every summer, dozens of people come from Ullŭngdo to catch sea lions. They build huts on this island

---

47   The divers with submersible gadgets went to Takeshi ma/Tokdo for fishing for two to three days on their way to Ullŭngdo, while some went there for two to three days in the good weather while fishing off Ullŭngdo Okura Hukuichi, *Takeshima oyobi utsuryoto* (Takeshima and Ullŭngdo), (Matsue, Japan: Hokosha, 1907), p. 11.

48   Kawakami, *op. cit.*, pp. 200-208.

49   Nakai Yozaburo, "Liancoto ryodo hennyu narabini kashisage negai (An Application for Territorial Incorporation of Liancourt Island and Its Lease)", *Foreign Ministry Records*, 1417.

and stay there for about 10 days each time.

Ullŭngdo, also called Matsushima [Dagelet Island]: Main activity is abalone gathering and a large quantity of dried abalones are exported. The sea animal called todo (sea lions) inhabit Takeshima southeast of this island and beginning in the 37th year of Meiji (1904) the people of this island began catching them. Sea lion catching is conducted for six months from April to September; at present three groups of fishing vessels are engaged in it (with each group catching about five head). Besides sea lions the Japanese are said to gather daily an average 1,130 kin (680 kg) of abalone by using two sets of diving apparatus and two steam boats.[50]

There was an argument between the governments of Korea and Japan as to whether "those people who came from Ullŭngdo" were Japanese or Koreans. Let's look at the data on which this is based as it is difficult to judge by this statement. The basic source of the above description is the reports by two Japanese warships, the *Niitaka* and the *Tsushima*. The former is more important. The logbook of the *Niitaka* in its entry on September 25, 1904, clearly states that the information was obtained from a man who actually saw [Liancourt] from Ullŭngdo and records as follows:

> Koreans call the Liancourt Rocks Tokdo, while Japanese fishermen call it Lianco. It is possible to moor vessels between the two rocks, but a small boat is usually pulled ashore. When the sea is rough and it is difficult to anchor, boats usually take refuge in Ullŭngdo until the weather calms down. Those who come from Ullŭngdo to catch sea lions use a Japanese vessel that can load 60 to 70 *koku* (307 to 358 U.S. bushels), and build huts to stay there for about 10 days each time; the catch is said to be

---

50   Japanese Navy Hydrographic Dept., ed., *Chosen suiroshi* (Korean Sealanes), 2nd revised ed., 1907, pp. 451-457.

plentiful; and the number of the crew sometimes exceeds 40 to 50, but they talk about the lack of fresh water.[51]

Another historical source is an article by Geographer Tanaka Akamaro based on various Navy reports and the report by the governor of Shimane prefecture on his inspection trip to Takeshima in August 1905 as follows:

On the East Islet, there are thatched-roof huts which belong to the Takeshima Fishing Company of Nakai Yozaburo and others. (Both the huts and vessel were washed away by a storm on August 8, 1905). These huts are for fishermen who come here in summers to catch sea lions but they are badly damaged and only traces remain now. The fishermen are based in Ullŭngdo and use wooden boats capable of loading 60 to 70 *koku,* and when fishing is over or when the boats cannot be berthed because of heavy seas, they take refuge at Ullŭngdo as soon as the weather calms down.[52]

Tanaka's article also contains the descriptions after Japan's incorporation of Takeshima/Tokdo. It is clear from these data that the sea lions hunting on Takeshima/Tokdo that began in 1903 was conducted mainly by Japanese. But, Koreans were not totally uninvolved with this hunting. The *Korean Sealanes* in its section on Ullŭngdo clearly distinguishes the Japanese from the Koreans but those who went to Takeshima/Tokdo for fishing are simply called the inhabitant of this island. Kawakami also acknowledges the fact that Koreans had taken part in Takeshima's sea lion hunting, although limiting them to

51   *Gunkan niitaka kodo nisshi* (The Logbook of Warship *Niitaka's* Operation), preserved in the History Dept. of Japan's Self-Defense Agency.

52   "*Okinokuni takeshima ni kansuru chirigakujono chishiki* (Geographical Knowledge on Takeshima of Oki Province)," *Journal of Earth Science,* no. 210, (1906).

those hired by Japanese.[53] There is no room for any doubt that it was mainly the Japanese fishermen who hunted the sea lions although some Koreans were involved.

What is noteworthy is that the Japanese fishermen such as Nakai Yozaburo were described as "inhabitants" of Ullŭngdo. They lived in Ullŭngdo and went out to Takeshima/Tokdo from their base in Ullŭngdo and promptly returned when a storm was gathering. In other words, those Japanese fishermen's activities on and off Takeshima/Tokdo would be viewed historically in the vein of the Japanese invasion of Ullŭngdo.

If that is the case, what kind of relationship did the Koreans on Ullŭngdo have with Takeshima/Tokdo? It was already stated that despite Kawakami's persistent denials, Takeshima/Tokdo can be seen from Ullŭngdo and that Koreans knew the island well. It is also clear through the warship *Niitaka*'s report that Koreans used the name of Tokdo before Japan incorporated it.[54]

In order to deny the possibility that Koreans on Ullŭngdo utilized Takeshima/Tokdo before Japan's incorporation of the island, Kawakami asserts that Koreans did not know about fishing. Mainly on the basis of the *Kankoku suisanshi* (Korea's Marine Products), Kawakami says that Koreans on Ullŭngdo started fishing after the Japanese taught them how to catch cuttlefish in 1907. He also observes that only Japanese gathered abalones, and no Koreans ever did it.

So, he concludes that it was not possible for Koreans to go to Takeshima/Tokdo for fishing even if they knew about the existence of the island.[55] But, Kawakami's assertion is disowned by the data he himself uses. For example, the *Navy's Kan'ei suiroshi* (The Sealanes of the World) writes about Ullŭngdo

53 *Kawakami, op. cit.*, pp. 188-190.

54 That "it is written as Tokdo" in the above mentioned data shows that the county chief who belonged to the intellectual class was cognizant of Takeshima/Tokdo. But, in some books, the name of Usando is still used. *Ibid*

55 *Kawakami op. cit.*, pp, 177-187.

as follows in Volume 2, Chapter 2:

> As for products, the island abounds in abalone and various kinds of fish in large quantity, and vegetables are found there too. In spring and summer, Koreans come to this island, build Korean-style boats and send them to the mainland and gather a large amount of crustaceans.[56]

Also, Secretary Takao Kenzo of the Japanese Foreign Ministry who was sent to Ullŭngdo in September 1899, reports[57]

> the island's native population at present is about 2,000 in some 500 dwellings, of them half are farmers and another half fishermen, and there are some carpenters making boats.

There are also records and documents between the mid-19th century and the early 20th century in Europe and Japan, which describe the fishing activities, particularly abalone gathering by the Korean fishermen in Ullŭngdo.[58] Ignoring all these would be too arbitrary.

Kawakami also refers to the crudeness of Korean navigational techniques of that time, but many Koreans were going between Ullŭngdo and the mainland every year, which is far more distant than between Ullŭngdo and Takeshima/Tokdo. It is quite natural for Korean fishermen who depended on abalone gathering for a living to go to an island rich in fish and located at a visible distance. Just as the Japanese fishermen recollected their fishing on and off Takeshima/Tokdo as mentioned already, an elderly Korean also gives his

---

56   *The Sealanes of the World, op. cit.,* p. 400.

57   Takao Kenzo, "The Report Dated Oct 3, 1899," *Foreign Ministry Records,* 3532.

58   Blakeney, William., R, N., "*On the Coasts of Cathay and Cipango, Forty Years Ago,*" (London: 1902); Griffis, William Elliot, *Corea, the Hermit Nation* (London: 1905).

246

firsthand experience of going to Takeshima/Tokdo for fishing.[59]

The Korean fishing on and off Ullŭngdo rapidly dwindled because of the invasion of many Japanese fishermen. The description in the *Records on Korea's Marine Products*[60] that "abalone gathering is entrusted to the Japanese and no native islanders are engaged in it" merely means that Korean fishermen formerly engaged in abalone gathering were pushed out of the fishing grounds by the new mode of Japanese fishing with such technology as diving apparatus.[61]

Accordingly, while even the indigenous fishing grounds off Ullŭngdo were robbed by the Japanese, the fishing rights on that distant islet could not become any problem. It was more than natural that the Japanese should lead the sea lion hunting on Takeshima/Tokdo from 1903.

If the concept of effective management is applied for form's sake, the Japanese side is clearly in an advanced position vis-a-vis Takeshima/Tokdo on the eve of the 1905 territorial incorporation. However, when viewed from the historical point of view, imperialism conducts "management" beyond its borders. The Japanese management of Takeshima/Tokdo in the early 20th century took place as a part of the Japanese advance to Ullŭngdo against the background of the government's aggressive policy.[62]

---

59 Hong Chae-hyŏn (born 1862) who moved to this island in 1883, recalled that "at the time of the development, the people on Ullŭngdo discovered Tokdo immediately, and went to Tokdo many times to gather seaweeds and abalones and catch sea lions. I myself went there several dozens of times." *Tokdo, op. cit.*, p. 30; also see, Yi Kyu-gyŏng (1764-1856), *Oju yŏn mun changjŏn san' go* (Random Expatiations of Oju), (Seoul: 1957), vol. 1, p. 655. He says that Koreans from Kangwŏndo, Ullŭngdo caught sea lions there.

60 Korea's Ministry of Commerce and Industry, ed., *Chosen suisanshi*. (Records on Korea's Marine Products), (Seoul: Nikkan Printing Co., 1910), vol. 2, p. 715.

61 Concerning the fishery dispute between Korea and Japan at Ullŭngdo, see Pak Ku- byŏng, "*Sipkusaegimal Hanilgan ŭi ŏŏp e chŏggyong doen younghae samhaeri wŏnch'ik e kwan hayŏ* (Concerning the Principle of Three-mile Territorial Waters Applied to Fisheries between Korea and Japan at the End of the 19th Century," *Hanil yŏn' gu* (Korea-Japan Study), vol. I, 1972.

62 The relations between Ullŭngdo and Takeshima/Tokdo were gradually strengthened and in the 1930s, 40 fishermen (including 2 to 3 Japanese) went fishing off Takeshima/Tokdo. Japan For-

The incorporation of Takeshima/Tokdo could have been justified only when the island had completely been a *terra nullius* and when the Korean government and people in the face of Japan's imperialist aggression had not raised an objection to the Japanese action of incorporation. The absence of the first condition has already been pointed out in the preceding chapter and the latter will be discussed in the following chapter.

It was in 1903 that Nakai started hunting sea lions on Takeshima/Tokdo, but as many competitors appeared the following year, the number of sea lions declined sharply. So, he thought of monopolizing the fishing ground by excluding competitors and went to Tokyo for maneuvering.

IV. Japan's Territorial Incorporation of Takeshima

A. Japanese Government's Military Demand

As the Russo-Japanese War broke out, the Japanese government found a new value in Takeshima/Tokdo from the strategic standpoint of war execution, quite apart from Nakai Yozaburo's personal plan.

The Japanese government had already decided at a cabinet meeting before the start of the war that "Korea should be placed under Japan's influence by force under whatever circumstances,"[63] and again made the Korean government acknowledge in the Korea-Japan protocol that Japan would temporarily expropriate the places needed for military purposes.[64] In reality, Japan went on tightening its military control over all of Korea without any treaties. In this

---

eign Ministry Asian Affairs Bureau, ed., *Takeshima gyogyo no henseng* (Changes in Fishiery off Takeshima) (Tokyo: 1953), pp. 17, 36, 37.

63   Japan Foreign Ministry, *Nihon gaiko nenpyo narabini juyo bunsho* (Chronicle of Japanese Diplomacy and Important Documents), vol. I (Tokyo: 1965), pp. 217-219, 223-224.

64   *Ibid.*

section, the Navy's military facilities will be taken up for discussion. Before the war, Japan was working on the military telegraphic communication lines and watchtowers, and decided to expand those facilities to Korea when the war started.

In June 1904, tension suddenly heightened in the Korean Strait as Russia's Vladivostok fleet showed up there and sank Japanese transports one after another. The Japanese Navy built the watch-towers on the coastal areas of Kyushu and Chugoku, in parallel with those of Chukpyŏn Bay, Ulsan, Kŏmŭndo, and Chejudo in southeastern Korea and linked them with submarine cables.

Chart3

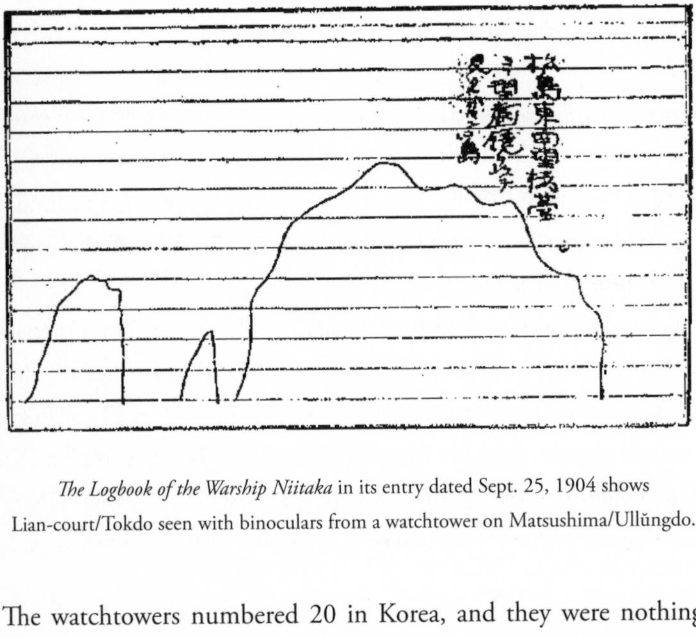

The *Logbook of the Warship Niitaka* in its entry dated Sept. 25, 1904 shows Lian-court/Tokdo seen with binoculars from a watchtower on Matsushima/Ullŭngdo.

The watchtowers numbered 20 in Korea, and they were nothing other than military occupation.[65] On July 5, 1904, watchtowers were built on Ullŭngdo and it was decided to link them with the Japanese Navy anchor-

---

65   Japan Naval General Staff, ed., *Gokuhi meiji sanju nana hachinen kaisenshi* (Top Secret History of Naval Battles in the 37th and 38th Years of Meiji), vol. 4, I-27, p. 218-276.

age in Chukpyŏn Bay on the Korean mainland by military submarine cables. Ullŭngdo's two watchtowers were one at the southeastern part (East Tower with six men posted) and the other at the northwestern part (West Tower with six men posted). Their construction started on August 3, 1904, and the operation began on September 2 of the same year. The submarine cable was installed under the threat of the Vladivostok fleet and completed on September 25 of the same year.[66] Through this cable, the watchtowers on Ullŭngdo were able to communicate directly with the Japanese naval base in Sasebo through the Korean mainland. The stationing of a Japanese military force on Ullŭngdo meant the further violation of Korean sovereignty over the island where the Japanese had already built its superior position.

In a series of construction work on Ullŭngdo as well as supply activities, and also in the course of patrol activities in these waters, a lot of information was gained about Takeshima/Tokdo.[67] Namely, the Navy already paid attention to the island's value well before Nakai Yozaburo submitted a request to the government, and had already started taking action even before the Japanese government officially decided to incorporate the island.

On November 13, 1904, the Japanese Naval General Staff ordered the warship *Tsushima* to inspect the Liancourt Island/Tokdo and see whether it was suitable for the installation of a telegraphic station (not radio station) there.[68] It was a survey to examine whether it was possible to build a watchtower there to be linked by submarine cable with Ullŭngdo. The *Tsushima* arrived at the Liancourt Island on November 20, and this was the first-ever survey of Takeshima/Tokdo by the Japanese government. The *Tsushima*'s captain reported that although there was some topographical difficulty, it was

---

66   *Ibid.* pp. 48-57.

67   The report by the warship *Niitaka* was made at the time of the work to install the cable on Ullŭngdo.

68   *Gunkan tsushima senji nisshi* (The Logbook of Warship *Tsushima* During the War), (kept in the Self-Defense Agency War History Department).

possible to build a structure on the East Islet.[69]

The Japanese government's interest in Takeshima/Tokdo at that time was only for its military value. As it was absolutely impossible to engage in construction work on Takeshima/Tokdo during the winter, Japan, without starting the work, faced the decisive battle with Russia's Baltic fleet. As the seas around Ullŭngdo and Takeshima/Tokdo became the main sea battleground, the island's military value came to be highly valued.[70]

The Japanese Navy drafted a plan on May 30 immediately following the sea battle, and on June 13, 1905, instructed the warship *Hashitade* to go to the island for a further detailed survey.[71] The Navy thus set up a plan for comprehensive facilities in the Sea of Japan (East Sea) including Ullŭngdo and Takeshima/Tokdo on June 24 of the same year. The plan called for (1) the construction of a large watchtower on the northern part of Ullŭngdo (nine men to be posted) and a wireless telegraphic station, (2) the construction of the long-pending watchtower on Takeshima/Tokdo (to be manned by four men), (3) the watchtowers of the two islands to be linked by submarin cables which are to be extended to the watch-tower on Oki Island. These were illegal military facilities without regard to national boundaries.

The construction of the new watchtower on Ullŭngdo started on July 14, 1905, and was completed on August 16, while that on Takeshima/Tokdo began on July 25 and completed on August 19. The original plan to link Takeshima/Tokdo with Oki Island by submarine cables were changed when the peace treaty with Russia was concluded in September 1905, and instead the line was set up between Takeshima/Tokdo and Matsue. This work was started at the end of October 1905, and a link from Ullŭngdo to Matsue via

---

69   Japan Naval General Staff, *op. cit.*, reference documents, pp. 366-367.

70   The name of Takeshima became widely known in Japan due to the newspaper reports about this naval battle.

71   *Gunkan hashitade senji nisshi* (The Logbook of the Warship *Hashitade* during the War), War History Dept., Japan Self-Defense Agency.

Takeshima/Tokdo was completed on November 9 of the same year.[72] Consequently in 1905, a network of military communication lines were completed from the Korean mainland (Chukpyŏn) to Ullŭngdo, Takeshima/Tokdo, and Matsue.

In short, for the Japanese government, Takeshima/Tokdo was nothing more than an object of military value, and it was closely related to and inseparable from military occupation of various parts of Korea at that time.

B. Opinions of Japanese Government Bureaucrats

In the early autumn of 1904, Nakai Yozaburo went to Tokyo to influence the Japanese government and obtain exclusive fishing rights to Takeshima/Tokdo. At that time, how Nakai regarded the territorial ownership of Takeshima/Tokdo was extremely important as he was in a position to know the local situation best.

The *Shimanekenshi* (Records of Shimane prefecture) published in 1922 by Shimane prefecture Education Board states in the Takeshima/Tokdo section: "There is a fear of many ill effects as many regions compete in overfishing in 1904. Believing this island to be Korean territory, and planning to apply to the government for lease of the island (dotted lines by the author), Nakai went to the capital to explain the situation at the Ministry of Agriculture and Commerce." In the Korea-Japan dispute, the Japanese government ignored this description in the historical data simply as the editor's misunderstanding.[73] Is it real?

There are two sources in which Nakai himself remarked about the territorial incorporation of Takeshima/Tokdo. First is the *Takeshima oyobi utsuryoto*

---

72   Japan Naval General Staff, *op. cit.*, pp. 20-21, 93-95.

73   Japan Foreign Ministry, *Kaigai chosa geppo* (Overseas Research Monthly), Nov. 1954, p. 68.

(Takeshima and Ullŭngdo) by Okuhara Hukuichi who narrates what he heard "personally from Nakai" on March 25, 1906 as follows:

> Nakai believed that the Liancourt island was Korean territory and decided to file a request with the Korean government for its lease. As soon as the fishing season ended in 1904, he went to the capital and met Fishery Bureau Director Maki at the Ministry of Agriculture and Commerce through an official of the Ministry named Fujita Kantaro from Oki. The Director supported his idea and took steps to ascertain the status of Liancourt Island from the Navy's Hydrographic Department. Nakai immediately went to see Director Kimotsuki of Hydro-graphic Department and heard from him that there was no definite evidence of the ownership of Liancourt, which is 10 nautical miles nearer to the Japanese mainland than the Korean mainland, and that so long as there is a Japanese who is engaged in management of the island, it is natural to incorporate it into Japanese territory. …

> Finally, Nakai made up his mind and submitted the request for territorial incorporation of Liancoiirt Island and its lease to the three Ministers of Home Ministry, Foreign Ministry and Agriculture-Commerce. Nakai presented himself to the Home Ministry Local Affairs Department and explained the situation to Secretary Inoue. He also went to the Foreign Ministry through a member of the House of Peers with the introduction of Doctor of Laws Kuwada from his native town and met Political Affairs Bureau Director Yamaza and discussed this problem with him. With Dr. Kuwada's active help, Nakai inquired at Shimane prefecture about its opinion. Then Shimane prefecture, after confirming the view of Oki Island, submitted a report to the higher authority and as a result, the incorporation of the island was decided at a cabinet meeting, with

Liancourt Island named Takeshima.[74]

From this data it is clear that: first, Nakai believed that Takeshima/Tokdo was clearly Korean territory and tried to apply to the Korean government for its lease; second, it was definitely the Japanese government which changed his request into that for incorporation of an ownerless land.

The second source is the personal history Nakai submitted to Oki Island. Nakai attaches a summary of his Takeshima management as follows:

> As I thought that the island was Korean territory attached to Ullŭngdo, I went to the capital trying to submit a request to the Residency-General. But, as suggested by Fishery Bureau Director Maki Bokushin, I came to question Korea's ownership of Takeshima. And at the end of my investigation with the matter, I convinced myself that this island was absolutely ownerless through the conclusion by the then Hydrographic Director Admiral Kimotsuki. Accordingly, I submitted an application through the Home Ministry to the three Ministers of Home Ministry, Foreign Ministry and Agriculture-Commerce Ministry for incorporation of this island into Japanese territory and for its lease to me.

> The Home Ministry authorities had an opinion that the gains would be extremely small while the situation would become grave if the acquisition of a barren islet suspected of being Korean territory at this point of time [during the Russo-Japanese War] would amplify the suspicions of various foreign countries that Japan has an ambition to annex Korea. Thus, my pertition was rejected.

---

74   Okuhara Hukuichi, *op. cit.*, pp. 27-32. Also Okuhara Hekiun (Hukuichi), "Takeshima enkaku ko (A Study of History of Takeshima)," *Rekishi chiri* (A Study of History & Geography), vol. 8, no. 6, 1906.

Undaunted, I rushed to the Foreign Ministry to discuss the matter in detail with the then Political Affairs Bureau Director Yamaza Enjiro. He said the incorporation was urgent particularly under the present situation, and it is absolutely necessary and advisable to construct watchtowers and install wireless or submarine cable and keep watch on the hostile warships. Particularly in terms of diplomacy, he told me not to worry about the Home Ministry view. He asked me in high spirits to urge the Home Ministry to refer his application speedily to the Foreign Ministry; in this way Takeshima came under our country's dominion.[75]

As this data was recorded several years after the incorporation, the Korean government was referred to as the "Residency-General" by mistake. But, it was written by Nakai himself and, therefore, describes in detail the Japanese government's posture to cope with the situation. The important points follow:

Firstly, the Home Ministry bureaucrats clearly opposed the incorporation of Takeshima/Tokdo. As stated above, the Home Ministry confirmed in 1877 that Takeshima/Tokdo was Korean territory the same as Ullŭngdo, and these records and this information were handed down to its bureaucrarts. Therefore, they hesitated to conclude that Takeshima/Tokdo was an ownerless island even when Japan started its aggression in Korea.

Secondly, it was the three men, Maki Bokushin, Kimotsuki Kenko and Yamaza Enjiro who forcefully carried out the incorporation over the opposition of the Home Ministry bureaucrats. The personal backgrounds of these three men are very interesting. Maki Bokushin, as mentioned before, had been the Fishery Bureau Director of the Agriculture-Commerce Ministry, the highest fishery administrator, for a long time and took the lead in develop-

75   Shimane ken koho bunshoka (Public Information & Document Div., Shimane prefecture), ed., *Takeshima Kankei Shiryo* (Materials on Takeshima), 1953, vol. I. From the end of Nakai's personal history, it is inferred to have been made in 1910.

ing Japan's stagnant fishing into a deep-sea industry.[76] However, that policy meant intrusion into the Korean coastal waters and expansion of its zone of operation.

Kimotsuki Kenko was a specialist bureaucrat who had spent his whole career in the Hydrographic Department and laid the firm foundation for Japan's waterway administration. In peacetime the department engaged in collecting and keeping ordinary hydrographic information and in time of war became a strategic organ providing necessary information for direct military operations. At the time of the Russo-Japanese War, Kimotsuki devoted himself to the military operations in the coastal waters of Korea and Manchuria, in the capacity of Hydrographic Department Director.[77]

Director Yamaza Enjiro of the Foreign Ministry Political Affairs Bureau was known to have been under the influence of the nationalist, rightist organization of the Genyosha and have pushed, together with Minister Komura Jutaro, for the Ministry's hardline external policy as well as the policy of advance into the Continent. Before becoming the director, he was assigned to the consulate and the legation in Korea and planned and worked busily to acquire various interests for Japan.[78] In the incorporation these bureaucrats forced, it is quite natural that Korea's sovereignty and claims were not taken into consideration.

Thirdly, the grounds for incorporation were clearly made known. Kimotsuki's claim that Takeshima/Tokdo was owned by no one at all in 1904 was totally different from the past position taken by the Navy's Hydrographic Department, as stated already. In spite of this, he suggested the application of the theory of "occupation of a *terra nullius*" on the basis of the simple fact that

---

76 "Hachinen mo tsutometa suisan kyokucho Maki Bokushin (Fishery Bureau Director Maki Bokushin Who Served for Eight Years)," *Suisankai* (Fisheries World), nos. 975, 1966.

77 Maritime Safety Agency, *op. ci.*, pp. 21-24, 83-88.

78 Hasegawa Shun, *Yamaza Enjiro* (1967); Ichiyu Masao, ed., *Yamaza enjiro den* (Biography of Yamaza Enjiro), 1974.

Nakai started fishing on this island in the previous year. But, this was only the superficial theory, and what motivated the Japanese government was the military need for the facilities to cope with the Russian naval fleet, as Yamaza said.

In the final analysis, the incorporation of Takeshima/Tokdo was similar to the military actions Japan took in many other parts of Korea at that time for the execution of the war, by infringing upon Korea's sovereignty. Only, it took advantage of an individual fisherman who sought to monopolize the fishing ground and did not end at its occupation but took the form of its incorporation. If Japan's military occupation of the Korean Peninsula was the prerequisite for the "annexation of Korea," the incorporation could be said to have been a step forward. Under the instruction of the three men mentioned above, Nakai submitted to the three Ministries of Home Ministry, Foreign Ministry and Agriculture-Commerce a "Request for Territorial Incorporation of Liancourt Island and Its Lease" on September 29, 1904, and the Japanese government decided at a cabinet meeting on January 28, 1905 on the incorporation of the island in the form of granting the application.

C. Japan's Public Notice and Korea's Response

On February 22, 1905, Shimane prefecture announced Public Notice No. 40, naming Liancourt Island Takeshima and placing it under the Chief of Oki Island. The Japanese government did not announce this decision in the official gazette, nor make a public announcement on the central government level. One can cite as a precedent of the Japanese government establishing territorial sovereignty over an island related to foreign countries, the case of the Ogasawara Islands in 1876. At that time, the Japanese government made the decision after negotiating with Britain and the United States which were deeply related with the islands, to win their understanding. Japan also notified

12 European countries and the U.S.A. of its action.[79]

As for the acquisition of Takeshima/Tokdo which some Japanese thought might belong to Korea, the Japanese government did not make inquiry of the Korean government, much less notify it of the action of incorporation afterwards. Korea learned of the Japan's incorporation in March 1906, one year after the measure was taken. A Shimane prefecture delegation led by an administrative official, Zinzai Yutaro, dropped by Ullŭngdo after making an inspection tour of Takeshima/Tokdo. On March 28, Zinzai Yutaro and his party visited Ullŭngdo County Chief Sim Hŭng-t'aek and notified him of the Japanese incorporation of Takeshima/Tokdo. Surprised at the unexpected news, Shim reported immediately to the central government the next day as follows:

Tokdo belonging to this county is located in the sea 100 *ri* from this county. A Japanese steamship moored at Todongp'o in Udo on the 4th day of the month about 8:00 a.m and a group of Japanese officials came to my office and said, "we came to inspect Tokdo since it is now Japanese territory." The group included official Zinzai, of Oki Island in Shimane prefecture, Director Yoshida Meigo of the Tax Supervision Bureau, police sub-station chief, Inspector Kageyama Iwahachiro, one policeman, one local assemblyman, a doctor and a technician and about a dozen followers. They have come for the purpose of finding out firstly, the number of households, population, and land production, and secondly, the number of personnel and expenditure. The record having being made, we submit this report for your reference.[80]

---

79   Yasuoka Teruo, *Meiji ishinto ryodo mondai* (The Meiji Restoration and the Question of Territory), 1980, pp. 196-213.

80   Yang T'ae-jin, *Han'guk kuggyong yongt'o kwan'gye munhŏnjip* (References on Korean Territory and Boundaries) (Seoul: n. p., 1979), p. 11 March 5 in the lunar calendar corresponds to March 29 in the solar calendar.

258

Lunar March 5, 10th year of Kwangmu (1906)

The visit to Ullŭngdo by the Zinzai party was well known, but this data has not been examined in Japan at all. In the dispute with Korea, the Japanese government even doubted the existence of this document itself. As its basis, a Japanese scholar writes that "one sea lion caught on Takeshima was presented to the County Chief, who thanked them for the gift. Such a treatment would not have happened if the County Chief had considered Takeshima as belonging to Ullŭngdo."[81]

But, that is to ignore the difficult situation Ullŭngdo was faced with at that time. As stated before, Japanese soldiers and police were permanently stationed on Ullŭngdo and more than 300 Japanese lived in and around Todong where the county office was located. The fact that Zinzai and his party investigated at will the number of households, population and geographical features in the foreign territory of Ullŭngdo graphically illustrates the one-sided power relations of that time.

If County Chief Sim did not openly raise objection to Zinzai and his party on the territorial problem, it was due to the pressure from the Japanese. His courteous treatment of the Japanese did not mean that he approved Zinzai remarks. This also does not justify the Japanese denial of this data itself.

Kawakami elaborates on the Zinzai visit to County Chief Sim, but does not refer to the county chief's report at all. As this data is widely used by Korean scholars in their research and contains extremely important contents, Kawakami's silence on this point can only be taken as a deliberate cover-up of the historical data.

County Chief Sim clearly states in his report that Takeshima /Tokdo belongs to Ullŭngdo. He reported on the unexpected movements of the Japanese officials who claimed the island as Japanese territory and asked the central government for instruction.

---

81   *Overseas Research Monthly, op. cit.*, November, 1954, p. 68.

Here, the island once called Usando is called Tokdo. There are many theories about the origin of the name of Tokdo, but Koreans already called and wrote the name of the island as Tokdo (獨島) before Japan's incorporation of the island as can be seen above.

Sim's report was delivered to the magistrate of Kangwǒn Province and Acting Magistrate Yi Myǒng-nae in turn reported it to the State Council (Ǔijǒngbu) Minister Pak Chae-sǒn. Minister Pak is said to have stated that the claim that Tokdo had become Japan's possession was groundless, and he instructed the officials to investigate in detail the Tokdo situation and report on what Japanese were doing there.

The administrative documents recording these facts are said to be still extant in Korea, but the full text has not been made public.[82] However, one can easily find the great repercussions triggered by Sim's report in the newspapers of that time.

Korea's representative newspaper of that time, the *Hwangsǒng sinmun* (Capital Gazette) reported an article entitled "Local Ullǔngdo Report to the Home Ministry" on May 9, 1906 about the Zinzai Incident by quoting the Ullǔngdo County Chief's report to the Home Ministry.[83] The content of the newspaper report is almost the same as the report from County Chief Sim, and appears to have originated from the Home Ministry. Therefore, there is no question about the existence of County Chief Sim's report.

Another national newspaper which existed at that time, *Taehan Maeil Sinbo* (Korea Daily News), a nationally circulated newspaper, also reported this incident. It carried the following story on May 1, 1906:

Unusually strange things are happening. Ullǔngdo County Chief Sim

---

82   "Haksǔl chwadam; tokdo munjae chaejomyǒng (Academic Round-Table: Reex- amination of the Question of Tokdo)," *Han'guk hakpo* (Journal of Korean Studies), vol. 24.

83   Han'guk munhwa kaebalsa (Korea Cultural Development Co.), ed., *Hwangsǒng sinmun* (Capital Gazette), vol. 13, (Seoul: 1976), p. 30.

Hŭng-t'aek reported to the Home Ministry that a party of Japanese government officials came to Ullŭngdo and professed that Tokdo belonging to Ullŭngdo was now Japanese territory, and took record of the topography, population and land size, etc. The Home Ministry sent a directive saying that it is strange for them to record the population of other country while on an excursion, and as their claim to Tokdo as Japanese territory is totally groundless, the story is really shocking.[84]

The first half of the article merely summarized County Chief Sim's report, but the second half is valuable in finding out the reactions of the central government. Namely, Korea's central government was recognizing from the beginning that Tokdo was Korean territory. Therefore, it harbors a suspicion of the movement of the Japanese officials who made incomprehensible remarks.

It is certain that many Korean people learned through this newspaper coverage of the Japanese move to incorporate Takeshi- ma/Tokdo into its territory and must have read it as an aggression into Korean territory. For example, Hwang Hyon who lived in Kurye, Chollado, at that time writes in a note that "the Japanese are making a false statement that Tokdo belongs to Japan while it is our own territory."[85]

In other words, Korea's central government, local Ullŭngdo County Chief and civilians all considered Japanese incorporation of Takeshima/Tokdo as aggression at that time. But, by that time, Japan had virtually started colonial rule over Korea, by establishing the Residency-General in Korea. That is why no further development could be made within the Korean government to cope with the problem of Takeshima/Tokdo. As the entire country was be-

84 Han'guk sinmun yon'guso (Korea Newspaper Research Center), ed., *Taehan maeil shinbo*, (Seoul: 1976), vol. 2, p. 1818.

85 Kuksa p'yonch'an wiwŏnhoe (National History Compilation Committee), ed., *Maech'ŏn yarok* (Personal Accounts of Maech'on), (Seoul; NHCC, 1971), p. 375.

ing robbed of its sovereignty and vanishing, the problem of the ownership of a small rocky island was hurled away. However, that the Korean people clearly raised objection to the Japanese action of incorporating Takeshima/Tokdo is a decisively important fact worthy of historical evaluation.

V. Conclusion

In 1905, the Japanese government incorporated Takeshima/Tokdo into its territory through administrative measures. To justify the measures there are two views: the majority opinion represented by Kawakami argues the island had continuously been Japanese territory since early modern times, and the measure of 1905 was nothing but its reconfirmation; and the minority opinion holds that the island had been completely a *terra nullius* in 1905 and was subject to prior occupation.

As to the former, this article has clarified that it is false, in view of the formal decision made by the Dajokan in 1877 that Takeshima/Tokdo was outside of the Japanese controlled territory. As for the latter, it is refuted by half of the facts cited in this article. In other words, Korea had been conscious of Takeshima/Tokdo as its territory since the 15th century and expressed its opposition immediately upon learning of the Japan's measure of 1905. The dispute started at the time of the Japanese incorporation, not in 1952.

Both the majority and minority opinions have one similar point that Japan's incorporation of Takeshima/Tokdo in 1905 was totally unrelated to Japan's aggression of Korea. However, the fishing at Takeshima/Tokdo which became the grounds for its incorporation cannot be separated from the Japanese advance into Ullŭngdo. Above all, the Koreans of the day considered the Japan's incorporation of the island similar to the infringement of its sovereignty and aggression taking place in other various parts of Korea.

A territorial problem should be examined individually and thoroughly from a historical viewpoint. In the case of Tokdo/Takeshima, the word "historical" should include the direct process leading to the incorporation of the island and also what kind of relationship Japan had with Korea in 1905.

Tokdo or Takeshima? The International Law of Territorial Acquisition in the Japan–Korea Island Dispute

Sean Fern

Researcher

Disputes over offshore territory in East Asia are commonplace and have proven difficult to resolve. The region's seas are relatively small in comparison to the size of the 11 bordering states, and complicating this fact is the existence of a number of small rocky islets that are the subject of competing claims to offshore sovereignty. For example, Japan's territorial disputes with the Soviet Union over the Kurile Islands and with China over the Senkaku Islands, are well known. Japan, however, has an equally long-standing, and perhaps even more entrenched, dispute with South Korea over two tiny rock islets in the Sea of Japan. To the Japanese, these rocks are known as Takeshima. To Koreans, they are Tokdo.

Since the end of World War II, Korea and Japan have contested ownership of these islets, given the name Liancourt Rocks by French whalers in the mid-1800s and called that by neutral observers to this day.[1] The area is currently occupied by South Korea, which maintains that it has always be-

---

1   For objectivity, in this paper Tokdo/Takeshima Island will be referred to as the Liancourt Rocks.

longed to the Republic of Korea. "Tokdo is our territory, historically and under international law," noted the South Korean Foreign Ministry in a press release dated February 9, 1996.[2] In response to that assertion, in June 1997 the Japanese countered that Liancourt belonged to Japan. "Takeshima Island is an integral part of Japanese territory and this has been our long-standing position on Takeshima Island. There is no question about this," said Foreign Ministry Spokesman Nobuaki Tanaka.[3]

Japan's claims to Liancourt are based mainly on historical documentation and inter- national law as evidenced by twentieth century agreements with Korea, formal declarations of ownership and protests against Korean activities on the islands. Conversely, South Korea claims that it originally discovered Liancourt and continues to administer and maintain a presence on the islands.[4] Moreover, the South Korean government argues that following its liberation from Japanese colonial rule, Japan returned Liancourt as a result of bilateral and multilateral treaties, including the two states' normalization agreements

Concomitant with these historical claims, economic interests also dominate any discussion of the Liancourt Rocks. With the introduction of the 1982 United Nations Convention on the Law of the Sea (UNCLOS), sovereignty over offshore territory has become increasingly important and complicated. Parties to UNCLOS are entitled to as much as 200 nautical miles of maritime and jurisdictional exclusivity. States that have established sovereignty over offshore territory are granted an exclusive economic zone (EEZ) around the area, giving the state exclusive fishing rights and mining access

---

2   Zeno Park, "South Korea Brushes Off Japanese Protests Over Disputed Islands," Agence France Presse, February 9, 1996.

3   "Press Conference by the Press Secretary June 3, 1997," Japanese Foreign Ministry, June 3, 1997. <http://www.mofa.go.jp/announce/press/1997/6/603.html#2>.

4   Benjamin Sibbett, "Tokdo or Takeshima? The Territorial Dispute Between Japan and Korea," *Fordham International Law Journal* 21 Fordham Int'l L.J. 1606 (April 1998), 1611.

to the seabed.[5] Both sides, therefore, serve to gain economically from formal ownership of the islands.

This dispute recently came to a head when South Korea began printing postage stamps showing pictures of flowers and seagulls. On January 16, 2004, South Koreans arrived en masse at post offices around the country to purchase the stamps. The series, "Nature of Tokdo," included a painting of a lonely gray island, topped with vegetation like a green toupee.[6] After three hours, 2.2 million stamps were sold, setting off a diplomatic row in which Japanese and South Korean leaders showed renewed hostility toward one another. Japanese officials said the issue violates the cooperative spirit of the Universal Postal Union and proposed that Japan counterattack with a "Takeshima" stamp.[7] The dispute set off a rash of nationalist sentiment in both countries, demonstrating the continued sensitivity of the issue.

Considering the evidence presented by both sides, South Korea establishes a stronger claim to the Liancourt Rocks because it has manifested greater affirmative acts of sovereignty—as necessitated by principles of international law—on and around the disputed area. Given the islands' ambiguous past, the dispute turns on which country has demonstrated affirmative ownership as set out by historical precedents. Nevertheless, the two sides are considered unlikely to bring this dispute before an arbitrator as such direct involvement would risk renewed hostilities and further divisions.

This paper sets out to demonstrate why South Korea has a stronger claim to the Liancourt Rocks. First, it provides a brief history of the islands in the context of Japan- Korea relations. Second, the international legal standards required for formal territorial acquisition and sovereignty over an island. Then,

---

5   Article 55 of the UN Convention of the Law of the Sea defines the exclusive economic zone as "an area beyond and adjacent to the territorial sea," which provides coastal states with various sovereign rights over living and non-living resources.

6   James Brooke, "A Postage Stamp Island Sets Off a Continental Debate," *The New York Times*, January 27, 2004, 4.

7   Ibid.

the paper analyzes each state's claims and sets out why Korea has a stronger title claim. Lastly, it concludes by assessing the security implications of Korea's possession of Liancourt.

Historical Perspectives on the Islands

Contemporary Japanese-Korean relations reflect the past to a large degree. Koreans feel an emotional need to anchor their modern day policies to recollections of former Japanese occupation and conduct. This view is manifested in the idea of *han*, which represents a combination of resentment, regret and renewed suffering. *Han* influences how Koreans reflect on the past and often stimulates the desire to revive past events as bargaining chips when dealing with Japanese businesses and government officials.[8] Japan, on the other hand, prefers to concentrate on the present and replace the past with a new, fruitful relationship.

The dispute over Liancourt serves to illustrate these antithetical approaches. Japan and Korea are similar geographically and culturally yet their pasts cast a dark shadow on the present. Michael Lev, a renowned international correspondent for the *Chicago Tribune*, attributes the Liancourt dispute to historical differences rather than a desire for money or territory. While the disagreement at first glance appears to be economic, in a deeper sense, Lev writes, it is "about history, a previous war, and what Koreans emotionally consider to be unfinished business with Japan." In this sense, Korea's status as a former Japanese colony has complicated efforts to resolve the dispute.[9]

---

8   Victor Cha, Georgetown University, lecture, February 17, 2004.

9   Michael Lev, "A Point of Contention in the Sea of Japan: Seoul Testily Asserts Old Claim," *Chicago Tribune*, March 4, 1996, pg. Lexis-Nexis.

Aftermath of Japan's Occupation of Korea

Following the Russo-Japanese War, Japan annexed Korea in a series of forced agreements made between 1905 and 1910. During this period, Japan laid claim to the islands by officially incorporating them into Shimane Prefecture. A notice issued on February 22, 1905 declared, "The island should be designated as 'Takeshima' and placed under the jurisdiction of Oki Islands."[10]

The end of World War II and the Japanese occupation of Korea did little to resolve the issue. The status of the Liancourt Rocks was not addressed in Article 2(a) of the 1951 San Francisco Peace Treaty, which forced Japan to recognize Korea's independence. Instead, the treaty provided that "Japan, recognizing the independence of Korea, renounces all right, title, and claim to Korea, including the islands of Qualpart, Port Hamilton, and Dagelet."[11] The Supreme Commander for the Allied Powers then removed the Liancourt Rocks from Japanese jurisdiction and put them under US armed forces control for use as a bombing range.

Shortly thereafter, on January 18, 1952, South Korean President Syngman Rhee issued the Korean Presidential Proclamation over the Adjacent Sea. The proclamation declared Korean sovereignty over a portion of the Sea of Japan, including the Liancourt Rocks, by creating the so-called Rhee Line. The text of the proclamation asserts "Korean jurisdiction over waters within a line running.

60 nautical miles from the Korean coast," thereby staking a direct claim to the disputed territory.[12] Japan responded by protesting Korea's claim and by declaring its non- recognition of the Korean claim to the rocks, thus sparking

---

10   "Mark Lovmo, "The Territorial Dispute Over Tokdo,"<http://www.geocities.com/mlovmo/page4.html>.

11   Seokwoo Lee, "The 1951 San Francisco Peace Treaty With Japan and the Territorial Disputes in East Asia," *Pacific Rim Law & Policy Journal*, 11 Pac. Rim L. & Pol'y 63 (2002), pg. Lexis-Nexis.

12   Brian Bridges, *Japan and Korea in the 1990s* (Cambridge, UK: University Press, 1993), 65.

the modern controversy.

Despite disagreement over the ownership of the Liancourt Rocks, in June 1965 the two claimants signed the Treaty on Basic Relations, which normalized their diplomatic relations. No mention was made of the status of Liancourt Rocks within the treaty's text. Instead, both sides agreed to disagree and deleted all direct mention of the islands from the final document.[13] The two sides did, however, pledge to seek a peaceful settlement of any future disputes through diplomatic channels.[14]

The International Law of Territorial Acquisition

The sea has always been a source of food, travel, communication links and trade. With modern technological innovations in offshore drilling and shipbuilding, the natural resources of the sea have become increasing- ly important. International law has thus focused on creating mechanisms for the equitable exploitation of marine resources. Subsequent international agreements, such as the 1982 Convention on the Law of the Sea, the International Maritime Organization and the International Seabed Authority, aim to govern the international use of the seas in order to prevent overexploitation and to set rules for the exclusive economic zones (EEZ) of states.

As of 2004, UNCLOS boasted 157 signatories, including Japan and the Republic of Korea. The convention entitles coastal states to 200 nautical miles of sovereign access to living and mineral resources within an exclusive economic zone. In addition, any islands and in some instances rocks that are capable of sustaining human life, over which states establish sovereignty, are

---

13   Ibid.

14   Kwan Bong Kim, *The Korea-Japan Treaty Crisis and the Instability of the Korean Political System* (New York: Praeger Publishers, 1971), 69.

also accorded individual maritime zones.[15] Within the EEZ, the coastal state has sovereign rights for the purpose of exploring and exploiting, conserving and managing the fish stocks of the zone. Concurrent with the convention entering into force in February 1996, Japan and South Korea created economic exclusion zones around their respective territories, and each of these zones included the Liancourt Rocks.[16] Among its other benefits, sovereign title to Liancourt would offer unilateral access to lucrative fishing areas in the Sea of Japan.

Economic Value of the EEZ

There is little information on fish catch and the status of stocks in the area surrounding the Liancourt Rocks. In 1985, before the Korea-Japan fisheries agreement of 1998 in which both states agreed to regard the waters around Liancourt as neutral territory, total fish production was about 12 million tons. Under the 2002 Korea-Japan Fishery Agreement, South Korea was allowed to catch 149,200 tons of fish while Japan was limited to 94,000 tons. In January 2002, the actual fishing industry output by Koreans was 149,218 tons, while the Japanese caught 93,773 tons.[17] The East-West Center projects that the total catch could be increased to about 13 million tons if the quotas were eliminated.[18] Furthermore, the species composition of the catch from

---

15   Article 121(3) of the UN Convention on the Law of the Sea (1982) states: "Rocks which cannot sustain human habitation or economic life of their own shall have no exclusive economic zone or continental shelf."

16   Peregrine Hodson, "Tokyo's Island Dispute with Seoul Worsens," *The Daily Telegraph*, February 21, 1996, pg. Lexis-Nexis.

17   Kunwoo Kim, "Korea-Japan Fish Dispute," *Inventory of Conflict & Environment Case Studies*, April 23, 2002, <http://www.american.edu/TED/ice/korea-japan-islands.htm>.

18   Mark Valencia (East-West Center) "Ocean Management Regimes in the Sea of Japan: Present and Future," *ESENA Workshop*, July 12, 1998 <http://www.nautilus.org/papers/energy/Valenci-

Liancourt's waters has changed over time. This may be due in part to the use of different fishing gear but it also implies changes in the ecosystem. Coastal fisheries stocks are in reasonable shape but there is specific concern about the stocks of flying fish, Pacific herring, sandfish, halibut, Alaska pollack, and Japanese sardine.[19]

Rightful Claims to Territory

International legal scholars do not have a consensual standard for determining legitimate territorial acquisition. "Once granted, however, sovereignty, in relation to a portion of the surface of the globe, gives a state a legal right to include such a portion into its territory," writes Douglas Shaw in *International Law*.[20] Customary international law provides the following five principles by which international tribunals can resolve sovereignty disputes.

Cession of state territory is the peaceful transfer of territory by the owner to another state. According to R.Y. Jennings in *The Acquisition of Territory in International Law*, "The cession of a territory means the renunci- ation made by one State in favor of another of the rights and title which the former may have to the territory in question. This is affected by a treaty of cession express- ing agreement to the transfer."[21] International treaties or bilateral agreements in which the ceding state must intend to relinquish and pass sovereignty to the other state conclude these transfers. Furthermore, the receiving state must willfully accept the territory. Agreements imposed by force are void because Article 52 of the Vienna Convention on the Law of Treaties nullifies treaties

---

aESENAY2.pdf>.

19   Ibid.

20   Douglas Shaw, *International Law* (Cambridge, UK: Grotius Publications Limited, 1991), 278.

21   R.Y. Jennings, *The Acquisition of Territory in International Law* (New York, NY: Oceana Publications, 1963), 16.

procured by the threat or use of force.[22]

Related to this standard is the principle of subjugation, which refers to title by conquest. It is the act by which one state acquires territory by annexation following military victory. Acquisition of territory following armed conflict, however, requires further action of an international nature in addition to domestic legislation to annex, including a treaty of cession or international recognition.[23]

Prescription is the process of acquiring territory through a "continuous and undisturbed exercise of sovereignty lasting long enough to create a widely held conviction that the possession conforms to the standards of the international community."[24] No general rules govern the length of time required to create this conviction, but if many other states protest the claim, the prescription standard is generally questioned.

Occupation is a state's intentional claim of sovereignty over territory treated by the international community as *terra nullius*, or territory that does not belong to any other state. It is, Jennings write, "the appropriation by a state of a territory, which is not at the time subject to the sovereignty of any other state."[25] Acquiring states substantiate their claim by establishing administration over the territory. In the Eastern Greenland case, the International Court of Justice stated that claims to sovereignty "based not upon some particular act or title such as a treaty of cession but merely upon continued display of authority, involve two elements, each of which must be shown to exist: the intention and will to act as sovereign, and some actual exercise or display

---

22   Article 52 states: "A treaty is void if its conclusion has been procured by the threat or use of force in violation of the principles of international law embodied in the Charter of the United Nations."

23   Shaw, 288.

24   Jennings, 21.

25   Ibid., 20.

of such authority."[26]

Empirical Examples and Case Law

In addition to the prescribed rules for establishing justified and legal claims to territory, a number of similar disputes shed light on the South Korea-Japan dispute. Resolving the Liancourt claims necessitates a comparison of the existing facts with relevant legal precedent, and several decisions by international adjudicatory bodies provide a framework for this analysis.

The Island of Palmas dispute between the United States and the Netherlands involved a case similar to Liancourt. The issue concerned ownership of the island of Palmas, located off the Philippine coast. The United States based its title to Palmas on discovery and Spain's subsequent cession of the Philippines to the US pursuant to the Treaty of Paris, which concluded the Spanish-American War. Spain had sovereign rights over the Philippines until the war, thus enabling the cession. The Netherlands, on the other hand, based its claim on the colonization of Palmas by the Dutch East India Company and on its subsequent uninterrupted and peaceful exercise of sovereignty over Palmas. The Netherlands claim that this sovereignty arose out of conventions entered into with the island's native princes.[27]

In the Permanent Court of Arbitration's decision, rendered by Justice Max Huber, the court stressed the importance of continuous and peaceful displays of sovereignty. Rejecting the United States' claims of discovery, the court awarded Palmas to the Netherlands, concluding that discovery is insufficient to establish sovereignty over an island. The court decided:

If a dispute arises as to the sovereignty over a portion of territory, it is customary to examine which of the States claiming sovereignty possesses a

---

26   "Legal Status of Eastern Greenland Case" P.C.I.J (1933), quoted in Shaw, 299.

27   Sibbett, 1625.

title—cession, conquest, occupation, etc.—superior to that which the other state might possibly bring forward against it. However, if the contestation is based on the fact that the other party has actually displayed sovereignty, it cannot be sufficient to establish the title by which territorial sovereignty was validly acquired at a certain moment; it must also be shown that the territorial sovereignty has continued to exist and did exist at the moment which for the decision of the dispute must be considered as critical. This demonstration consists in the actual display of State activities, such as belongs only to the territorial sovereign.[28]

Thus the court held that effective occupation completed title of the territory claimed to have been part of the Netherlands. Mere discovery of land cannot compete against the continuous and peaceful display of sovereignty by another state.

In another case, the Clipperton Island dispute between France and Mexico, the court applied the *Palmas* rules to Clipperton, an unpopulated island in the Pacific Ocean. In the dispute, Mexico claimed that Spain originally discovered the island and as the successor of the Spanish state, Mexico should be awarded full title to the land. France, for its part, argued that it obtained Clipperton in November 1858 as a result of a French Navy lieutenant's discovery of the island and the subsequent proclamation, declaration, and notification of the French consulate.[29]

The arbitrator found no decisive proof that Spain discovered Clipperton. It concluded that even if one assumes that Spain discovered Clipperton, Mexico did not support its claims with the requisite manifestations of sovereignty. Consequently, Clipperton Island was *terra nullius* when France staked its original claim. Therefore, the question posed to the court was whether either claimant had completed its ownership claims by actual manifestations of sovereignty as determined by the *Palmas* case.

---

28   Jennings, 92.

29   Shaw, 296.

According to Shaw's *International Law*, "The arbiter concluded that the actual, and not the nominal taking of possession was a necessary condition of occupation."[30] Since Mexico engaged only in the symbolic act of hoisting its flag, it did not display the requisite peaceful and continuous acts of sovereignty. In granting Clipperton to France, the arbiter found that France manifested its sovereignty over the island by a formal proclamation of sovereignty, a formal protest to Mexico's assertions of title, a formal naval landing on the island and the creation of a guano procurement station. As such, Shaw writes, both the *Palmas* and *Clipperton* decisions demonstrate that "in the case of uninhabited areas, little is required by way of displaying actual physical authority over the territory to effectuated possession."[31] These acts, however, are necessary to complete a state's title to any territory.

International Legal Claims to the Liancourt Rocks

As noted above, Japan's claims to Takeshima are based on historical documentation and international law. The Japanese government points to agreements with the Korean government, formal declarations of ownership, and formal protests against Korea's activities on the island. In response, Korea argues that it originally discovered Liancourt and continues to administer and maintain a presence on the island. It contends that Japan only acquired title to the island during its illegal occupation of the Korean peninsula and that Korea's subsequent liberation gives it a legal claim to the land.

---

30   Ibid., 296.

31   Ibid., 297.

Japan's Claims to Takeshima

The earliest Japanese records documenting the existence and ownership of Takeshima date to 1650 and indicate the granting of the territory to what is known today as Tottori Prefecture. Japan also asserts that numerous pre-nineteenth century documents provide a sound basis for its historical claim. The Japanese Ministry of Foreign Affairs, for example, points to a 1779 map by Sekisui Nagakubo, which represents the location of Takeshima as part of Japan. Furthermore, the Foreign Ministry points to historical documents dating to 1618, which purport to provide evidence of Japanese fishermen's use of the Liancourt Rocks. Japan also contends that it occupied Takeshima during the Seven Yeas' War and the Russo-Japanese War.

Most important for Japan's case, however, was its annexation of Korea between 1905 and 1910. The Japanese claim to have incorporated Liancourt—land they considered to be *terra nullius*—into Shimane Prefecture on February 22, 1905. After having declared Takeshima as a part of Imperial Japan in February 1905, Japanese officials registered the island in the State Land Register for Okinokuni, District 4.[32]

Japan contends that as part of its annexation of Korea, all Korean territory became Japanese. It asserts, "the measures to incorporate Takeshima reaffirmed the intention of the Japanese government to claim territorial rights as a modern nation over Takeshima. In addition, the incorporation of Takeshima was reported in the newspapers and was not undertaken secretly, hence it was implemented validly."[33] Accordingly, in Japan's view the annexation of Korea consisted of a peaceful, voluntary, and negotiated merging of both countries.

Following Japan's defeat in World War II, the Allied Powers invalidated Japan's title to Takeshima. The Supreme Commander for the Allied Powers

---

32   Lovmo.

33   "The Issue of Takeshima," The Japanese Ministry of Foreign Affairs, March 2004 <http://www.mofa.go.jp/region/asiapaci/takeshima/position.html>.

(SCAP) issued SCAPIN 677, which outlined Japanese territory and specifically instructed that the disputed islets were to be excluded from Japanese administrative authority. The directive included a caveat, however, stating that the document would not represent a final decision regarding the attribution of Japanese sovereign territory.[34] Japan therefore maintains that Takeshima rightfully belongs to it and ought to be returned.

During negotiations over the 1951 San Francisco Peace Treaty, Japan tried to regain administrative ownership of Takeshima. These efforts were unsuccessful, however, and the issue remained off the table largely because of Syngman Rhee's announcement of the "Rhee Line" just months before the San Francisco talks.

Japan's confidence in its position resurfaced in September 1954 when it threatened to refer the matter to the International Court of Justice. Since then, Japan dispatches an annual notice to Seoul to remind the Korean government of Japan's claims to the island. It also regularly sends Maritime Safety Agency vessels to the area in order to hoist the Japanese flag.

South Korea's Claims to Tokdo

The South Korean claim to Tokdo is based on earlier, more numerous precedents than that of Japan. Korean experts claim that numerous eighth-century historical records prove that the area was first incorporated into the Korean Shilla Dynasty in 512 A.D. In addition, Korea asserts that numerous maps, including one by Japanese cartographer Dabuchi Tomohiko, verify its title to Tokdo.[35]

"The Japanese government cites the *Onshu Shicho Goki* (Records on Observation in Oki Province) edited by Saito Hosen in 1667 as the first record

---

34   Ibid.

35   Lovmo.

on Tokdo," writes Yong-Ha Shin in *A Historical Study of Korea's Title to Tokdo*. "Saito was a retainer of the *daimyo* of Izumo and at his lord's behest made an observation trip to Oki Island. In Saito's report, Tokdo and Ullungdo were both ascribed to Korea and Oki to Japan as its westernmost border. This first Japanese record on the islands clearly places Oki within Japan's territory and Tokdo within Korea's."[36]

Korea also maintains that it was in a weakened position vis-à-vis Japan in 1905, when Tokdo was incorporated into Shimane Prefecture. The South Korean government argues that Korea was unable to protest the Japanese move at the time because Japan had forcibly taken control of Korea's foreign affairs under the Protectorate Treaty. Furthermore, South Korea claims that after World War II, Japan returned Tokdo as part of the 1943 Cairo Declaration and the 1945 Potsdam Proclamation, which ended Japanese control of Korea. The Cairo Declaration pledged that Korea would be free and independent after declaring, "Japan shall be stripped of all the islands in the Pacific which she has seized or occupied . . . Japan will also be expelled from all other territories which she has taken by violence and greed."[37]

In 1946 SCAP issued Directives No. 677 and No. 1033, in which Japan is defined as including the four main islands and approximately a thousand smaller adjacent islands. The directive, however, specifically excluded Ullungdo, Chejudo and Tokdo. Given that the directive was made without the participation of Korean diplomats, Tokdo was clearly recognized as Korean territory by the international community.[38] Furthermore, the Treaty of Peace with Japan stated in its territory clause that Japan, "recognizing the independence of Korea, renounces all right, title and claim to Korea, including Chejudo, Ko-

---

36   Yong-Ha Shin, "First Japanese Record on Tokdo," from *A Historical Study of Korea's Title to Tokdo* <http://www.tokdo.com/english/tokdo_02.htm>.

37   "Cairo Declaration of 1943," from the National Diet Library of Japan <http://www.ndl.go.jp/constitution/e/etc/c03.html>.

38   Sun Myong Kim, "Tokdo," University of Tennessee-Knoxville, 1996. <http://enigma.phys.utk.edu/~kim/tokdo.html>.

mundo and Ullungdo."[39] The names of the islands were cited as illustrations but obviously not as an exhaustive enumeration. Therefore, all other small islands around the Korean Peninsula, including Tokdo, were not mentioned but should not be considered as excluded.

Subsequent to the end of the Japanese occupation, Tokdo saw its first Korean inhabitants. Since then, there has been a continual Korean presence of at least one or two fishing families and a permanent coast guard. The South Korean government has also taken steps to develop the area. In 1995 for example, the government began building harbor facilities and announced plans to install a desalinization plant to provide drinking water for Tokdo's inhabitants. Beginning in March 1996, tourists were allowed to visit the island and upgraded navigational facilities made access to Tokdo easier.[40] Such measures are part of a larger campaign to make the South Korean government's claims to territory clear and to establish a permanent presence on Tokdo.

Superior Claims Under International Law

In order for either state to gain the exclusive economic zone afforded by Liancourt, it must first establish internationally recognized sovereignty over the island. Considering the claims of both sides to the Liancourt Rocks, Korea has established the stronger claim because it has manifested greater acts of sovereignty in the area. While Korea offers limited arguments that it acquired Liancourt as a result of a particular method of territorial acquisition, it has demonstrated ownership by manifesting relevant, affirmative acts of sovereignty as necessitated by the *Palmas* and *Clipperton* decisions.

Despite Japan's reliance on the 1905 and 1910 annexation treaties by which it argues that all Korean territory became Japanese, it is questionable

---

39   Ibid.

40   "Lighthouse Planned on a Disputed Islet," *Wall Street Journal*, December 13, 1996.

whether Korea intended to give up its title and pass sovereignty to the Japanese, as is required for a valid cession. Indeed, Korea resisted the annexation
period with uprisings, protests, and a continual struggle to gain independence. Additionally, when news of Japan's incorporation of Tokdo reached
Korea, the Minister of Home Affairs rejected the Japanese claim, stating, "it is
totally groundless for the Japanese to lay claim to Tokdo and I am shocked at
the report."[41] The Korean State Council responded by issuing Directive No.
III on April 29, 1906, wherein the council denounced the Japanese claim as
groundless.

Japan points to the absence of any actionon the part of the Korean government when the area was annexed but does not acknowledge that the Japanese Resident- General in Korea was responsible for foreign affairs, leaving the
Korean government no diplomatic channel for disputing the Japanese claim.
Protestations of a peaceful transfer reflect more on the harsh control of the
Japanese over Korea during the occupation period than on actual events. Finally, any argument that Korea voluntarily merged into Japan as a result of
peaceful negotiations has been refuted repeatedly by a variety of documentary
sources. As such, Japanese claims to title based on cession fail.

Japan and South Korea would have difficulty propounding any claims
under the prescription standard. South Korea continually protests Japan's
annexation rule and Japan continuously protests South Korea's presence on
Takeshima. These protests undermine prescription's requirement of an undisturbed exercise of sovereignty and a general conviction that the claim
conforms to the international order. While Japan could argue that the international community did not protest its occupation of Tokdo or the entire
peninsula between 1905 and 1945, Japan cannot demonstrate that its sovereignty remained undisturbed after granting Korea independence.[42]

41　Yong-Ha Shin, "Korean Government's Reaction," from *A Historical Study of Korea's Title to
Tokdo* <http://www.tokdo.com/english/tokdo_07.htm>.

42　Sibbett, 1641.

Japan has a strong claim to acquiring Liancourt by subjugation. By issuing a formal annexation order following its conquest of Korea, Japan established sovereignty over the peninsula and its holdings. An international adjudication body might consider this a handover of title to Japan. If, however, South Korea can prove that Japan forced Korea to cede Liancourt to Japan, such an act would be cession rather than subjugation. As noted earlier, since Korea did not intentionally relinquish title to Japan, Japanese claims based on cession are likely to fail.

Japanese claims to sovereignty based on occupation are also weak. Occupation presumes that the occupied territory did not already belong to a state. Liancourt's history, however, appears to show that the island initially belonged to Korea. Furthermore, Japanese claims to sovereignty based on the annexation treaties negate any claim to have discovered Takeshima because the treaties concede a lack of initial ownership. If, on the other hand, South Korea can prove that it had original title based on discovery, then it has a good chance of establishing complete title by effective occupation as set by the *Palmas* decision. Under the *Palmas* and *Clipperton* standards, Korea's manifes- tations of sovereignty, including permanent Korean inhabitants and the construction of infrastructure, should prove sufficient to demonstrate effective occupation.[43] Japan's occupation, by contrast, was not continual and only occurred during times of unrest. There is no indication of a Japanese presence on the island since World War II ended.

South Korea has an enormous advantage over Japan because it has *de facto* possession of the islands and has undertaken a variety of infrastructure projects and improvements. As the *Palmas* decision shows, international judicial bodies highlight establishing sovereignty through positive acts, especially when occupying a territory. Effective possession of the Liancourt Rocks generally entitles Korea to the claim.

Japan may claim that formal protests such as hoisting the Japanese flag on

---

43   Ibid.

the island and sending ships to the area are sufficient signs of sovereignty, but a judicial body might find otherwise. In the *Clipperton* case, Mexico tried to substantiate its claim by raising a Mexican flag on the island and by sending a warship to defend the island from takeover. Nonetheless, the court in the case found these acts insufficient to substantiate Mexico's claim.

Ultimately, South Korea has a stronger claim to Liancourt than does Japan. Japan's claims rest largely on numerous agreements with the Korean government, implying that the islands originally belonged to Korea. Accordingly, assuming Korea originally possessed Liancourt and can prove that it completed its original claims by subsequent affirmative manifestations of sovereignty, a judicial body should find in its favor.

An Atmosphere of Compromise

Throughout the post-World War II history of Korea and Japan, the two governments have been embroiled in disputes over Tokdo/Takeshima. Central to this dispute are the economic implications of access to the island's exclusive economic zone. Both states believe that the area is one of their most important fishing fields given the size of fish stocks in its waters. For this reason, the longstanding issue will likely feature in bilateral discussions and cause frictions in the years to come, although neither country seems willing to break off relations over a minor territorial dispute. Despite a history of tensions related to the island, none has risen to the level of extreme discord. Instead, both states appear willing to compromise and cooperate. Negotiations, including agreements granting the Japanese access to Tokdo's fishing areas, are one way in which the South Korean government is trying to mend relations with its former colonizer.

Flare-ups do occur periodically, however, as in the 1999 example in which Tokyo and Seoul tried to register permanent addresses on the islands. Seoul reacted by sending a letter to Tokyo calling for "immediate cancellations of the registrations." Tokyo responded by stating it "cannot bar its residents from shifting census registrations, as the island is part of its territory."[44] Despite this exchange of letters, neither country was willing to escalate tensions and each dropped the issue within days.

Additionally, after South Korea announced plans to construct a lighthouse and permanent coast guard stations on the Liancourt Rocks, Japan protested by sending a formal letter to Seoul but quickly dropped the issue. The postage stamp dispute mentioned above, while initially a matter of contention, has subsided; both sides have essentially agreed to disagree. Thus, while both states maintain their claims to the islands and are angered by measures to assert title by the other side, they are willing to compromise.

In November 1998, South Korea and Japan agreed to renew a 1965 treaty that set a provisional fishing zone around the islands. Under the agreement, fishing boats from Japan and South Korea were allowed to operate in each other's 200 nautical mile exclusive economic zones if they obtained permits, while fishing quotas and conditions for such operations were to be decided by the two countries every year.[45] This agreement laid the foundation for a subsequent 2002 fisheries accord in which each state agreed to lower its catch quota in order to preserve depleting fish stocks around the islands.

Despite this paper's conclusion that South Korea has a better legal claim to Tokdo, the two states are unlikely to bring the issue before an international arbitrator. Instead, Japan will likely remain adamant in its claim but not push the issue formally as long as other, more important territorial disputes exist. Given the need for a close bilateral relationship between Japan and South Korea, the two sides will likely resolve any remaining disputes related to Tokdo by compromise and agreement. Korea will likely maintain possession of the islands in order to protect its historical claims. Since Japan is mainly concerned

---

44   Roger Dean Du Mars, "Address Registration Revives Islands Dispute," *South China Morning Post*, December 28, 1999.

45   "South Korea, Japan Agree Fisheries Treaty," *BBC Monitoring Asia Pacific*, November 28 1998.

with its economic interests, however, it will continue to pursue fishery agreements similar to the 2002 pact to ensure its continued access to the lucrative waters of the Sea of Japan.

Territorial Issue between Japan and Korea:
Case of Takeshima / Dokdo
– A Critique of the "10 Issues of Takeshima"
Published by the MOFA of Japan

Seichu Naito

Professor Emeritus, Shimane University

Preface

The confrontation between Korea and Japan surrounding the issue of sovereignty over Dokdo/Takeshima has recently intensified. What touched off the latest friction was the Japanese Government announcement of July 14, 2008 that it would include the Takeshima issue in a new guidebook for junior high school teachers and textbook publishers.

The guidebook, which was published in line with the revised teaching guidelines of March 2008, is expected to lead to an increase in the number of textbooks that will explain the issue of Takeshima. Currently, one of six geography textbooks and three of eight social studies textbooks are reported to deal with the issue.

Until now, the section on the northern territories (islands disputed between Japan and Russia) in the guidebook has merely stated, "It is necessary to accurately handle the fact that the Japanese Government is demanding Russia to return them." The revised guidebook, however, adds the statement, "Just

Seichu Naito   Territorial Issue between Japan and Korea: Case of Takeshima / Dokdo   **285**
                      – A Critique of the "10 Issues of Takeshima" Published by the MOFA
                      of Japan

like the northern territories, it is necessary to deepen the understanding of domains and territories of Japan by making reference to differences in claims between Japan and Korea surrounding Takeshima."

In the revised guidebook, it is clearly stipulated that the northern territories are an "inherent part of the territory of Japan." Though the guidebook does not go as far as to contain the same explanation for Takeshima, it is implicitly instructing teachers to teach that Takeshima is an inherent part of the territory of Japan "just the same as the northern territories."

As there is an obvious controversy over whether Takeshima can be referred to as an "inherent part of the territory of Japan" just like the northern territories, this booklet is aimed at elucidating in detail the truth of the matter. Aside from that, it is known that the Japanese Government decided not to include the unequivocal expression about Takeshima being an inherent part of its territory in deference to the Korean Government.

In Japan, there has been strong criticism from the Liberal Democratic Party and others that school textbooks deal with the Takeshima issue insufficiently. In response, the Ministry of Education, Culture, Sports, Science and Technology demanded that authorized textbooks stipulate that Takeshima is an inherent part of Japanese territory. At the parliamentary hearings in March 2005, Minister Nariaki Nakayama of the same ministry also remarked that Takeshima should be clearly explained in the teachers' guideline. However, the revised guideline posted on the government gazette in March 2008 intentionally avoided any reference to Takeshima and continued to contain the existing statement. Just before March, Korean President Lee Myung-bak took office and reinstated shuttle diplomacy with Japanese Prime Minister Yasuo Fukuda, sending a signal of improvement in Japan-Korea relations. The renewed bilateral ties had to be protected from being strained all over again, and it is reported that the Japanese Government took such an action for that reason.

This action invited a backlash from some lawmakers in the Liberal Democratic Party. The Ministry of Education had promised that it would clarify the main point of the issue in the guidebook, making it a fait accompli. As a result, Korea mounted yet more fierce opposition against the series of such movements in Japan.

At the expanded meeting on the sidelines of the Hokkaido Toyako Summit on July 9, President Lee directly asked Prime Minister Fukuda to ensure that the Japanese Government would not include an explanation of the Takeshima issue in the guidebook. It is not known how Prime Minister Fukuda responded at that time, but later he said," How can a request from a head of state be disregarded" and instructed the Ministry of Education to review if they could come up with any alternative. It is reported that the ministry prepared more than 100 different versions of the explanation. Based on these, Chief Cabinet Secretary Nobutaka Machimura, Minister of Education Kisaburo Tokai and Minister of Foreign Affairs Masahiko Komura decided on a final version after consultations on the night of July 13 and announced it on the following day. However, Koreans lodged strong nationwide protests against the announcement of the Japanese Government.

After 5 o'clock in the afternoon of July 14 when the announcement was made, Minister Yu Myung-hwan of Foreign Affairs and Trade of Korea called in Japanese Ambassador to Korea Toshinori Shigeie to deliver an intense protest. The Korean minister said, "The action is very regrettable in that it goes against the Korean Government's efforts to march toward the future." His expression implied that Korea felt it had been betrayed even after President Lee asked Prime Minister Fukuda for a fair handling of the issue. President Lee also commented, "I cannot but express profound disappointment and regret in light of the relationship between the two leaders who agreed to work together for future-oriented Korea-Japan ties."

Despite serious concerns expressed from Korea in advance over the issue, the Japanese Government never imagined that the situation would end up spiraling out of control. The circumstances following the July 14 announcement point to that fact. Japanese newspapers played it up in the morning editions the next day, but relevant articles were scarcely found after July 16, reflecting the extremely low public interest in the issue. On the contrary, public opinion

Seichu Naito   Territorial Issue between Japan and Korea: Case of Takeshima / Dokdo   **287**
– A Critique of the "10 Issues of Takeshima" Published by the MOFA
of Japan

in Korea boiled over, escalating popular pressure against Japan. A variety of scheduled exchange programs were put on hold.

In addition, there arose another problem on July 28. The U.S. Board on Geographic Names (BGN) changed Takeshima's designation from "Korean Territory" to "Undesignated Sovereignty." In connection with this issue, deputy spokesman for the State Department Gonzalo Gallegos explained at a press conference that the U.S. Government's longstanding position is not to support either Japan or Korea, both of which are claiming sovereignty over the island. He added that the BGN's decision did not mean a policy change but was intended to be compatible with that policy. A newspaper article from Washington quoted him as saying, "A renewed interest in the issue has prompted the Government agency to review the description on its own discretion." The paper expounded that all this insinuated that the recent movement in Japan surrounding the guidebook triggered the change.

Prodded by subsequent strong protests from Korea, the U.S. State Department announced that it had restored the designation to "Korean Territory" from "Undesignated Sovereignty" in accordance with President Bush's political judgment just days before his scheduled visit to Korea.

The latest happening sparked a firestorm of criticism in Korea that the Korean Government had taken insufficient action. As part of countermeasures against the explanation of Takeshima in the guidebook for teachers in Japan, Korean Prime Minister Han Seungsoo visited Dokdo on July 29 to showcase Korea's control of the island. During the first visit to Dokdo by an incumbent Korean Prime Minister, he erected a stone monument on the heliport reading that Dokdo is Korean territory.

The Japanese Government never anticipated that the situation would escalate to such a point. Thus, it still says it did its best to consider Korea's position by mentioning the differences with Korea or only adding the new phrase of "being illegally occupied" in reference to the northern territories even though it did not change the overall policy of including some explanation about Takeshima. At a press conference, Vice Minister Masami Zeniya of

Education, Culture, Sports, Science and Technology explained three reasons why an explanation about Takeshima had to be included: 1) the revised Japanese education law was designed to foster an attitude of love for country and the land; 2) the number of questions from the Diet about education in relation to Takeshima had increased, and local municipalities had also been making demands to add the topic; and 3) the Japanese Government had published a pamphlet about Takeshima.

What matters here is the government-compiled pamphlet on Takeshima, which was published in February 2008 by the Northeast Asia Division of the Asian and Oceanian Affairs Bureau of the Ministry of Foreign Affairs of Japan. Under the title, 10 Issues of Takeshima, the pamphlet was published in Korean, English and Japanese. It is the first publication that clarifies the official position of the Japanese Government on the Takeshima issue. In addition, as explained by the vice minister of education, this pamphlet has played an important role in the decision about whether to include the explanation about Takeshima in the guidebook. It is expected that teachers will utilize this publication at school in the future. The pamphlet on Takeshima, however, is filled with indisputably sloppy explanations, containing no valid points. In addition, I cannot but point out that no proof has been produced even for the most important claim that Dokdo is "an inherent part of the territory of Japan."

The pamphlet says, "Japan thus established its sovereignty over Takeshima by the mid 17th century at the very latest." This claim to sovereignty over the island, however, does not make any sense because the Bakufu (Shogunate) came to know of the existence of Matsushima (present-day Takeshima/Dokdo) and confirmed that both Takeshima (present-day Utsuryo/Ulleung-do) and Matsushima were not under the jurisdiction of Tottori-han (鳥取藩) domain in 1696.

Furthermore, the Japanese Government says that the incorporation of Takeshima into Japan's territory in 1905 was a reaffirmation of its intention to claim sovereignty over the island. The decision by the Cabinet, however, does not contain such explanations. In the decision, the Cabinet cited that there

Seichu Naito   Territorial Issue between Japan and Korea: Case of Takeshima / Dokdo   **289**
– A Critique of the "10 Issues of Takeshima" Published by the MOFA
of Japan

was no evidence of its being occupied by any country, confirming that Lyanko Island (present-day Takeshima) was terra nullius (land without owners). If that is the case, the island cannot constitute an inherent part of the Japanese territory. This fact contradicts the Japan's assertion that it was an inherent part of its territory.

In the pamphlet, the Ministry of Foreign Affairs made critical mistakes on the most crucial issues without expressing any doubt, thus it cannot be used as an official view. If Japan claims that Takeshima is Japanese territory, it is necessary more than anything else to produce convincing grounds that can be accepted by everyone. This booklet discusses the problems of each point in the pamphlet. I hope this booklet will be used to illuminate the truth about the issue in question.

August 2008
Seichu Naito

Foreword

The Ministry of Foreign Affairs of Japan published a 14-page pamphlet titled, 10 Issues of Takeshima in February 2008.[1]

It was the first publication about Takeshima by the Foreign Ministry that has so far promoted its assertions only through a website, which provides the public free and easy access to information. Despite its advantage, the website has a problem in that it is simple to revise the content without leaving a record of what changes were made or when. Regarding the issue of Takeshima, three

---

1   A PDF version is available on the Internet.

     http://www.mofa.go.jp/mofaj/area/takeshima/pdfs/pmp_10issues.pdf (Japanese)

     http://www.mofa.go.jp/region/asia-paci/takeshima/pamphlet_e.pdf (English)

revisions were made over the past three years. The Government assertions should not have been changed so furtively or so easily. Printed materials remain as a record, but websites on the Internet never leave any trace. I thought the website was a very inappropriate means for keeping a historic record. On that point, I welcome the issuance of the publication by the Foreign Ministry.

The pamphlet was made in an attempt to supplement some of the contents of the current website. Of course, the claim by the Japanese Government that "Takeshima is clearly an inherent territory of Japan, in light of historical facts and based upon international law" has remained consistent and unchanged.

The pamphlet, however, is based on a misunderstanding of historic facts. In addition, I should point out some other problems, such as a disregard for or omission of crucial facts.

Shimane Prefecture passed a local ordinance in March 2005 designating "Takeshima Day."[2] On this occasion, new historic documents related to the Takeshima issue were unveiled and the results of relevant research were made public. These efforts notwithstanding, it is particularly worrisome that the Japanese Government does not seem to take such research trends into consideration at all. The pamphlet on Takeshima by the Ministry of Foreign Affairs of Japan is indisputably exposing a dearth of study on the part of government authorities. Worse yet, the view of the Ministry of Foreign Affairs can be said to have played a great part in encouraging the Ministry of Education, Culture, Sports, Science and Technology to include explanations about Takeshima in the teachers' guidebook.

This booklet discusses each issue point by point as it appears in the Ministry of Foreign Affairs' pamphlet.

---

2   (2) The prefectural assembly enacted an ordinance (no. 36) to mark February 22 as "Takeshima Day" to celebrate the island's territorial "incorporation" into Shimane prefecture in 1905. (It was proclaimed on March 25, 2005, the centennial anniversary of the "incorporation.")

Seichu Naito   Territorial Issue between Japan and Korea: Case of Takeshima / Dokdo   291
                      – A Critique of the "10 Issues of Takeshima" Published by the MOFA
                      of Japan

Point 1. Japan has long recognized the existence of Takeshima.
→ Is this true?

Present-day Takeshima (Dokdo) was known as "Matsushima" from the old days and Utsuryo (Ulleungdo in Korean) was formerly called "Takeshima" or "Isotakeshima." The pamphlet states, "Although there has been a period of temporary confusion concerning the names of Takeshima and Utsuryo Island due to an error in the charting of Utsuryo Island by European explorers and others, it is obvious from a variety of written documents that Japan has long recognized the existence of Takeshima and Matsushima." As a representative example of those documents, the pamphlet cited *Kaisei Nihon Yochi Rotei Zenzu* (改正日本輿地路程全圖,[3] Complete Revised Map of Japanese Lands and Roads, 1779) by Sekisui Nagakubo (長久保赤水).[4]

According to a Japanese history book, Ulleungdo was recorded as Uruma Island in the 11th century. Since then, the island was called "Isotakeshima," but after the 17th century when families from Yonago-cho in the region of Houki-no-kuni[5] made passage to the island, it began to be known as "Takeshima." The present-day Takeshima (Dokdo), which was discovered during the passage to Ulleungdo and named "Matsushima," was known to only a limited number of relevant officials at that time. The Shogunate also did not recognize the existence of Matsushima (present-day Takeshima) near Takeshima (present-day Ulleungdo) until it issued a directive prohibiting all Japanese from making passage to Takeshima.

Inshu Shicho Gakki (隠州視聴合紀, A Collection of Observational Re-

---

3   Colored woodblock maps printed by Suharaya Mohei and Asano Yahei.

4   Real name: Harutaka, Lay name: Gengobe. 1717-1801. Sinologist and geographer of the Edo era. The major book mentioned above, Kaisei Nihon Yochi Rotei Zenzu, was completed in 1775. The first edition was published in 1779.

5   Old name for the central western part of present Tottori prefecture. Also known as "Hakushu."

cords of Inshu, 1667) by Kansuke Saito (斎藤勘介)[6] from Matsue-han explains that Matsushima and Takeshima were located northwest of Oki-no-kuni (present-day Oki Island), but that they were not part of Oki-no-kuni. On a map appended to that publication, Matsushima and Takeshima were also excluded from Japan's territory, marking only Tozen and Togo as part of its territory.

Sekisui Nagakubo's Kaisei Nippon Yochi Rotei Zenzu (Complete Revised Map of Japanese Lands and Roads), which the Ministry of Foreign Affairs of Japan regards as the most prominent cartographic Takeshima are shown on the map, the first edition leaves these two islands uncolored as if they belonged to another country. Why is it that the Foreign Ministry presented it as the representative map recording Takeshima? The intention of the ministry is hard to comprehend.

Aside from this, Sangoku Setsujozu (三國接壤圖, Map of Three Adjoining Countries), which was appended to Sangoku Tsuran Zusetsu (三國通覧圖說, An Illustrated General of Three Districts, 1785) published by Shihei Hayashi (林子平),[7] reveals in a note that Takeshima is under the jurisdiction of Joseon Dynasty (朝鮮) and does not show Matsushima. It means that neither Takeshima nor Matsushima were recognized as Japanese territory after 1696 when the directive was issued to prohibit all Japanese from making passage to Takeshima.

It stands to reason that *Kanpan Jissoku Nihon Chizu* (官板實測日本地圖, A Government Map of Japan Based on Real Survey, 1867), which was the only government map produced during the Edo period, does not include Takeshima and Matsushima. This map was made on the basis of a map pub-

---

6   Also known as Saito Toyonobu. A retainer of the Matsue domain. Oki magistrate at the time.

7   1738-1793. Given name: Tomonao. Critic and political scholar in the latter Edo era. He was born in Date (Sendai) domain and received education in Nagasaki and Edo. He is also known as Rokumusai Shujin. Other major works include Kaikoku Heidan (Treatise on military matters of a maritime nation).

Seichu Naito   Territorial Issue between Japan and Korea: Case of Takeshima / Dokdo   **293**
                                  – A Critique of the "10 Issues of Takeshima" Published by the MOFA
                                  of Japan

lished by Japanese cartographer Tadataka Ino (伊能忠敬).[8]

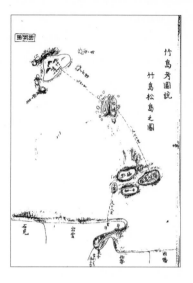

"Takeshima-Matsushima-no-Zu" (Map of Takeshima and Matsushima) in *Takeshima-Kou*
written by Okajima Masayoshi (1828), (in collection of Tottori Prefectural Museum)

In the pamphlet, the Japanese Foreign Ministry states, "on many maps…
the locations of Utsuryo Island and Takeshima are accurately recorded at their
current positions between the Korean Peninsula and the Oki Islands." The
truth is, however, that there are no other maps than Kaisei Nippon Yochi
Rotei Zenzu that contain such records. Thus, it cannot be said that Japan has
long recognized Takeshima as part of its territory.

---

8   1745-1818. Childhood name: Sanjiro. Geographical surveyor and father of modern Japanese
      surveying. Conducted surveys in various areas starting from Oshu (Tohoku) and Ezo (Hok-
      kaido). These surveys formed the basis for *Dai Nihon Enkai Yochi Zenzu* (Maps of Japanese
      coastal areas) (completed in 1821. Also known as "Ino Daizu").

Point 2. There is no evidence that the ROK has long recognized the existence of Takeshima.
   → What is the truth?

Many parts of the explanations in the pamphlet are identical to those on the website of the Ministry of Foreign Affairs of Japan. This particular point, however, was completely revised reflecting a new theory advocated by a few researchers. The revision represents the position of the Japanese Foreign Ministry. The following is what can be found on the ministry's website:

Recognition of Takeshima in the Republic of Korea

1. Overview

The ROK claims that the islands, that appeared in old Korean documents with names such as Usan-do and other islands, are the current Takeshima. However, nothing can be found to firmly support their claim that those islands such as Usan-do correspond to the current Takeshima.

2. Claims by the ROK
   (1) The ROK claims that, based on what is recorded in old Korean texts such as the *Sejong Sillok Jiriji* (世宗實綠地理志,[9] Geographical Appendix to the Veritable Records of King Sejong: 1454) and *Sinjeung Dongguk Yeoji Seungnam* (新增 東國與地勝覽, A Revised Edition of the Augmented Survey of the Geography of Korea: 1531), Koreans had long been aware of the existence of the two islands of Ulleungdo and Usan-do, and that this very Usan-do is the current Takeshima.
   (2) However, even in A Revised Edition of the Augmented Survey of the Geography of Korea, although a theory of two islands of Usan-do and Ulleungdo is asserted, there are sentences that suggest the possibility of

---

9   Volume 153, Geography.

Seichu Naito   Territorial Issue between Japan and Korea: Case of Takeshima / Dokdo   295
                     – A Critique of the "10 Issues of Takeshima" Published by the MOFA
                     of Japan

these being two different names for only one island. In addition, there are other ancient Korean documents which point out that Usan-do is another name for Ulleung (Utsuryo) Island and these two names are meant for the same island.

(3) Moreover, in records concerning Usan-do in ancient Korean documents, the island is described as a place in which many people live, and where large bamboo groves are cultivated. Such description does not represent the realities of Takeshima and rather reminds us of Ulleungdo Island.

(4) In the map attached to A Revised Edition of the Augmented Survey of the Geography of Korea, Ulleungdo Island and Usando are described as two separate islands. If, as the ROK Claims, Usan-do were the current Takeshima, then it should have been described as a much smaller island than Ulleungdo Island situated east of Ulleungdo Island. However, the Usando is portrayed on the map as being roughly the same size as Ulleungdo Island, and situated between the Korean Peninsula and Ulleungdo Island (west of Ulleungdo Island). This clearly shows that that is an island that does not exist in reality.

On the other hand, the pamphlet states: (1) The ROK claims that, based on what is recorded in old Korean texts..., Koreans had long been aware of the existence of the two islands of Utsuryo and Usan Island, and that this very Usan Island is the Takeshima of today. (2) However, whereas in *History of the Three Kingdoms* (三國史記, 1145),[10] there is a description that Ulleungdo Island, which belonged to Usan Country, became a part of Silla (新羅) in the year of 512, but there is no mention of Usan Island. Moreover, in records concerning Usan Island in ancient Korean documents, the island is described

---

10   The oldest Korean historiography in the Kiden-tai style. It was completed in 1145, with 50
      volumes. Covers the period from the time of the Three Kingdoms of Korea to the end of Unified
      Silla.

as a place in which many people lived, and where large bamboo groves were cultivated. Such description does not represent the realities of Takeshima and rather reminds us of Ulleungdo Island. (3) The ROK side claims that Usan Island is what the Japanese called Matsushima (present-day Takeshima), based on the description in *Yeojiji* (輿地志, Record of Geography: 1656) cited in *Study of Korean Documents* (東國文献備考, 1770), *Augmented Study of Documents* (增補文献備考, 1908) and *Handbook of State Affairs* (萬機要覽, 1808). However, there is a study which argues that the original text in Record of Geography indicates that Usan Island and Ulleungdo Island are two names for the same island and that the description in the documents such as Study of Korean Documents are indirect and inaccurate quotations from Record of Geography. The study makes the point that the description in those documents were copied from *Ganggyego* (Study of National Boundary) (part of Ganggyeji [Record of National Boundary: 1756]), which had uncritically borrowed from the unreliable deposition by An Yongbok. (4) The map attached to the *A Revised Edition of the Augmented Survey of the Geography of Korea* (same map on the website).

There are problems with explanations (2) and (3) in the pamphlet. As stated in claim (2) there is no Korean who ever asserted that there is an explanation about Usando in the *History of the Three Kingdoms*. Why then did the Japanese Foreign Ministry bring up this issue? A record about Ulleungdo can be found in this Korean document, but there is no mention about other islands. Some people make the interpretation, based on the records in the *History of the Three Kingdoms*, that present-day Takeshima did not belong to Usan Country. It is, however, unreasonable to assert that Usando did not belong to Usan Country just because there is no mention about it in that particular document.

Concerning the issue surrounding the citation from the *Record of Geography* presented in (3) above, the pamphlet claims that the original text in the *Record of Geography* indicates that Usan Island and Ulleungdo Island are the

Seichu Naito   Territorial Issue between Japan and Korea: Case of Takeshima / Dokdo   **297**
                      – A Critique of the "10 Issues of Takeshima" Published by the MOFA
                      of Japan

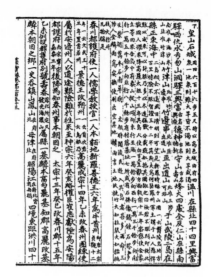

Annals of King Sejong, Geography

same based on the contention that the two names refer to one island.

An article on Ulleungdo in the *Ganggyego* (疆界考, Study of National Boundary, more accurately translated as Study of Territorial Borders, 1756) says, "Thinking about *Yeojiji* (Record of Geography), it says that there is one theory that Usan and Ulleung were the same island, but considering many maps, it must be two islands. One of them must be what Japan calls Matsushima, and probably the two islands made up Usan-guk." While citing a phrase from the *Record of Geography* that says, "There is a theory that Usan and Ulleung is the same island," the *Study of Territorial Borders* takes account of the theories of many other maps as well. In addition, there is an explanation in *Yeojigo* (Study of Geography) found in the *Dongguk Munheon Bigo* (東國 文献備考, Study of Korean Documents, more commonly translated as Reference Compilation of Documents on Korea, 1770) stating, "*Yeojiji* (Record of Geography) says that Ulleung and Usan are all Usan-guk. Usan is so-called by the Japanese Matsushima." It is not understandable why the Japanese Foreign Ministry has to mention a different view only in the pamphlet by saying,

"However, there is a study which criticizes…"

The explanation about a map attached to the Revised Edition of the Augmented Survey of the Geography of Korea discussed in (4) seems to be in line with an assertion by Kenzo Kawakami[11] (Editor's note: He is a Japanese Foreign Ministry researcher, who wrote an extensive study of Takeshima/Dokdo in 1966). He claimed that Utsuryo Island and Usan Island were depicted as two separate islands because someone who had never seen them in reality made the map using his imagination. The map, however, was hand-drawn in the 16th century and it is natural that the location and the size of islands are depicted inaccurately. With regard to this map, the pamphlet says, "This clearly shows that that island (Usan) does not exist at all in reality," but this claim is nothing but an obsession with the theory of Usan and Ulleung being the same island, which is already discussed in (3).

Japan's intention here is to deny the claim by Korea that Usan is the present-day Takeshima, but the explanations in the above are not convincing at all.

Point 3. Japan used Takeshima as a stopover port en route to Utsuryo (Ulleungdo) Island and as a fishing ground. It thus established its sovereignty over Takeshima by the mid 17th century at the very latest.
→ What are the grounds for this argument?

Under the title" Outline of the Issue of Takeshima" on the website of the Ministry of Foreign Affairs of Japan, there is a subtitle on the "Sovereignty of Takeshima." In the explanation about "Permission for Passage to Utsuryo

---

11   A diplomat in the Treaties Bureau of the Ministry of Foreign Affairs of Japan who mainly dealt with the Takeshima issue. His major works include *Takeshima no Rekishi Chirigakuteki Kenkyu* (Historical and geographical study on Takeshima), Tokyo: Kokon Shoin, 1966.

Seichu Naito   Territorial Issue between Japan and Korea: Case of Takeshima / Dokdo   **299**
                         – A Critique of the "10 Issues of Takeshima" Published by the MOFA
                         of Japan

Island," no mention of "sovereignty" can be found despite its subtitle. In the pamphlet, however, a new sentence is added saying, "Therefore, we firmly believe that Japan has established the sovereignty of Takeshima (Dokdo) by the early Edo Period (1603-1867) in the mid 17th century at the very latest." By doing this, the Japanese ministry tries to highlight the establishment of sovereignty over Takeshima, but it never explains on what grounds sovereignty of Takeshima was established.

Jinkichi Ohya and Ichibei Murakawa of Yonago in the province of Houki-no-kuni received a permit of passage to Takeshima from the Shogunate. (Editor's note: Today, Japan calls Dokdo "Takeshima," as in the above paragraph, but in the 17th century, Japan was still calling Ulleungdo "Takeshima"). The two families took turns in traveling to the island once every year to catch abalone and hunt sea lions.

In response to the application for the license by the two families of Yonago, the document was issued to the Lord of Tottori-han domain by the Shogunate for the license of voyage to the island contains the date May 16, but there is no record of the year. The two merchants of Yonago had initially applied for the license. The pamphlet claims that it is 1618, but that year is merely a commonly presumed date based on a document of the Ohya family, not an official record. It was not until 1622 that all four Shogunate officials who signed the license had been promoted to *roju* (老中), the position directly under the Shogun during the Edo period that took overall responsibility for general government affairs. In light of this fact, it is certain that the permit was issued after 1622. As of 1618, only two of the four co-signees had taken the position of roju, thus it is impossible for the roju document to have been co-signed by the four in 1618. The Japanese Foreign Ministry added a note saying, "Some believe that it was in 1625," but this issue should not be dealt with in such a light manner.

The license of voyage states that the application for passage to Takeshima from Yonago in the region of Houki-no-kuni was granted because the applicants had already made passage by ship to the island in the previous year and

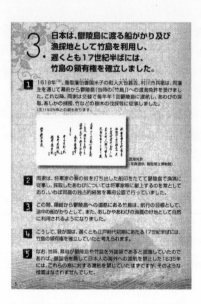

Ministry of Foreign Affairs of Japan, Takeshima (pamphlet)

wanted to make another passage. However, what the Shogunate allowed then was a voyage for "this one time." Despite the fact, the merchants of Yonago kept making passage to Takeshima after that, taking advantage of the hollyhock crest (of the Tokugawa family) that they emblazoned on the ship. The Japanese Foreign Ministry claims without any doubt that the permit of passage to Takeshima was a license of voyage to Ulleungdo. Ulleungdo belonged to Joseon Kingdom. Even though Joseon enforced a vacant island policy for Ulleungdo and made it an uninhabited island, it does not mean that Joseon gave up sovereignty over the island. How is it possible for the Shogunate to approve passage to Ulleungdo that belonged to Joseon? It is needless to say that the permit cannot be regarded as valid. The truth is that the Shogunate named the new island (present-day Ulleungdo) "Takeshima" and approved exclusive fishing rights for the people of Yonago. Japan at that time called Ulleungdo "Isotakeshima." In 1614, Tsushima-han plotted to claim sovereignty over Ulleungdo and began negotiations with Joseon. Under that situation, Japan needed another name for the new island (present-day Ulleungdo) than

Seichu Naito   Territorial Issue between Japan and Korea: Case of Takeshima / Dokdo   **301**
– A Critique of the "10 Issues of Takeshima" Published by the MOFA
of Japan

Isotakeshima and named it as "Takeshima." The appellation of Takeshima in reference to Ulleungdo as Takeshima was one of the issues during the negotiations over Takeshima Ikken (竹島一件, the Affairs of Takeshima) that started from 1693 between Japan and Joseon.

On a previous website of the Japanese Foreign Ministry, it said that a license of voyage to Ulleungdo issued by the Shogunate to merchants of Yonago was *hairyo* (拝領), a bestowal of sovereignty over land from the lord. However, Ulleungdo was not under the jurisdiction of the Shogunate, and it is nonsense from a historic perspective to say that the Shogunate issued a document directly to the local merchants to recognize their possession of the island without going down the proper hierarchical chain, such as *han* and *kuni*.

The same goes for present-day Takeshima (Matsushima at that time). Takeshima (Dokdo) is situated on the passage route to Ulleungdo, and it is evident that the island was used as a stopover port and fishing ground. On these grounds, the Japanese Foreign Ministry states "It thus established sovereignty over Takeshima," but it obviously doesn't make any sense. With regard to Takeshima, there is a document of the Ohya family that expounds that Shirogoro Abe, a *hatamoto* (a samurai in the direct service of the Tokugawa Shogunate), acted as broker for the two merchants of Yonago in 1661 and received the informal consent from the Shogunate for passage to *Matsushima* (present-day Takeshima). Citing this document, Kenzo Kawakami exaggerated the consent as Matsushimahairyo (松島拝領, a bestowal of Matsushima), on which the Japanese Foreign Ministry erroneously bases its assertion. Again, it cannot be said that Japan established its sovereignty over the island.

The Foreign Ministry also contends that the Shogunate took no action about passage to Ulleungdo or Takeshima when it issued a directive of *sakoku* (closed-door policy) in 1635 because it did not consider those two islands as foreign territory. If the Shogunate had recognized Ulleungdo as being an island of Joseon, a license of voyage should have needed a *shuinjo* (朱印状, the official seal of the Shogun). Because there was only one route to Busan from Japan, this could not have applied to voyaging to Jukdo. Under these circumstances, it should be understood that the Shogunate gave a new name of Takeshima to Ulleungdo to treat it as Japanese territory and issued a permit of voyage to the island.

In this case, the closed-door policy would not have applied. The island that Japan renamed Takeshima so that the Shogunate could issue a permit of voyage was the island that Joseon claimed as Ulleungdo. This caused the two countries to get embroiled in a dispute. This incident is referred to as Takeshima Ikken, and it was resolved when Japan recognized Ulleungdo as Joseon's territory in 1696.

Point 4. At the end of the 17ᵗʰ century Japan prohibited passage of ships to Utsuryo Island, but not to Takeshima.
→ **What are the historic facts?**

With the permission of the Shogunate to make passage for Utsuryo (Ulleung-do) Island, the Ohya and Murakawa families of Yonago engaged in a monopolistic business enterprise without any hindrance for approximately 70 years.

In 1692 when the Murakawa family traveled to Utsuryo Island, they encountered many Koreans on the island engaged in fishing. The following year, when the Ohya family made the journey to the island, they also met with many Koreans and decided to take two of them, An Yong-bok[12] and Pak Eo-dun,[13] back with them to Japan.

The feudal clan of Tsushima (which was the point of contact with the Korean Government at that time), following directions from the Shogunate after

---

12 A Korean fisherman from Busan, Dongnae, Gyeongsang-do. In 1693, he encountered Japanese fisher folk in Ulleungdo and was taken to Japan and interrogated. He came to Japan on his own will in 1696 and protested the Japanese occupation (seizure) of Ulleungdo. He also clarified that Takeshima was called Ullengdo and that Matsushima was called Jasando, and that both of them belonged to Gangwon-do in Korea.

13 A Korean fisherman from Ulsan, Dongnae, Gyeongsang-do.

Seichu Naito   Territorial Issue between Japan and Korea: Case of Takeshima / Dokdo   **303**
– A Critique of the "10 Issues of Takeshima" Published by the MOFA
of Japan

an investigation by the Lord of Tottori-han domain in Yonago, repatriated An and Pak to Korea, and initiated negotiations with Korea requesting it to prohibit its fishermen from going to Utsuryo Island. However, these negotiations failed to end in an agreement, given the difference in opinions between the two countries concerning the ownership of Utsuryo Island.

The negotiations between Korea and Japan lasted for three years and were concluded in 1696. In *10 Issues of Takeshima*, the pamphlet of the Ministry of Foreign Affairs of Japan, it is written, "Having received a report from the Tsushima clan concerning the breaking off of negotiations, the Shogunate decided to prohibit passage to Utsuryo Island in January 1969, judging that it is in the best interest of Japan to maintain favorable relations with Korea." However, the facts are significantly different from this explanation.

The diplomatic incident concerning the ownership of Utsuryo Island is known as the Takeshima *Ikken* (竹島一件, the Affair of Takeshima). It began when Japan, arguing that it had sovereignty over the island that it called Takeshima, suggested a prohibition against Korean fishermen making a voyage to Utsuryo Island. This Japanese claim collided with the Korean assertion that Utsuryo Island belonged to Korea as specified in the *Dongguk Yeoji Seungnam* (東國輿地勝覽, Survey of the Geography of Korea) which had also been introduced to Japan. Finally, the issue came to an end with Japan acknowledging that Utsuryo Island was the sovereign territory of Joseon and banning Japanese people from making passage to the island, the opposite conclusion from the Japanese claim.

Concerning the conclusion of the incident, the Foreign Ministry of Japan explained: "Having received a report from the Tsushima clan concerning the breaking-off of negotiations, the Shogunate decided to prohibit passage to Utsuryo Island in January 1969, judging that it is in the best interest of Japan to maintain favorable relations with Korea." However, this explanation is not true. Details of the proceeding of the negotiations over three years are clarified in Takeshima Kizi (竹島紀事, Detailed Account of the Incidents Surrounding

Takeshima),[14] which was compiled by the Tsushima clan. However, the focus here shall be confined to the progress leading up to the conclusion of the incident explained in the pamphlet of the Ministry of Foreign Affairs of Japan.

In a bid to seek a breakthrough in the stalled negotiations, the Lord of Tsushima (対馬藩主) came to Edo (now Tokyo) to consult with the Shogunate. During the consultations, the Lord of Tsushima did not report the failure of the negotiations. Although the he was seeking the opinions of the Shogunate by briefing it on the progress of the negotiations, he was just trying to solidify the policy of demanding the prohibition of voyage by Korean fishermen to Takeshima considering it as Japanese territory.

In the meantime, the Shogunate raised the question with the Lord of Tottori-han domain who was directly involved in the issue of making passage to Takeshima. In answering the inquiry, the Lord of Tottori-han made it clear that Takeshima did not belong to the provinces of Inaba-no-kuni nor Houki-no-kuni. On the basis of these answers,[15] the Shogunate established its policy. Thus, the Lord of Tottori-han applied for a permit for domain merchants to make voyage to Takeshima and, on January 9, 1696, was given permission to do so. This was not an attempt to claim the island of the Joseon Kingdom as belonging to Japan.

The Shogunate decided to prohibit the Japanese from making passage to Takeshima, remarking, "No one from our country resides on Utsuryo Island, and considering the distance to the island, it is considered to be part of the territory of Korea … it is therefore better to simply prohibit travel to it." On January 28, 1696, the Shogunate officially notified the domains of Tottori-han and Tsushima-han of the prohibition on going to Takeshima. On August 1, Tottori-han belatedly informed the Ohya and Murakawa families of Yonago of the prohibition while Tsushima-han notified Dongnae-bu of the Joseon

---

14   A Tsushima domain document on negotiations with Korea, compiled in 1726 by retainers of the domain, Matsuura Giemon and Koshi Tsuneemon.

15   The eastern part of present Tottori prefecture. Also called "Inshu."

Seichu Naito   Territorial Issue between Japan and Korea: Case of Takeshima / Dokdo   **305**
– A Critique of the "10 Issues of Takeshima" Published by the MOFA
of Japan

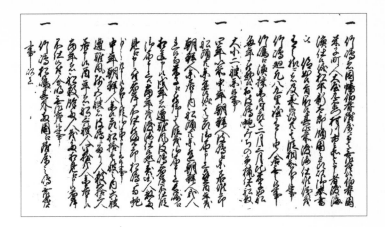

The final (sixth clause reads, "There are no islands, including Takeshima and
Matsushima, that belong to either of the both provinces." Response of the Tootori domain
to the Shorgunate on December 8, 1695 (in collection of Tottori Prefectural Museum)

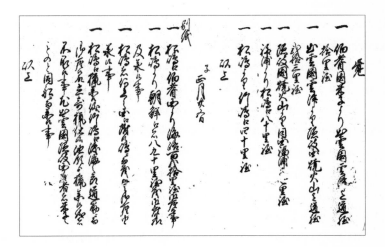

The third item in the appendix reads "We understand that Matsushima belongs to no
province." Response of the Tottori domain in the Shogunate in January 25, 1696
(in collection of Tottori Prefectural Museum)

Kingdom of the fact on October 16, 1696.

The prohibition by the Shogunate at that time only mentioned passage to Takeshima (Ulleung-do), and it did not mention Matsushima (current Takeshima/Dokdo). As a result, the pamphlet states, "On the other hand, passage to Takeshima (referring to Matsushima) was not banned. This clearly shows that Japan has regarded Takeshima as its territory since then." This explanation was excluded from the website of the Ministry of Foreign Affairs.

From the answers of the Lord of the Tottori-Han, the Shogunate first came to know of that Matsushima (Dokdo), the current Takeshima existed near Takeshima (Ulleungdo). Asked on December 24 whether, in addition to Takeshima, there were any other islands which did belong to the provinces of Inaba-no-kuni or Houki-no-kuni, the Lord of Tottori-han answered that there were no other islands than Takeshima and Matsushima. After hearing the answer, the Shogunate suddenly inquired to the Lord of Tottori-han the details of Matsushima. The answer explained the distance from Houki-no-kuni to Matsushima and the facts that Matsushima was not under the jurisdiction of Tottori-han, that fish were caught around Matsushima on the way to Takeshima and that nobody from provinces other than Inaba-no-kuni or Houki-no-kuni visited the island.

Upon hearing the answers, the Shogunate came to confirm the fact that both Takeshima and Matsushima did not belong to Tottori-han. Consequently, as long as nobody from provinces other than Inaba-nokuni or Houki-no-kuni of Tottori-han went fishing around Takeshima, the Shogunate seemed to have jugded that it would be enough to ban fishermen from Tottori-han from making passage to Takeshima. In this aspect, there was no need of mentioning Matsushima, a stopover on the way to Takeshima. Accordingly, it does not make any sense to argue that Matsushima was not mentioned in the prohibition as Japanese people regarded Matsushima as their own territory.

In 1837, the Shogunate issued an order banning passage to the seas of other countries. The ban was triggered by Aizuya Hachiemon (会津屋八右衛

Seichu Naito   Territorial Issue between Japan and Korea: Case of Takeshima / Dokdo   **307**
                      – A Critique of the "10 Issues of Takeshima" Published by the MOFA
                      of Japan

門),[16] who was caught smuggling on Takeshima (Ulleungdo) in 1836. He was from Matsuharaura of Hamadahan domain, Iwami-no-kuni province. It was known that he had engaged in smuggling on Takeshima after arriving there under the pretext of making a voyage to Matsushima (Dokdo) since passage to Takeshima was prohibited. The incident is cited as an example showing that passage to Takeshima was banned while there was no problem in travelling to Mastushima since it was not prohibited. On the basis of this fact, many Japanese people today agree with Kenzo Kawakami (川上健三) in advocating that Mastushima, the current Takeshima (Dokdo), belonged to Japan.

According to the passage ban in 1837, however, it was stated, "The prohibition of passage to Takeshima was ordered when the island was handed over to the Joseon Kingdom during Genroku period (1688-1703)." At the same time, it was also mentioned that "Fishermen are required to refrain from going too far out to sea, if possible, in order to avoid an encounter with vessels from other countries." In other words, the ban was intended to call the attention of fishermen to the need to avoid a voyage far out to sea. Needless to say, Matsushima could only be reached after a long-distance voyage from Japan. In this context, it does not make any sense to argue that Matsushima was excluded from the passage ban. On top of this, only Tottori-han, a directly related party, was notified of the passage ban during the Genroku era. In the Tenpo period (1830-1843), however, the ban was made public all across the country by being posted on bulletin boards.

---

16   1798-1836. A cargo ship owner of the Hamada Domain, Iwami province (present Hamada city, Shimane prefecture). He was a designated merchant of the domain. In 1836, his smuggling was reported to the authorities by Mamiya Rinzo, an undercover agent of the Shogunate. He was prosecuted by the Osaka Nishimachi magistrate and sentenced to death. (Takeshima Smuggling Incident 「竹島渡海一事件」)

Point 5. The deposition by An Yong-bok, on which the ROK side bases its claim, contains many points that conflict with factual evidence.
→ What is the important fact?

An Yong-bok from Busan went to Japan two times in 1693 and 1696. Since the incidents involving An took place in Japan, much of the historical records about him remain in Japan. When he returned to Korea, An was investigated by the *Bibyeonsa*[17] (Border Defense Council), and his statements are recorded in the *Joseon Wangjo Sillok* (朝鮮王朝實録,[18] Annals of the Dynasty of Joseon). In Korea, scholars have recently carried out research concerning him using documents of both the Korean and Japanese sides. Thus, current studies do not make assertions about An Yong-bok based solely on Korean documents.

When An Yong-bok and Pak Eo-dun were fishing around Ulleungdo in 1693, they were captured by some members of the Ohya family, residents of Yonago, and taken to Japan against their will. After being 44 questioned at Tottori-han domain, they were repatriated to Busan from the Tsushima-han. An Yong-bok's second visit to Japan was made voluntarily in order to protest that Japanese had trespassed on Ulleung-do (Takeshima) and Jasando (子山島, Matsushima/Dokdo), both of which were Joseon territory. On May 1696, he arrived at Tottori-han via Oki Island. After staying for two months, he departed from Karo in Tottori-han to return to Korea and was captured in Gangwon-do province. His words and activities during this period are recorded in the documents of Tottori-han and Tsushima-han while his explanations and activities in Korea are documented in *Sukjong Sillok*, (肅宗實録,[19] Annals

---

17   Also called "Bikyoku" or "Chushi." One of the Korean military administrative posts at the time.

18   Also known as *The true record of the Joseon Dynasty*. A historiography compiled by the government in chronological form, covering the Joseon Dynasty period.

19   A historiographical record on King Sukjong (1661-1720) (ruled 1674-1720) of the Joseon Dynasty.

Seichu Naito   Territorial Issue between Japan and Korea: Case of Takeshima / Dokdo   **309**
– A Critique of the "10 Issues of Takeshima" Published by the MOFA
of Japan

of King Sukjong) and other historical records.

The pamphlet of the Ministry of Foreign Affairs of Japan only touches on the visit of 1696. However, it goes without saying that the An Yong-bok incident was triggered when he was taken to Japan in 1693. From then on, he came to harbor a big question about why he had been captured by Japanese people and taken to Japan when Ulleung-do was Joseon territory. This unresolved question served as an occasion for him to make up his mind to visit Japan to protest in 1696.

The second visit of An Yong-bok took place on May 1696. The Foreign Ministry's pamphlet states that some comments of An Yongbok were inconsistent with the factual evidence; "An Yong-bok is reported to have stated on his 1696 visit to Japan that there were many Japanese on Utsuryo Island. However, his visit to Japan on the occasion was after the Shogunate had decided to prohibit passage to Utsuryo Island, and neither the Ohya nor Murakawa family went to the island at that time." In other words, according to the Foreign Ministry, it means that no Japanese made passage to the island after January 1696.

However, the Shogunate's ban in January 1696 did not immediately come into effect nationwide. As it was August 1696 when the residents of Yonago were informed of the prohibition from Tottori-han, they might have made a voyage to Utsuryo Island as they did in previous years. The Foreign Ministry pamphlet thus wrongly states, "The deposition contains many points that conflict with factual evidence... these descriptions have been cited by the ROK side as one of the foundations for sovereignty over Takeshima."

In addition, the pamphlet also states, "...An Yong-bok confessed that while in Japan he had acquired a written document from the Edo Shogunate that indicated the Shogunate's acceptance of Utsuryo Island and Takeshima as territories of Korea... there are no records that a written document such as that claimed by the ROK side was ever given to An Yong-Bok." It was 1693 when he received the written document from the Edo Shogun. It is also known that after being transferred from Tottori-han to Edo and treated well by the Shogunate, An received a written document that was later confiscated by the Lord of Tsushima. None of these statements are totally accurate.

As illustrated by the documents of the Murakami (村上) family on Oki Island,[20] An Yong-bok maintained on his 1696 visit that Takeshima (Ulleung-do) and Matsushima (Usando/Dokdo) were a part of Gangwon-do (province) by showing *Joseon Paldo Jido* (朝鮮八道之圖, Map of Eight Provinces of Joseon). It has added significance that An Yong-bok had Japanese officials record that the two islands concerned belong to Korea.

Afterwards, he planned to go to Tottori-han to protest to the Lord of Tottori, but to no avail. According to the records of Takeshima Kizi, a letter to the Shogun and a letter to the Lord of Inaba-han, which were written on the voyage were confiscated by the Lord of Tottori-han. However, it is believed that the letter to the Shogun was delivered through Tottori-han, which is corroborated by the dialogue between the magistrate of Dongnae and the Lord of Tsushima-han in February 1697.

The lord of Tsushima-han asked, "Last fall, your countryman tendered a document to a government of fice of Japan. Was it delivered by the order of the royal court?" In response, the magistrate of Dongnae answered, "The royal court knew nothing of it. A civilian adrift on the sea might have submitted it at his own discretion." In addition, a document in March 1698 states, "The submission of a written document makes one guilty of a reckless behavior." All these combine to demonstrate that both Japan and the document states that Gangwon-do "includes Takeshima and Matsushima" (Murakami Document). Joseon Kingdom recognized that An Yong-bok submitted a written document to the *kanpaku* (関白, chief advisor to the emperor). Though impossible to find out what was written in the document, it is safe to assume that the document stated that Takeshima and Matsushima were under the jurisdiction of the Joseon Kingdom.

An Yong-bok was the first Korean to make it clear that Matsushima (Us-

---

20   A group of island to the north of Shimane peninsula.

Seichu Naito   Territorial Issue between Japan and Korea: Case of Takeshima / Dokdo   **311**
– A Critique of the "10 Issues of Takeshima" Published by the MOFA
of Japan

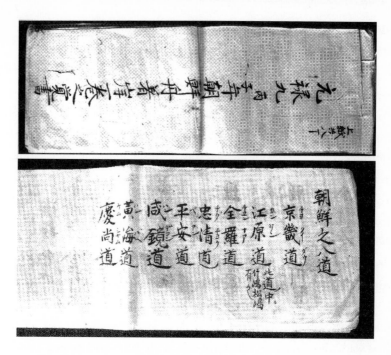

The document states that Gangwon-do "includes Takeshima and Matsushima"
(Murakami Document).

ando) was a part of Gangwon-do (province) as an administrative dependency
of Takeshima (Ulleung-do) after seeing the islet firsthand. As a result, the
awareness about Usando in Joseon increased so that the *Ganggyego* (疆界考,[21]
Studies on Territorial Borders, 1756) and *Dongguk Munheon Bigo* (東國文献備
考, Reference Compilation of Documents on Korea, 1770) record as follows:
"Usando refers to Matsushima mentioned by the Japanese."

---

21   Historical maps of Korean territories compiled by Sin Gyong Jun, along with Dongguk Mun-
      heon Bigo (Reference Compilation of Korean Documents).

Point 6. Japan reaffirmed its intention to claim sovereignty over Takeshima by incorporating Takeshima into Shimane Prefecture in 1905.
→ What does "reaffirmed its intention" mean?

Amidst a sea change triggered by the Meiji Restoration in 1868, the new Meiji Government was faced with the necessity of reexamining the issue surrounding Takeshima and Matsushima in its relations with Joseon. In *Chosenkoku Kosai Shimatsu Naitansho* (朝鮮國交際始末内探書,[22] A Confidential Inquiry into the Particulars of Foreign Relations of Korea) filed in April 1870, three Japanese Foreign Ministry officials dispatched to Joseon Kingdom reported the results of their survey under the category of "The particulars of how Takeshima and Matsushima have come under Joseon's (Korea's) possession" as follows:

"Matsushima (Dokdo) in this case is a neighboring island of Takeshima (Ulleungdo). No document has been filed concerning Matsushima so far. There was a case in which Takeshima had been leased from Joseon for settlement for some time during the Genroku era. At that time, it was still an uninhabited island, as it had been."

In addition, in the section on Oki-shoto (Oki Islands) of Nihon *Chishi Teiyo* (日本地誌提要,[23] The Epitomized Regional Geography of Japan) published by the *Seiin Chisika* (正院地誌課, Land Register Division) of the Dajokan (Grand Council of State) in 1875, it was noted that a total of 179 small islands of Oki belonged to Honshu, the main island of Japan. It also recorded that besides those islands, there were Matsushima and Takeshima,

---

22 A mission report submitted by a group including Sada Hakuga, a government clerk of the Ministry of Foreign Affairs of Japan who stayed at Korea until December of the previous year.

23 The first geographical record compiled by the Meiji government. It was written by Tsukamoto Akitake in 1872-1873. At the time of publication, manuscripts were sent to each prefecture for correction, and were thus checked and revised. Publication began in 1874 and was completed in 1879. The areas included Fusanokuni, the two capitals (Tokyo/Kyoto), Goki-Shichido (the five provinces and seven circuits), the Ryukyu islands, Hokkaido and Sakhalin.

Seichu Naito   Territorial Issue between Japan and Korea: Case of Takeshima / Dokdo   **313**
                      – A Critique of the "10 Issues of Takeshima" Published by the MOFA
                      of Japan

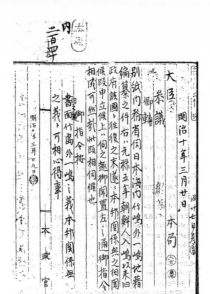

Minister of State's order on March 29, 1877 (in National Archives of Japan)

which means that those two islands did not belong to Honshu.

When *Nihonkainai Takeshimahoka Itto Chiseki Hensankata Ukagai* (日本海内竹島外一島地籍編纂方伺, A Note of Inquiry about the Compilation of the Land Register on Takeshima and Another Island in the Sea of Japan) was submitted by the Shimane Prefecture, the Grand Council of State concluded on March 29, 1877 that "Regarding Takeshima (Ulleungdo) and 'another island' (Dokdo), it is to be understood that our country has nothing to do with them." As the highest decision-making body of the Japanese Government, this organization's decisions had great significance.

In the Yuraino Gairyaku (由来の概略, Broad Explanation on the Origin) which was attached to the Shimane Prefecture's note of inquiry, an explanation about Takeshima is followed by a description of Matsushima (Dokdo); "There is another island called Matsushima (Dokdo). Lying along the same route toward Takeshima (Ulleungdo), its circumference is 30 *cho* (町) or 3.3 km, and is located 80 ri (里) or 320 km, from Oki Island. Trees or bamboos are rare, but there are fish and animals." In the *Isotakeshima Ryakuzu* (磯竹島略圖, A Rough Sketch of Isotakeshima), a map attached to the Grand Council of State Directive, Matsushima is marked along with Isotakeshima (Takeshima).

However, Takeshima and Matsushima were not shown on the *Dai-nihonkoku Zenzu* (大日本國全圖, The Complete Map of Great Japan, produced by the Interior Ministry in 1880) and *Dai-nihon Fuken Bunkatsuzu* (大日本府県分割圖, The Complete Map of Prefectures of Great Japan, 1881). In addition, *Dai-nihonkoku Zenzu* (大日本國全圖, The Complete Map of Great Japan, 1877), published by the Japanese Staff Bureau of the Ministry of the Army, does not include Takeshima and Mastushima. In *Shusei Nijumanbunnoichizu Ichiranhyo* (輯製二十万分一圖一覧表, A List of Maps Compiled on a Scale of One to Two Hundred Thousand, 1885), only Takeshima is marked with a dotted line without a name and Matsushima is not shown. In *Kanei Suiroshi* (寰瀛水路誌, The Hydrographic Chart of Japan, 1883) compiled by the Hydrographic Department of the Ministry of the Navy, Takeshima is referred to as Liancourt Rocks under the section of the "East Seashore of Joseon and Islands."

As shown above, the Foreign Ministry of Japan totally disregards significant historic facts that were ascertained in the process of land registration and topographical compilation during the period from 1870 to 1880 right after the launch of the new Meiji Government. It is because those facts constitute a fundamental contradiction to the views of the Foreign Ministry that "Takeshima is clearly an inherent territory of Japan, in light of historical facts…" The position of the Foreign Ministry of Japan disregarding historical facts must not be overlooked.

Regarding the incorporation of Liancourt Rocks into the Japanese territory in 1905, the Foreign Ministry's pamphlet notes, "With this Cabinet Decision, Japan reaffirmed its intention to claim sovereignty over Takeshima." However, the Cabinet Decision on January 28, 1905 notes, "Regarding a *terra nullius* where there is no evidence of its being occupied by any country, it

Seichu Naito
Territorial Issue between Japan and Korea: Case of Takeshima / Dokdo
– A Critique of the "10 Issues of Takeshima" Published by the MOFA
of Japan
315

decided to incorporate into Japan's territory recognizing Yozaburo Nakai's[24] engagement in fishing off the island as an occupation under the international law." In other words, it based its explanations on the theory of international law, an occupation of terra nullius. It should be highlighted that the Cabinet Decision did not mention the reaffirmation of intention to claim sovereignty by the Japanese Government.

According to Yozaburo Nakai's records, he thought that the uninhibited island, Lyanko Islands, was under the jurisdiction of Korea. In the *Jigyo Keiei Gaiyou* (事業経営概要, A Summary of Business), a book describing the hunting of sea lions off Lyanko Islands, Yozaburo Nakai wrote, "As I believed that the island was Korean territory being attached to Ulleungdo, I came up to the capital after being informed that I might need to consult with the Japanese Residency-General (統監府) in Korea." After hearing personally from Nakai, Hekiun Okuhara (奥原碧雲)[25] notes in his publication *Takeshima Oyobi Ut-suryoto* (竹島及鬱陵島, Takeshima and Ulleungdo, 1907) that" Nakai believed that the Lyanko Islands was Korean territory and decided to file a request with the Korean Government for its lease."

It was high-ranking Japanese Government officials who persuaded Nakai to change his request for the lease into that for territorial incorporation. Naomasa Maki (牧朴眞), Director of the Fisheries Bureau of the Ministry of Agriculture and Commerce expressed doubt about the fact that Lyanko Islands belonged to Korea. Kaneyuki Kimotsuki (肝付兼行),[26] Director of the

---

24   Born in Ogamo-village, Tohaku-district, Tottori prefecture and moved to Saigotown, Suki-district, Shimane prefecture. He was a pioneer of diving fishery and purse-seine fishery. Founded *Takeshima Gyoryo Goshi Gaisha* (Takeshima Fishing Company) and became its president.

25   Also known as Okuhara Fukuichi. A local historian (1873-1935) of Matsue, Shimane prefecture. His other major works include Okinoshima-shi (Records of Oki islands) and Aikason-shi (Records of Aika village).

26   1853-1922. Served as a member of the House of Peers and as mayor of Osaka city. His major achievement in the field of surveying was the telegraphic determination of Japan's location. He was a baron and a navy vice admiral.

Hydrographic Department of the Imperial Navy stated his opinions as follows: "Lyanko Islands are located 85 nautical miles from Oki Island and 55 nautical miles from Ulleung-do. And, they are 108 nautical miles away from Takobana (多古鼻) of Izumo-no-kuni (出雲国) while 118 nautical miles away from the Cape of Krudner (ルツドネル岬), thus being 10 nautical miles nearer to Japanese mainland than the Korean mainland. As long as there are Japanese fishermen engaged in fishing off the islands, it is natural to incorporate them into Japanese territory." Accordingly, Nakai came to the conclusion that "Based on the decision of Director of the Hydrographic Department Vice Admiral Kimotsuki, it was reconfirmed that there was no definite evidence of ownership of the island."

However, the petition for territorial incorporation of Lyanko Islands and their lease submitted to the three Ministers of Home Affairs, Foreign Affairs and Agriculture-Commerce Affairs was turned down. Concerning the reason behind the opposition, Nakai himself stated, "At this time, if the acquisition of a barren islet suspected of being Korean territory would amplify the suspicions of various foreign countries watching the situation that Japan had an ambition to annex Korea, the gains would be extremely small while the situation would become grave." However, Enziro Yamaza (山座円次郎, the Director of Political Affairs Bureau at the Foreign Ministry), expressed his views to Nakai that "Under the present circumstances, it is imperative that the island be incorporated. And it is absolutely necessary to construct Cabinet decision on January 28, 1905 (in collection of Japan Center for Asian Historical Record) observation posts and install wireless connections or submarine cables for the surveillance of enemy ships. Particularly, diplomacy is free of such considerations as required in the Home Ministry." In sum, he was stressing that the territorial incorporation should be done as quickly as possible highlighting the strategic importance of Lyanko Islands at a time when the situation was rapidly changing.

As such, the incorporation of Lyanko Islands was hastened as part of preparations for battles with the Russian fleet in the Sea of Japan (East Sea).

Seichu Naito   Territorial Issue between Japan and Korea: Case of Takeshima / Dokdo   **317**
– A Critique of the "10 Issues of Takeshima" Published by the MOFA
of Japan

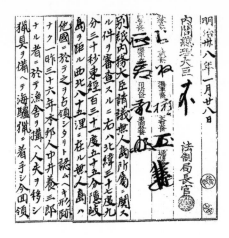

Cabinet decision on January 28, 1905
(in collection of Japan Center for Asian Historical Record)

In other words, the incorporation was pushed not because of Nakai's request to hunt sea lions but because of the request from the military. As a matter of fact, the authorities accepted Nakai's petition on September 29. Prior to the acceptance, however, the construction of an observation post on Ulleung-do was completed, and it was to be connected with an observation post on Lyanko Islands through submarine cables. It was the Cabinet decision made on January 28, 1905 at the height of the Russo-Japanese war. At that time, the Japanese army has already placed Hanseong (Seoul), the capital of The Korean Empire (大韓帝國), under its domination. According to the Korea-Japan Protocol (日韓議定書)[27] in February 1904, the administration of state affairs of the Korean Empire came under the control of the Japanese army. In signing a further Korea-Japan Agreement in August 1904, it was decided that advisors for Korea's diplomatic and financial affairs would be appointed out

---

27   Treaty signed by Japan and Korea in 1904 against the background of the Russo- Japanese War. This treaty led to three treaties between Japan and Korea and further to the Japan-Korea Annexation Treaty (1910).

of those recommended by the Japanese Government. Under these circumstances, Japan did not consult with the Korean Government, disregarding any possible doubt that Ryanko Islands might be Korean territory. It did not even inform the Korean Government of the incorporation. The Foreign Ministry of Japan insists that under international law, a nation is not obliged to notify a foreign country of territorial incorporation measures. Still, it is more natural to reckon that Japan was completely disregarding the Korean Government.

The Japanese Government did not publish the incorporation of Takeshima in its Official Gazette. It just ordered Shimane Prefecture to issue the public notification within the jurisdiction of the prefecture. On February 22, 1905, Shimane Prefecture announced that Takeshima had come under the jurisdiction of the Okinoshima branch of the Shimane Prefectural Government in the Official Gazette of Shimane Prefecture. On top of this, the Sanin Shimbun (山陰新聞),[28] a local paper of Shimane Prefecture, reported the incorporation in an article on February 24 entitled "A New Island of Oki Island." It cannot be said that these measures were taken in a completely secret manner, but it must be pointed out that the notification was far from being valid from the standpoint of the international law.

In 1900, five years before the incorporation of Lyanko Islands by the Japanese Government, the Korean Government carried out the reorganization of administrative districts to change the name Utsuryo Island into Utsu Island (pronounced Uldo in Korean) and create Uldo-gun by incorporating Jukdo and Seokdo in accordance with the Imperial Edict No. 41. Under this edict, Jukdo and Seokdo refer to current Jukseodo and Dokdo, respectively. Accordingly, the Imperial Edict made clear Korea's sovereignty over Dokdo.

In those days, Dokdo was referred to as Matsushima, Liancourt Rocks, Lyanko and Yanko by the Japanese people. However, it came to be called

---

28   Founded in 1882. Merged with Shoyo Shimpo in 1942. The name was later changed to Shimane Shimbun, Sanin Shimpo and then to current The San-in Chuo Shimpo. http://www.sanin-chuo.co.jp/.

Seichu Naito   Territorial Issue between Japan and Korea: Case of Takeshima / Dokdo   **319**
                      – A Critique of the "10 Issues of Takeshima" Published by the MOFA
                      of Japan

Korean Empire's "Edict 41" of 1900. Ishijima corresponds to Takeshima/Dokdo.

Seokdo (literally meaning stone island). A majority of the people who settled on Ulleung-do was from Jeolla-do (province). In the dialect of that region, *dol* (石 in Chinese character) was also pronounced *dok* (獨). Thus, the rocky island far off from Ulleungdo was called dol-seom. However, it came to be registered as Seokdo (石島 in Chinese characters). When it is pronounced as written, it becomes Dokdo.

On September 25, 1904, Koudou Nitshi (行動日誌),[29] the logbook of the Japanese warship Niitaka (新高) recorded, "Koreans refer to the Liancourt Rocks as Dokdo while Japanese fishermen call them Lyanko for short." This entry was based on information it got from the people who saw Liancourt Rocks from Ulleung-do. On the other hand, the pamphlet of the Foreign Ministry states, "…there is no evidence that Korea had ever exercised effective control over Takeshima around the time of the promulgation of the Imperial Ordinance. Therefore, it is considered that Korea had never established sovereignty over Takeshima." In 1900, the name of Joseon was *Daehan Jeguk* (the Korean Empire) while "Takeshima" was dubbed as Matsushima, Lyanko

---

29   The Imperial Navy of Japan, *Gunnkan niitaka koudounisshi* 37 (Naval Ship Niitaka, Daily report of activities 37), 1904.

Islands or Yanko Island. In several Japanese publications, which were used as a guidebook for advancement into Korea, Yanko Island was introduced as an island attached to Ulleung-do, Gangwon-do province. They include *Kankai Tsuryo Shishin* (韓海通漁指針, Guide to Fishing in the Korean Sea, 1903) by Shusuke Kuzu (葛生修亮), *Saishin Kankoku Zitsugyo Shishin* (最新韓國實業指針, Updated Manual for Doing Business in Korea, 1904) by Shigeka Iwanaga (岩永重華) and Kankoku Shin Chiri (韓國新地理, A New Korean Geography, 1905) written by Tomohiko Tabuchi (田淵友彦). The fact that Dokdo was regarded as Korean territory being called Yanko Island, means that Korea had established sovereignty over Dokdo. In addition, it was Naomasa Maki and Enziro Yamaza who wrote the prefaces to Kankai Tsuryo Shishin and Saishin Kankoku Zitsugyo Shishin, respectively. Accordingly, it is only natural to conclude that Lyanko (Yanko) Islands were regarded as attached to Utsuryo Island (Ulleungdo) by Yozaburo Nakai who submitted the petition for territorial incorporation of Lyanko Islands and their lease.

On March 1906 when the Japanese officials from Shimane Prefecture visited Ulleung-do, Sim Heung-taek (沈興澤), the County Magistrate of Uldo-gun, immediately reported what he had heard from the Japanese to the Governor of Gangwon-do Province. In his report, he wrote about the incorporation of Takeshima into Shimane Prefecture stating, "Dokdo, which belongs to this county…" His records clearly show that Dokdo was undisputedly under the jurisdiction of Uldo County.

Point 7. In the drafting process of the Treaty of Peace with Japan, the United States rejected the request by the ROK that Takeshima be added to the relevant article of the Treaty as one of the areas which Japan would renounce, asserting that Takeshima had been under the jurisdiction of Japan.

→ What was the basic position of the Allied Powers and the United States?

Seichu Naito   Territorial Issue between Japan and Korea: Case of Takeshima / Dokdo   **321**
– A Critique of the "10 Issues of Takeshima" Published by the MOFA
of Japan

What Point 7 of the Japanese Foreign Ministry's pamphlet states is that the San Francisco Peace Treaty determined territories that Japan must renounce while stipulating the recognition of the independence of Korea from Japan. The pamphlet argues that because the treaty did not mention Takeshima/Dokdo specifically, "It is evident that Takeshima was affirmed as part of the territory of Japan."

To support its position, Japan lists two documents. The first is a letter that Yang You-chan, Korean ambassador to the United States, sent in July 1951 to Dean G. Acheson,[30] U.S. Secretary of State. The other is a letter that David Dean Rusk,[31] the U.S. Assistant Secretary of State for Far Eastern Affairs, sent to Ambassador Yang You-chan in the following month.

Rusk's letter[32] states, "As regards the island of Dokdo, otherwise known as Takeshima or Liancourt Rocks, this normally uninhabited rock formation was according to our information never treated as part of Korea and, since about 1905, has been under the jurisdiction of the Oki Islands Branch Office of Shimane Prefecture of Japan. The island does not appear ever before to have been claimed by Korea."

This letter written by Rusk on August 10, 1951 became the basic position of the U.S. Government on the Takeshima/Dokdo issue. And this influenced CHAPTER II: TERRITORY of the San Francisco Peace Treaty that was prepared the following month.

It should be noted, however, that the Peace Treaty did not cite Takeshima/Dokdo as belonging to Japan specifically. What happened is that the United States simply refused to accept the Korean Government's request for the reason that Takeshima/Dokdo did not seem to be Korean territory. But,

---

30   1893-1971. American lawyer and politician. Served as Secretary of State (in office 1949-1952) under President Harry S. Truman.

31   1909-1994. American lawyer and politician. Served as Secretary of State under Presidents John F. Kennedy and Lyndon B. Johnson.

32   Document sent by Dean Rusk, the United States Assistant Secretary of State mentioned above, to the Korean government on August 10, 1951.

it should be noted that the U.S. action does not constitute an endorsement of Japan's position, either. Despite this fact, the Japanese Government argues that "Takeshima has been affirmed as part of the territory of Japan." Is this argument acceptable?

Rusk's letter, written "according to our information" was bound to cause controversy. How could he have reached such a conclusion saying, "…the island of Dokdo … was never treated as part of Korea" and" The island does not appear ever before to have been claimed by Korea." The historic facts point to a totally different conclusion as this critique has expounded so far.

It would be useful to take a look at how Takeshima/Dokdo was treated in the course of preparing the drafts of the San Francisco Peace Treaty.

It is noteworthy that in the first draft of March 20, 1947 through the fifth draft of November 2, 1949, Takeshima/Dokdo was on the list of specific islands to be renounced by Japan. But the territorial right over Takeshima/Dokdo was shifted to Japan in the sixth draft of December 29, 1949. Then the seventh draft of August 7, 1950 dropped the list of islands that would remain as Japanese territory altogether. The final draft was prepared by the United States and Britain jointly in May 1951, becoming part of the Peace Treaty as Article 2 (a).

Here, it is necessary to delve into how and why the territorial right over Takeshima/Dokdo shifted between Korea and Japan in the course of preparing the Peace Treaty. Until November 1949, Japan was required to renounce the island, and in December 1949 the island was suddenly shifted to Japan. And then, from August 1950, the Japanese right over the island was nowhere to be found in the Treaty.

The fact is that until December 1949, Takeshima/Dokdo was treated as Korean territory. Under SCAPIN[33] (Supreme Commander for the Allied Powers Instruction) No. 677, issued on January 29, 1946, the island was under

---

33 Supreme Commander for the Allied Powers Instruction (SCAPIN). Referred to as "SCAPIN" in the body text.

Seichu Naito   Territorial Issue between Japan and Korea: Case of Takeshima / Dokdo   **323**
– A Critique of the "10 Issues of Takeshima" Published by the MOFA
of Japan

the control of the U.S. Army Military Government in Korea. When the independent Republic of Korea was established in 1948, the jurisdiction over the island was transferred to Korea as a matter of course.

Now, about the sudden change that happened regarding the status of the island on December 8, 1949, it was found that the person behind the change was William J. Sebald, the Political Advisor in Japan. What happened was that Mr. Sebald suggested to the U.S. State Department that Japan's claim to the island appeared to be valid and that for security reasons, the United States might consider the installation of weather and radar stations on the island.

In this connection, it is helpful to understand the international situation in the Far East at the time. On September 23, 1949, the Soviet Union revealed that it possessed atomic bombs. On October 1 the same year, the Communist People's Republic of China was established. In this way, the Cold War in the region was intensifying. In his 1950 New Year Statement to the Japanese people, Gen. MacArthur, the Supreme Commander of the Allied Forces, emphasized Japan's right to self-defense. On January 31 the same year, Gen. Omar N. Bradley,[34] the Chairman of the U.S. Joint Chiefs of Staff, declared that the U.S. bases in Okinawa and Japan would be beefed up. The Allied Commander in Japan instructed Japan to create the National Police Reserves, which later developed into Japan's Ground Self-Defense Force and Marine Self Defense Force, and to strengthen the Marine Safety Agency, the predecessor of the Coast Guard. Rearmament of Japan was starting in earnest. On November 1, 1949, the U.S. State Department announced that the Allied Powers were preparing a Treaty of Peace with Japan.

This is the situation surrounding Sebald's suggestion concerning Takeshima/Dokdo. It was obvious that the issue of the island began to be dealt with from the perspective of U.S. interests and security needs. Takeshima/Dokdo became part of Washington's Far East strategies and was initially to serve as a

---

34   1893-1981. U.S. Army general. First chairman of the Joint Chiefs of Staff. First chairman of the NATO (North Atlantic Treaty Organization) committee.

radar station. In April 1950, John Foster Dulles[35] was appointed special representative of the U.S. President, with the rank of ambassador, to negotiate the Treaty of Peace with Japan. In an apparent move to make the draft concerning Japanese territory a little simpler, he opted not to mention Takeshima/Dokdo in the document.

In April 1951, Britain produced a draft plan depicting a line around Japanese territory using longitudes and latitudes. Under the plan, Takeshima/Dokdo was excluded from Japan's territory. Britain and the United States consulted each other over the British plan and produced a final joint draft that did not have descriptions in longitudes and latitudes. Some people argue that the elimination of longitudes and latitudes in the final draft implied inclusion of the island into Japanese territory. But the argument is not persuasive as the list of names of all the islands had been removed in the seventh draft of August 1950. The final draft simply represented the British plan without descriptions in longitudes and latitudes.

Although negotiations between the Allied Powers and Japan on the peace treaty were in full swing, Korea knew little about it initially. In fact, Korea was embroiled in a civil war.[36] The Korean War broke out on June 25, 1950. On October 25 the same year, China joined the war in aid of the Communist North. Protracted Armistice Talks began near Gaeseong on July 10, 1951. Although fully occupied in war, South Korea felt strongly the need to reflect its position in the San Francisco Peace Treaty and submitted an 11-point request to the United States. The Republic raised the Takeshima/Dokdo issue on July 19, 1951 for the first time. On that day, in a second meeting with John Foster Dulles, Korean Ambassador Yang You-chan made an official request that the

35   1888-1959. American lawyer and politician. Served as Secretary of State under President Dwight D. Eisenhower (in office 1953-1959). Visited Japan, the Philippines, Australia and other countries as a peace envoy in 1956.

36   Began with the North Korean Army's invasion of the South on June 25, 1950. An armistice agreement (de facto cease-fire) was signed on July 27, 1953, solidifying the division of the Korean Peninsula.

Seichu Naito   Territorial Issue between Japan and Korea: Case of Takeshima / Dokdo   **325**
          – A Critique of the "10 Issues of Takeshima" Published by the MOFA
          of Japan

Peace Treaty clarify that Japan specifically renounce its claim to Takeshima/ Dokdo. In a reply on August 10, Dean Rusk, the Assistant Secretary of State for Far Eastern Affairs, responded negatively to the request.

Dean Rusk clearly rejected the Korean Government's demand. It is obvious that Rusk made the reply based on Sebald's recommendations of December 1949. As mentioned earlier, Sebald's recommendations in turn were made based on the information fed to him by the Japanese Government as well as his concept of America's impending security interests in the region.

Now, the Japanese Foreign Ministry seems to think that Rusk's letter is about the only evidence that matters in the controversy. Furthermore, Tokyo has come to the rash conclusion that the United States regarded Takeshima/ Dokdo as Japanese territory and that the San Francisco Treaty made the island Japanese territory beyond question. Does it make sense, though? Japan has all along tried to influence the United States so that Washington would support and enhance Tokyo's position. But Washington's basic stance is not to get involved in the controversy between Japan and Korea. Washington's policy of noninvolvement is quite natural, as it is not the United States that can determine who has sovereignty over Takeshima. As evidenced by the Foreign Ministry's pamphlet, the Japanese government seems to rely on the United States for the resolution of the Korea-Japan problem. With this kind of approach, there is no possibility of resolving the Takeshima/Dokdo issue.

Point 8. In 1952, Takeshima was designated as a bombing range for the U.S. Forces stationed in Japan, which shows that Takeshima was treated as a part of the territory of Japan.
    → What was the background of this U.S. action?

Takeshima/Dokdo was designated as a bombing practice range in a U.S.-Japan Joint Committee meeting on July 26, 1952. But the designation was repealed by the U.S-Korea Joint Committee on March 19, 1953.

The reason the designation was repealed in less than a year's time was that the Korean Government protested against the U.S. military action. The repeal was made after the Seoul Government, which learned about the designation belatedly, sent an official protest letter to the U.S. military authorities on February 27, 1953. Accordingly, it doesn't make any sense for the Foreign Ministry pamphlet to state, "…the fact that the Island was designated as an area for use by the U.S. Forces stationed in Japan clearly shows that Takeshima is part of the territory of Japan."

In fact, the U.S. military's use of Takeshima/Dokdo as a practice bombing range was nothing new because the island had been used as an aerial bombing range before 1952. Although before that time, there were serious issues of the same kind, in both cases the U.S. Air Force in Korea and the Korean Government made a negotiated settlement. This is good evidence that the island is Korean territory. (At least the U.S. military authorities and the Allied Forces as well as the Korean Government had a firm understanding of this.)

The initial designation of Takeshima/Dokdo as a U.S. military bombing range came on September 16, 1947 under SCAPIN No. 1778. On June 30, 1948, at least 30 Koreans were killed while engaged in fishing near the island because of a bombing exercise of the U.S. Air Force.

Korea established an independent government in 1948. On April 25, 1950, the country protested to the U.S. Air Force holding it accountable for the 1948 incident. But the U.S. Forces replied that it had not used the fishing boats as targets of the bombing. Eventually, however, compensation was paid to the Korean victims.

The U.S. military reasserted the designation of Takeshima/Dokdo as a practice bombing range on July 6, 1951 under SCAPIN No. 2160. Then on July 26, 1952, the U.S.-Japanese Joint Committee again made a similar designation. On September 18, 1952, the Korea Alpine Association received approval from the U.S. Forces in Korea to conduct a second academic survey of Takeshima/Dokdo.

However, while heading for the island, the mountain climbers found

Seichu Naito   Territorial Issue between Japan and Korea: Case of Takeshima / Dokdo   **327**
– A Critique of the "10 Issues of Takeshima" Published by the MOFA
of Japan

that a U.S. bombing practice was going on there. So they gave up their trip, returned home and reported to the government what had transpired. On November 10, 1952, on the basis of the report, the Korean Government sent a letter to the American Embassy in Korea requesting that the Embassy take steps to prevent a recurrence of any such incident. The next month, on December 24, the Commander of the U.S. Far East Air Force sent a letter promising that his forces would no longer engage in bombing practice near the island. Then came the decision to repeal the designation on March 19, 1953 by the U.S-Korea Joint Committee. In light of this, it is obvious that the United States had taken a series of actions on the basis of its recognition that Takeshima/Dokdo is Korean territory.

The website of the Japanese Foreign Ministry does not mention salient actions that took place in Korea in connection with the repeal of the bombing range designation. Instead, it just states as follows: "However, receiving strong requests from local residents for sea lion hunting, abalone fishing and seaweed harvesting in the waters around Takeshima, and given that in the winter of 1952 the U.S. Forces had ceased using Takeshima as a bombing range, the Joint Committee, at a meeting in March 1953, decided to remove Takeshima from the list of military exercise areas."

This part of the Japanese government's website is confusing because Shimane Prefecture had already submitted a petition requesting the deletion of Takeshima from the list of U.S. military training sites. The petition was addressed to the Japanese Minister of Foreign Affairs and Minister of Agriculture and was submitted on May 20, 1952 in time for the U.S.-Japan Joint Committee meeting that was scheduled for about two months later on July 26. According to the minutes of the subcommittee on maritime exercise sites of the U.S.-Japan Joint Committee of March 19, 1953, it was decided that the U.S. Air Force in Japan would not require Liancourt Rocks (Takeshima/Dokdo) as a bombing range any longer. This bilateral agreement reached at the subcommittee was reported to the joint committee and approved on that same day.

As such, the Japanese Foreign Ministry's explanation above regarding the

U.S. forces' repeal of the designation of Takeshima/Dokdo as a training site shows obvious sequential discrepancies.

Point 9. The ROK is illegally occupying Takeshima, against which Japan has been consistently making strong protests.
→ What are the Japan's protests about?

The Japanese Foreign Ministry's pamphlet states as follows: "The occupation of Takeshima by the ROK is an illegal occupation undertaken on absolutely no basis of international law. No measure taken by the ROK during its illegal occupation with regard to Takeshima has any legal justification."

The crux of Japan's claim to Takeshima/Dokdo appears to be that the country made a proclamation annexing the island in 1905, and has exercised jurisdiction over it. But, after World War II under the U.S. military rule, the island was put outside Japanese jurisdiction in accordance with SCAPIN No. 677. Furthermore, SCAPIN No. 1033[37] established the MacArthur Line,[38] prohibiting Japanese ships and crew members from approaching 12 nautical miles from Takeshima/Dokdo. SCAPIN No. 1033 was rescinded on April 25, 1952. However, SCAPIN No. 677 has never been rescinded. Therefore, Korea maintains that SCAPIN No. 677 is still valid, constituting a sole legal basis about the status of the island. The ensuing San Francisco Peace Treaty does not have specific provisions about Takeshima/Dokdo, so the validity of SCAPIN No. 677 excluding the island from Japanese jurisdiction still stands, according to Korea. Meanwhile, the Japanese Government believes that validity of SCAPIN No. 677 was automatically lost with the signing of the San Francisco Peace Treaty and that Takeshima/Dokdo belongs to Japan despite a lack of

---

37   Titled "Area Authorized for Japanese Fishing and Whaling."

38   The sea zone authorized for Japanese fishing and whaling, designated by the above mentioned SCAPIN 1033 "Area Authorized for Japanese Fishing and Whaling."

Seichu Naito   Territorial Issue between Japan and Korea: Case of Takeshima / Dokdo   **329**
– A Critique of the "10 Issues of Takeshima" Published by the MOFA
of Japan

any provision on it in the San Francisco Treaty. Accordingly, Japan regards the current status of the island as an "illegal occupation" by Korea. But, Japan has failed to produce solid, specific reasons why the current status represents "illegal occupation."

Also, the Japanese Government criticizes that the "Syngman Rhee Line[39] was a unilateral act in contravention of international law." But the Rhee Line is basically the successor of the MacArthur Line that was drawn according to SCAPIN No. 1033. The MacArthur Line, too, prohibited Japanese boats from fishing near Takeshima/Dokdo, and it is worthwhile to delve into why the U.S. military government in the Far East established the maritime line.

One possible explanation is that there was a need to protect Korean fisheries as Japan had long been firmly controlling Korean fishing equipment, technology and capital. Although Korea was liberated from the Japanese colonial rule, the fledgling Korean fishing industry needed nurturing and protection. The MacArthur Line was necessary for the protection of Korean fishermen from their Japanese counterparts. Furthermore, before the breakout of the World War II, Japanese fishermen were the object of international complaints because they were engaged in arbitrary fishing operations without heeding the needs of neighboring countries. The MacArthur Line was the response to the international demand to regulate Japanese fishing operations. But the Japan fishing associations were persistent in requesting abolition of the MacArthur Line[40] long before the San Francisco Peace Treaty was concluded.

The Tokyo Government criticized the Rhee Line as contravening the principle of freedom on the high seas. The principle sounds fair enough. But the reality changed after the war. Contrary to the prewar practices, it has be-

---

39   A military boundary line declared and established by South Korean President Syngman Rhee (1875-1965, in office 1948-1960) on January 18, 1952. It was based on his Proclamation of Sovereignty over Adjacent Seas. The line was abolished under the Japan-Korea Fishery Agreement of 1965.

40   Japan Fisheries Association, National Federation of Fisheries Co-operative Associations (Zengyoren), etc.

come a general principle that priority should be given to coastal countries and newly emerging nations. That is why the Peace Treaty, in Article 9, stipulates, "Japan will enter promptly into negotiations with the Allied Powers so desiring for the conclusion of bilateral and multilateral agreements providing for the regulation or limitation of fishing and the conservation and development of fisheries on the high seas."

Syngman Rhee Line

Korea was not one of the Allied Powers, but on the basis of Article 21 of the San Francisco Treaty depicting benefits of certain parties, Korea was entitled to the benefits provided in Article 9. In other words, Japan was required by the Treaty to conclude a fishing agreement with Korea. So Korea naturally expected that Japan would conclude a fishing agreement, giving due attention to Korea's need to protect its fishing right, refraining from fishing in the seas near the new republic and putting all these things in writing in a bilateral agreement. However, the Tokyo Government did not show any intention of imposing any self-restriction. Therefore, Korea had no choice but to take a self-protective measure, which was the Syngman Rhee Line, the successor of the MacArthur Line.

Seichu Naito   Territorial Issue between Japan and Korea: Case of Takeshima / Dokdo   **331**
– A Critique of the "10 Issues of Takeshima" Published by the MOFA
of Japan

The Japanese Government may see the Rhee Line as abrupt and unilateral. Japan argued that the Rhee Line was against freedom on the high seas and that it was illegal, unjustified and one-sided. But the decision of the Korean State Council on the Rhee Line clarifies this point. The Republic says that the Rhee Line was established based on concrete international precedents such as the Truman Declaration.[41] The Korean Government explained that after the war, the international community was moving toward firmly establishing the principle that the rights of countries adjacent to the seas should be respected. Seoul also pointed out the growing trend that a country does not necessarily need the consent of neighboring countries in proclaiming its maritime zones. To this, the Japanese Government has only made emotional protests regarding the inclusion of Jukdo within the Syngman Rhee Line, as was the case for the MacArthur line. Japan has rarely proposed constructive measures for protecting and utilizing fish and other marine resources in the Sea of Japan (East Sea).

The Foreign Ministry pamphlet stated, "In July of the same year … demanded Koreans engaged in illegal fishing to leave the vicinity of Takeshima…" As mentioned earlier, on March 19, 1953, the U.S.-Korea Joint Committee decided to repeal the measure allowing the United States to use Takeshima/Dokdo as a bombing range. On the same day, the same kind of decision was made at the U.S.-Japan Joint Committee.

It was also mentioned earlier that in 1952, the Korea Alpine Association members obtained permission to explore Takeshima/Dokdo from the U.S. military authorities in Korea that were using the island as a bombing range. The alpinists found that bombing practice was still being conducted on the island. After the Korean Government protested about the incident, the U.S. military decided to stop using the island for air raids. From this fact, it is obvious that the U.S. military recognized Korea's territorial right over the island.

41   "Exclusive Economic Zone" (sea zone defined based on the United Nations Convention on the Law of the Sea, over which a state has economic sovereignty) announced by U.S. President Harry Truman. With this the United States set its jurisdiction (sovereignty) over international fishery resources. Also known as Presidential Proclamation No. 2667.

With the U.S. military's decision to delist the island as a training site, Korean fishermen resumed their activities there. Now, how can anyone call this" illegal fishing?"

When Korea became an independent republic in 1948, jurisdiction over Dokdo was handed over to Korea from the U.S. Army Military Government. But Japan did not obtain any right over the island in writing when it signed the San Francisco Peace Treaty. How, then, can it be Japanese territory? Sometime after the beginning of 1953, clashes took place on the sea between fishermen of the two countries. Then Korean volunteer guards landed on the island and began effective control of it. Since December 1956, the Korean National Police has been guarding the island. Since 1953, the Governments of the two countries have been exchanging protest statements off and on involving the island.

Point 10. Although Japan proposed to the ROK that the dispute over Takeshima be referred to the International Court of Justice, the ROK rejected this proposal.
→ What are the untold stories?

On September 25, 1954, the Japanese Government proposed in a *note verbale* that Japan and Korea jointly refer the issue of the territorial right over Takeshima/Dokdo to the International Court of Justice, but Korea rejected it on October 28 at the same year.

The Japanese pamphlet does not give any reason why Korea rejected its proposal, giving the wrong impression that Korea is dodging the issue. Korea has clarified that Takeshima/Dokdo has always been Korean territory, and so there is no need to get confirmation about its territorial right from the International Court of Justice.

Meanwhile, at the Korea-Japan Diplomatic Normalization Talks that started in 1951, the two countries did not deal with the Takeshima/Dokdo

Seichu Naito   Territorial Issue between Japan and Korea: Case of Takeshima / Dokdo   **333**
                – A Critique of the "10 Issues of Takeshima" Published by the MOFA
                of Japan

issue. But in 1965, they produced an Exchange of Memorandum Concerning Resolution of Disputes, which states as follows: "Except for the cases agreed on otherwise, bilateral disputes between Korea and Japan should be resolved through diplomatic channel primarily. If a solution cannot be reached in this way, the two sides will attempt to make resolution through mediation according to the procedures they concur."

In light of this, any referral of this case to the International Court is unthinkable by just one side as some Japanese ruling party members advocate. The issue can only be resolved through bilateral diplomatic negotiations or mediation by a third party when the two sides agree to that.

The Foreign Ministry pamphlet also states as follows: "According to the report of Special Envoy Van Fleet[42] who visited the ROK in 1954, ...the United States concluded that Takeshima is Japanese territory, and took the position that the dispute might properly be referred to the International Court of Justice. Special Envoy Van Fleet reports that though the United States conveyed this suggestion to the ROK the ROK argued that .Dokdo was part of Ulleung (Utsuryo) Island."

Around that time, Japan was lobbying for the support of the U.S. Department of State for the purpose of having the UN Security Council make a recommendation to the effect that the Takeshima/Dokdo issue be referred to the International Court of Justice. Concerning Japan's expectation about the role of the United States as a mediator, however, the important fact is that the United States made it clear that it did not want to get involved in the issue and that the two countries should solve the problem between them. (Source: The final version of the "Investigative Research Report on Takeshima Issue." Relevant content I: November 16, 1954 minutes of the meeting on the "Japanese Proposal to Refer the Liancourt Rocks Dispute to the UN Security Council."

---

42   1892-1992. U.S. Army general. After a tour in 1954 to Japan, South Korea, Taiwan, Philippine and other countries as Special mission ambassador of President Eisenhower, he submitted a report (Report of Van Fleet Mission to The Far East), 1954 to the president.

Relevant content II: November 17, 1954 memorandum entitled, "Liancourt Rocks").[43]

As evidenced by the Japanese Government's activities with reference to the 1951 letter from Dean Rusk and the 1954 report of Special Envoy Van Fleet, the Ministry of Foreign Affairs of Japan appears to have totally relied on the U.S. Department of State in trying to solve their own problem concerning the Takeshima/Dokdo issue. But Japan should realize that it cannot rely on a third party to solve a territorial issue; fundamentally, the issue has to be settled between the two parties concerned. In this connection, it is hard to understand why the Japanese Government does not mention the existence of the 1965 Exchange Memorandum Concerning Resolution of Disputes. Maybe that's because the Korean Government's position is that Takeshima/Dokdo has always been Korean territory, that it is a non-issue and that it has nothing to do with the Exchange Memorandum Concerning Resolution of Disputes. However, regardless of the Korean position, the Tokyo Government needs to produce firm evidence that the island belongs to Japan. The contents of this Foreign Ministry's pamphlet are not persuasive at all.

Afterword

The feeling I had after reading the Foreign Ministry's pamphlet was that "This is just too much. This is too much to bear." It was obvious the Japanese Government was refusing to face history squarely but was only trying to use part of it to fit its needs. The Government was ignoring facts that did not seem to fit its own cause, never wanting to consider them. By presenting what it claimed to be the Government's basic position on the issue, the Government just confused the Japanese public. The Government even published its posi-

---

43   Shimane prefecture website http://www.pref.shimane.lg.jp/soumu/webtakeshima/takeshima04/takeshima04_01/.

Seichu Naito   Territorial Issue between Japan and Korea: Case of Takeshima / Dokdo   **335**
                             – A Critique of the "10 Issues of Takeshima" Published by the MOFA
                             of Japan

tion in English and Korean and is just advertising worldwide its lack of research on the issue.

As a Japanese citizen and historian, I appeal to the Japanese Government to use complete facts more than anything. The Takeshima/Dokdo issue should be resolved based on historic facts.

If the Japanese Government approaches the issue arbitrarily without seeking historic facts as the Foreign Ministry has done, there will be no answer to the question. I have written this booklet based on historic facts and in the belief that it will serve the cause of an honorable Japan. The most serious problem of the content of the Foreign Ministry's pamphlet is that it failed to prove its points based on a correct reading of history while maintaining that Takeshima is "inherently Japanese territory." Substantial discussion has been made in the main body of this booklet. However, for the sake of a concise summary, it would be worthwhile to repeat some of the salient facts as follows:

First, the Shogunate learned about the existence of Matsushima (present day Takeshima/Dokdo) in January 1696 for the first time during questions and answers with the Lord of Tottori-han domain. Therefore, it is not reasonable for the Government to argue that Japan had established territorial right over the island in the middle of the 17th century.

Second, the Shogunate exchanged questions and answers with the Lord of Tottori-han from December 1695 through January 1696 and confirmed the fact that both Takeshima (present-day Utsuryo/Ulleungdo) and Matsushima (present-day Takeshima/Dokdo) do not belong to Tottori-han. After concluding that present-day Takeshima/Dokdo was not Japanese territory, it prohibited Japanese subjects from sailing to the island in January 1696.

Third, in 1877, the Dajokan (Japanese Grand Council of State) of the Meiji Government received an inquiry about jurisdiction over Takeshima/Dokdo from Shimane Prefecture. After having government officials investigate the issue, it replied that "Takeshima and the other island (present-day Takeshima/Dokdo) do not have anything to do with Japan."

Fourth, the Foreign Ministry states that Japan incorporated Takeshima/

Dokdo in 1905, reaffirming that it was Japanese territory. This is wrong because neither the Shogunate nor the Meiji Government had ever maintained that the island belonged to Japan. On the contrary, the two entities clarified in 1696 and 1877 respectively that the island was not Japanese territory. In the Cabinet decision for incorporation of the island, the Japanese Government stated that it was taking the action on the basis of terra nullius. *Terra nullius* means it is not possessed by anybody. Now, if the island had not been possessed by anybody until that time, how can Japan claim that the island has been inherently Japanese territory? It is important, indeed, to find out if the island was possessed by any entity at that time.

Again, if the Japanese Government intends to maintain that Takeshima/ Dokdo is inherently its territory, it should answer the questions above. In the absence of diligent research and solid evidence on the issue, the Government is likely to keep producing such mediocre pamphlets as the Foreign Ministry's. The good news is that a number of new historic materials on Takeshima/ Dokdo are available today. The two countries even have a system for sharing the materials they have. Times have changed, and it is incumbent on the two nations to begin to work together and enhance common historical recognition as it relates to their long relations. The Governments of the two countries, in turn, will have to humbly accept results from the research founded on historic facts. The Error-ridden pamphlets of the Government will only bring international shame on the Japanese people, and such practices should be put to an end once and for all.

Finally, I would like to express deep appreciation to the many people who supported publishing this booklet. Particularly, Publisher Ko I-sam of Shinkansha has been most helpful and I thank him immensely.

Seichu Naito
August 2008